Frommer's®

Florence & Tuscany
day BY day®

3rd Edition

by Donald Strachan

WILEY

John Wiley & Sons, Inc.

Contents

Published by:

John Wiley & Sons, Inc.

111 River St.
Hoboken, NJ 07030-5774

ISBN 978-1-118-16717-5 (paper); 978-0-470-47478-5 (ebk);
978-1-118-21933-1 (ebk); 978-1-118-21934-8 (ebk)

Editor: Jennifer Reilly
Production Editor: Eric T. Schroeder
Photo Editors: Cherie Cincilla & Alden Gewirtz
Cartographer: Andrew Murphy
Production by Wiley Indianapolis Composition Services

For information on our other products and services or to obtain technical
support, please contact our Customer Care Department within the U.S.
at 877/762-2974, outside the U.S. at 317/572-3993 or fax 317/572-4002.

Wiley also publishes its books in a variety of electronic formats. Some
content that appears in print may not be available in electronic formats.

Manufactured in China

5   4   3   2   1

A Note from the Editorial Director

Organizing your time. That's what this guide is all about.

Other guides give you long lists of things to see and do and then expect you to fit the pieces together. The Day by Day guides are different. These guides tell you the best of everything, and then they show you how to see it *in the smartest, most time-efficient way*. Our authors have designed detailed itineraries organized by time, neighborhood, or special interest. And each tour comes with a bulleted map that takes you from stop to stop.

Hoping to relive the glory days of the Florentine Renaissance, or to tour the highlights of Siena? Planning a drive through Chianti country, or a tour of Tuscany's most charming small towns? Whatever your interest or schedule, the Day by Days give you the smartest routes to follow. Not only do we take you to the top attractions, hotels, and restaurants, but we also help you access those special moments that locals get to experience—those "finds" that turn tourists into travelers.

The Day by Days are also your top choice if you're looking for one complete guide for all your travel needs. The best hotels and restaurants for every budget, the greatest shopping values, the wildest nightlife—it's all here.

Why should you trust our judgment? Because our authors personally visit each place they write about. They're an independent lot who say what they think and would never include places they wouldn't recommend to their best friends. They're also open to suggestions from readers. If you'd like to contact them, please send your comments our way at feedback@frommers.com, and we'll pass them on.

Enjoy your Day by Day guide—the most helpful travel companion you can buy. And have the trip of a lifetime.

Warm regards,

Kelly Regan

Kelly Regan, Editorial Director
Frommer's Travel Guides

About the Author

Donald Strachan is a London-based writer and journalist. He has written about Italian travel for publications including the *Sunday Telegraph, Independent on Sunday, Sydney Morning Herald*, and *Guardian*, and is the co-author of Frommer's *Florence, Tuscany & Umbria, Italy 2013,* and *Tuscany & Umbria with Your Family*.

Advisory & Disclaimer

Travel information can change quickly and unexpectedly, and we strongly advise you to confirm important details locally before traveling, including information on visas, health and safety, traffic and transport, accommodations, shopping, and eating out. We also encourage you to stay alert while traveling and to remain aware of your surroundings. Avoid civil disturbances, and keep a close eye on cameras, purses, wallets, and other valuables.

While we have endeavored to ensure that the information contained within this guide is accurate and up-to-date at the time of publication, we make no representations or warranties with respect to the accuracy or completeness of the contents of this work and specifically disclaim all warranties, including without limitation warranties of fitness for a particular purpose. We accept no responsibility or liability for any inaccuracy or errors or omissions, or for any inconvenience, loss, damage, costs, or expenses of any nature whatsoever incurred or suffered by anyone as a result of any advice or information contained in this guide.

The inclusion of a company, organization, or website in this guide as a service provider and/or potential source of further information does not mean that we endorse them or the information they provide. Be aware that information provided through some websites may be unreliable and can change without notice. Neither the publisher nor author shall be liable for any damages arising herefrom.

Star Ratings, Icons & Abbreviations

Every hotel, restaurant, and attraction listing in this guide has been ranked for quality, value, service, amenities, and special features using a **star-rating system.** Hotels, restaurants, attractions, shopping, and nightlife are rated on a scale of zero stars (recommended) to three stars (exceptional). In addition to the star-rating system, we also use a **kids** icon to point out the best bets for families. Within each tour, we recommend cafes, bars, or restaurants where you can take a break. Each of these stops appears in a shaded box marked with a coffee-cup-shaped bullet ☕.

The following **abbreviations** are used for credit cards:

AE	American Express	DISC	Discover	V	Visa
DC	Diners Club	MC	MasterCard		

Travel Resources at Frommers.com

Frommer's travel resources don't end with this guide. Frommer's website,
www.frommers.com, has travel information on more than 4,000 destinations. We update features regularly, giving you access to the most current trip-planning information and the best airfare, lodging, and car-rental bargains. You can also listen to podcasts, connect with other Frommers.com members through our active-reader forums, share your travel photos, read blogs from guidebook editors and fellow travelers, and much more.

A Note on Prices

In the "Take a Break" and "Best Bets" sections of this book, we have used a system of dollar signs to show a range of costs for 1 night in a hotel (the price of a midseason standard double-occupancy room) or the cost of a midpriced *a la carte* entree at a restaurant. Use the following table to decipher the dollar signs:

Cost	Hotels	Restaurants
$	under 75€	under 8€
$$	75€–150€	8€–16€
$$$	150€–225€	16€–24€
$$$$	225€–300€	24€–32€
$$$$$	over 300€	over 32€

How to Contact Us

In researching this book, we discovered many wonderful places—hotels, restaurants, shops, and more. We're sure you'll find others. Please tell us about them, so we can share the information with your fellow travelers in upcoming editions. If you were disappointed with a recommendation, we'd love to know that, too. Please write to:

Frommer's Florence & Tuscany Day by Day, 3rd Edition
John Wiley & Sons, Inc. • 111 River St. • Hoboken, NJ 07030-5774

18 Favorite
Moments

18 Favorite **Moments**

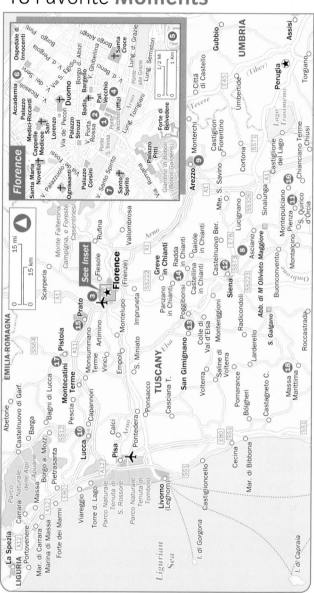

Previous page: Brunelleschi's dome and Giotto's campanile are standout features of the Florence skyline.

The treasures of the Uffizi and Michelangelo's *David* are just the start of an unforgettable journey into Tuscany: There is so much more to the region than the magnificence of Florence. Beyond the city that cradled the Renaissance lie snow-capped peaks, dramatic cypress-studded ridges, the turquoise Tyrrhenian Sea, and silver-green olive groves. With Chianti's vineyards, Pisa's errant Tower, San Gimignano's medieval "skyscrapers," and a wealth of Florentine and Sienese art and architecture, it's difficult to single out 18 highlights—but this list is my best attempt to do just that.

Piazza della Signoria.

❶ **Eating the world's best gelato.** At Florence's **Carapina,** San Gimignano's **"di Piazza,"** or Siena's **Kopa Kabana,** the ice cream is most definitely not just for kids. You name the flavor, you'll probably find it somewhere. Vespa-riding ravers and contessas alike come for their daily fix. *See p 19, 163, and 173.*

❷ **Drinking in the full 360-degree view of Piazza della Signoria.** Find a comfortable perch on Florence's grandest square—the site of Savonarola's infamous "Bonfire of the Vanities"— and take in Benvenuto Cellini's *Perseus* with the head of Medusa, a replica of Michelangelo's *David*, the Uffizi, and the Palazzo Vecchio. It's the best free show in town. *See p 13.*

❸ **Walking the road of the ancients from Fiesole to Florence.** Start at Etruscan Fiesole's Piazza Mino and follow the road through San Domenico to Florence, below. Untamed vegetation pours over the high walls that line the way past gnarled olive groves, ordered gardens, and 18th-century villas— and a panoramic vista of the city that opens suddenly. *See p 23.*

❹ **Catching a glimpse of where Tuscan art was born.**

A small sampling of the divine gelato available in Tuscany.

A copy of the David, *at the Piazzale Michelangiolo.*

In Room 2 of the Uffizi the great *Madonnas* of Cimabue, Duccio, and Giotto are displayed side by side. Between them, these three painters shaped Florentine and Sienese art for generations. *See p 25.*

⑤ Basking in the lights of the Renaissance, at twilight, from San Miniato al Monte. The climb up here is a stiff one, but the view of the city twinkling from the steps in front of this ancient church will rank among the greatest you've seen. *See p 15.*

⑥ Standing in awe at the foot of Michelangelo's *David.* The massive genius of Michelangelo's masterpiece in marble, at the Accademia, may bowl you over— even from behind its Plexiglas barrier. After 5 centuries, he is still

miraculously alive, embodying the ideals of the Tuscan High Renaissance. *See p 13.*

⑦ Hitting San Frediano after dark. I love the buzz of this fashionable, left-bank neighborhood that stretches west along the River Arno from the Ponte Santa Trinita to and through the Porta Pisana. Once a working-class, artisan's borough, it is now where young Florentines head for the buzziest bars and most creative restaurants in the city. *See p 66 and 133.*

⑧ Seeing Siena for the first time—from the hills of Le Crete. The S438 from Asciano to Siena traverses Tuscany's most photogenic landscape. And that first, unmistakable sight of the 102m (335-ft.) Torre del Mangia piercing the horizon in the distance is one you won't forget. *See p 87.*

⑨ Following the Piero della Francesca trail. His iconic work is Tuscany's best fresco cycle, the *Legend of the True Cross* in Arezzo's San Francesco. But the Piero trail continues to Monterchi for a rarity in Italian art, a pregnant *Madonna.* His hometown of Sanselpolcro still holds the painting Aldous Huxley claimed was the greatest ever

Biking the walls of Lucca.

Tuscan tomatoes, a key part of any Tuscan al fresco *meal.*

painted, his 1463 *Resurrection of Christ. See p 89 and 125.*

⑩ Biking the walls of Lucca.
Kids and octogenarians alike peddle Tuscany's greatest cycle track, 5km (2¾ miles) in length, on 16th-century ramparts so thick they now function as a tree-lined promenade and public park. The chestnut and ilex trees are compliments of Marie-Louise of Bourbon, from the 1800s. *See p 133.*

⑪ Dining *al fresco* in autumn.
What could be finer than a *bistecca alla fiorentina* dripping with olive oil and fresh herbs, grilled over a chestnut-wood fire? One served outdoors, of course, in Tuscany in autumn. When the leaves are turning red and gold, regional delicacies—black truffles, roast pheasant, foraged porcini mushrooms—taste their best. Try La Porta, in Montichiello close to Pienza and Montepulciano. *See p 149.*

⑫ Attending the Palio, Italy's grandest medieval spectacle.
This breakneck, bareback horse race around Siena's dirt-packed Piazza del Campo takes place twice a year, in July and August, in honor of the Virgin Mary. Beyond the race, it's bacchanalia—with days of parades, pageantry, and partying. *See p 171.*

⑬ Wandering San Gimignano's historic center at dusk.
Its unique skyline pierced by 14 towers (sometimes nicknamed "skyscrapers") is what makes this place the #1 spot on the hilltown trail. When the tour buses have left, the quiet streets exude a haunted, medieval air quite unlike anywhere else in Tuscany. *See p 73.*

⑭ Tasting the wine in Chianti Country. The vine-studded hills between Florence and Siena nurture

One of the many excellent wines available in Chianti country.

a glass of the sweet wine, take one of the hard almond cookies, and dip. My favorite places just leave the bottle, the biscuits, and plenty of time. For the originals, correctly known as *biscotti di Prato,* visit Mattei, the best biscuit-maker in their home city. *See p 93.*

⑯ Discovering your favorite Tuscan hilltown. My vote goes to Montepulciano: Not just for its noble red wine first cultivated here by the Etruscans, nor for its *palazzi* by High Renaissance masters like Sangallo. I just love the pace of the place, the welcoming nature of its inhabitants, and the fact that I know I'll find Tuscany's best steak right in the center. *See p 128.*

⑰ Riding the train from town to town. There's no better way to fit right in than arriving like a local on Italy's cheap and easy rail network. Prato and Pistoia are perfect destinations for your day on the train. *See p 98.*

⑱ Squeezing into La Tana del Brillo Parlante for a memorable lunch. This tiny restaurant in sleepy Massa Marittima is the best place to get acquainted with the flavors of the Maremma, the fertile terrain that stretches along Tuscany's coast. *See p 141.* ●

Montepulciano, one of Tuscany's most beautiful hilltowns.

one of Italy's most famous exports. Against a backdrop of ancient villages and crenellated castles from the Middle Ages, you can sample the *vino* from cantinas around Castellina, Greve, and Radda. *See p 91.*

⑮ Rounding out lunch with cantuccini and vin santo. Pour

Prato, which boasts a stunning Duomo, is an ideal day trip via Tuscany's rail network.

1

Strategies for Seeing **Tuscany**

Strategies for Seeing **Tuscany**

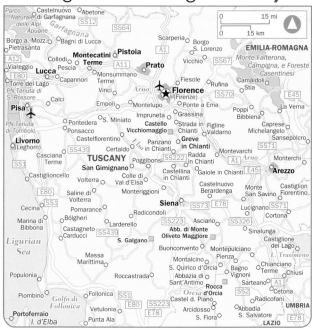

Tuscany isn't Tokyo or New York; racing around trying to "see" everything runs against the grain of the place, and might prevent you from really *experiencing* it. It's tempting to make tracks, given that there is so much to see within a relatively small region easily traversed by car. But structuring a relaxed itinerary makes for a memorable trip. In the chapters that follow I've shown you how to maximize your time here, but remember: Just about everywhere in this glorious corner of Italy is improved by taking 1 extra day to see it.

Previous page: A sunflower field in Tuscany.

Rule #1: Slow down.
Consider the experience of two couples I know who visited the region. One fashioned an aggressive itinerary that encompassed most of the major towns I cover in chapter 6. And while they were able to say they saw town after town, church after church, and artwork after artwork,

they spent 2 or 3 hours a day in the car, fighting the heat and crazy truck drivers. The other couple decided to take on less turf and, naturally, didn't see as much; they even missed Cortona and some of my other favorite towns. Instead, they spent an entire afternoon in a Montepulciano cafe, splitting a bottle of Vino Nobile, staring over a wrought-iron balcony at a church in the distance. In hindsight,

Sangiovese vines growing in a vineyard near Montalcino.

they considered that stop the pinnacle of their trip.

Rule #2: Remember, distances between towns are short.

Visiting Tuscany is as easy as traveling around a small U.S. state or midsize Mediterranean island. You can drive from Florence to San Gimignano, Lucca, Pisa, or Siena in around an hour. The entire Chianti wine country is only 48km (30 miles) from north to south, and 32km (20 miles) at its widest point. Once you veer off the autostrada, the roads become slower, but unless you're taking a *strada bianca* (unsurfaced road) to a remote hamlet, they're generally well maintained and signposted (if sometimes erratically). The only problem in summer will be occasional traffic caused by visitors aiming for the same towns as you.

Rule #3: Consider staying in one place over a daily hotel hop.

Checking in and out of hotels is often a tedious hassle—involving packing and unpacking, registering and checking out, and other technicalities that can drain pleasure from a trip. Because many Tuscan towns are within easy reach of one another, you can set up camp in the same hotel for 3 nights—in Siena, for example—and

venture to smaller towns nearby on day trips. From Siena, you can easily visit San Gimignano, Pienza, Colle di Val d'Elsa, Montepulciano, Montalcino, or the Chianti wine country without wasting too much time in the car. You'll save a lot of wear and tear on your soul with this tack, reserving your energy for hotel switches required by longer hauls.

Rule #4: Plan your excursions around lunch.

If you're driving from town to town, plan to reach your destination by noon, which gives you time to hit the tourist office before it closes for the *riposo*. Restaurants usually serve lunch until 2 or 2:30pm, and you'll also need time to park (which is sometimes tricky) and to locate the address of your restaurant (ditto). If you don't want to be beholden to such a schedule, pack a picnic before setting out.

Rule #5: Every now and then, let the train take the strain.

It's cheaper, greener, and hassle free arriving in your Tuscan town for the day by train. The Italian network is inexpensive, accessible, and easy to use—even for beginners. Not every town is handily reached by rail, but the highlights of the region's northwest like Lucca, Pisa, Pistoia, and Prato are all built for seeing by train.

Strategies for Seeing Tuscany

Cheese, a key component of any Tuscan lunch.

Rule #6: The tourist office is the best (and often the friendliest) free resource in any town—so use it.
This guidebook arms you with just about everything you need

to plan an amazing trip to Tuscany. But there's no substitute for the 100 percent local savvy you'll find in most Tuscan destinations, particularly for information on what's happening around town on the day you show up. See p 182 for contact details of Tuscany's tourist offices.

Rule #7: Don't follow these ideas to the letter; use them as building blocks for your trip.
This is a *guidebook,* not a rule book, and was designed to help you piece together your own getaway. You can plan your time in Florence using one section and then hop about Tuscany, in the next few days, using another. It's like an a la carte menu—select one item from column A and another from column B, then mix according to your own tastes and interests, to make the most of my advice. ●

Pick Your Point of Entry

The logical start to your Tuscan adventure is Galileo Galilei airport in Pisa. Flights on regular and budget airlines connect it with most of Europe—and there's a direct flight to New York's JFK Airport between 3 and 6 days a week. However, if you're already touring near Milan, Venice, or Rome, there's no need to think about connecting to Pisa by air. All are well linked to Tuscany by rail or autostrada. Rome and Milan are alternative, hassle-free intercontinental air gateways—both about 1¾ hours from Florence by high-speed train. From Rome, a 277km (172-mile) drive north to Florence on the fast-moving A1 takes you right past some of the highlights of southern and eastern Tuscany: Break your trip in Montepulciano, Cortona, or Arezzo. Milan is slightly farther—298km (183 miles) northwest of Florence—but worth the minimal extra distance if you find a cheaper connection there. A drive down to Florence can pleasantly be broken in Pisa or Lucca. For more about reaching Tuscany by plane, and the options for getting between airports and your final destination, see the "By Plane" section in "Getting There/Getting Around," p 187.

Florence **in One Day**

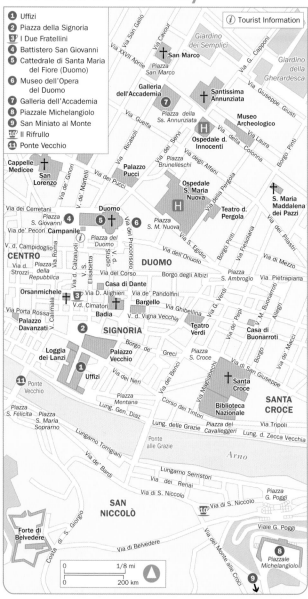

1. Uffizi
2. Piazza della Signoria
3. I Due Fratellini
4. Battistero San Giovanni
5. Cattedrale di Santa Maria del Fiore (Duomo)
6. Museo dell'Opera del Duomo
7. Galleria dell'Accademia
8. Piazzale Michelangiolo
9. San Miniato al Monte
10. Il Rifrullo
11. Ponte Vecchio

i Tourist Information

Previous page: Florence's Duomo.

Florence in a day? "Impossibile," a Florentine might tell you before throwing up her hands in despair and striding away, convinced you are mad. But 1 day in Florence is better than none—provided you rise with the roosters and move with discipline and stamina, to make the most of it. This "greatest hits" itinerary begins with the highlights of the Uffizi, the most rewarding and time-consuming stop. After lunch in the Centro Storico, you'll take in the city's majestic ecclesiastical complex, including the Duomo and Baptistery. Round out the day with a trek to Michelangelo's *David* at the Accademia, followed by an *aperitivo* on the city's lively Left Bank and a stroll across the Ponte Vecchio as night falls. START: **Bus C1 to the Uffizi.**

The Rape of the Sabines.

❶ ★★★ **Uffizi.** This is one of the world's great museums, and its single best repository of Renaissance art. In room after room, you'll confront masterpiece after masterpiece—including Leonardo da Vinci's *Annunciation* (with an angel that could be Mona Lisa's brother), Michelangelo's *Holy Family*, Botticelli's *Birth of Venus*, Giotto's *Ognissanti Madonna*, and more. In old Florentine, *uffizi* means offices, and that's what Vasari deigned this building to be in 1550. But it's come a long way, *bambino*. These Uffizi will dazzle you. (Serious art devotees may want to spend an entire day here.) ⏲ *3 hr.* See p 25.

❷ ★★ **Piazza della Signoria.** The monumental heart of Florence (and Tuscany's most famous square) is an open-air museum of sculpture, dominated by Michelangelo's *David* (a copy of the original, which used to stand here). The powerful mass of the Palazzo Vecchio dominates one side of the square; another is defined by the 14th-century **Loggia dei Lanzi,** filled with ancient and Renaissance statues (the most striking being Bevenuto Cellini's bronze *Perseus* holding aloft the severed head of Medusa). Also check out Giambologna's *Rape of the Sabines*, which marks the point (1584) when Tuscan tastes abandoned drama in favor of melodrama. ⏲ *30 min.*

The Battistero San Giovanni (see p 14).

The Cattedrale di Santa Maria del Fiore.

③ ★ I Due Fratellini. This old-fashioned hole-in-the-wall fiaschetteria sells central Florence's favorite lunch on the move. Choose a tasty sandwich from the long list, wash it down with a "shot" of chianti, and continue on the sightseeing trail. *Via dei Cimatori 38R.* ☎ *055-2396096. www.idue fratellini.com. $. Bus: C2.*

④ ★★★ Battistero San Giovanni. On a hurried first-day tour of Florence, you need invade the inner precincts of the Baptistery only to take in the magnificent 13th-century mosaics lining the inner dome. The major excitement is outside, on the world-famous bronze doors that face the Duomo. Sure, they're replicas (the originals are in the Museo dell'Opera del Duomo; see bullet **⑥**, below); but even the copies are masterpieces. Ghiberti's north doors—a commission he won in 1401 in a public competition against Brunelleschi, Donatello, and Jacopo Della Quercia—are said to mark the start of the Renaissance. ⏱ *30 min. See p 32,* **⑨**.

⑤ ★★ kids Cattedrale di Santa Maria del Fiore (Duomo). Consecrated in 1436, one of Europe's most majestic cathedrals rests under Filippo Brunelleschi's revolutionary dome, a triumph of engineering over gravity. As the symbol of Florence itself, it's a tourist stamping ground of horrendous proportions—but justifiably so. It's part church, part candy cane, part zebra—in stripes of marble-white, bottle-green, and pink. The interior, by contrast, is spartan but has one of Europe's classic views from the top of the cupola. ⏱ *45 min. See p 31,* **⑦**.

⑥ ★ Museo dell'Opera del Duomo. For connoisseurs of Renaissance sculpture, this museum opposite the rear of the Duomo is a shrine, hosting everything from an unfinished, heart-wrenching *Pietà* by Michelangelo to its premier attraction—the restored panels of Lorenzo Ghiberti's *Gates of Paradise*. The works here were deemed too precious to be left to the elements, and so were moved inside from their positions adorning the ecclesiastical monuments. ⏱ *1 hr. See p 42,* **⑦**.

⑦ ★★ Galleria dell'Accademia. You've seen replicas of Michelangelo's *David* all over the world. This gallery has the real thing (1501–04)—a monumental icon of youthful male beauty and a stellar example of Michelangelo's humanism. His four unfinished *Slaves* are equally expressive. Admission can require an hour-long wait, unless you reserve space. ⏱ *30 min., without wait. Via Ricasoll 58–60.* ☎ *050-294883 to reserve* tickets (in English). *www.firenze musei.it. Admission 6.50€–11€ (higher price is during regular special exhibitions). Tues–Sun 8:15am–6:50pm. Bus: C1, 6, 11, 14 or 23.*

Ride bus 23 from Piazza San Marco across the Arno to alight at the Porta San Niccolò, then walk directly uphill.

❽ ★ kids Piazzale Michelangiolo. For a fine view over Florence, head for its panoramic piazza, laid out in 1885. From the balustraded terrace, the city of the Renaissance unfurls before you. In the center of the square is yet another replica *David.* 🕐 *15 min. Bus: 12 or 13.*

❾ ★★★ San Miniato al Monte. As the shadows lengthen, there's no better spot to drink in the views, and the silence, than this ancient Romanesque church surrounded by its monumental graveyard. Time it right and you'll catch the Benedictine monks who still inhabit the complex celebrating Vespers with Gregorian chant. 🕐 *30 min. See p 34, ❶.*

🔟 ★ Il Rifrullo. This laid-back bar is right at the social center of a buzzy Oltrarno corner just downhill from Piazzale Michelangelo. Join

The Ponte Vecchio.

locals and visitors for an aperitivo. *Via San Niccolò 55R.* ☎ *055-2342621. www.ilrifrullo.com. $–$$. Bus: 12 or 13.*

⓫ ★ Ponte Vecchio. The Ponte Vecchio, as its name suggests, is the city's oldest bridge; its latest incarnation dates to 1345, but the shops along it have been taking advantage of the foot traffic since at least the 12th century. Originally occupied by blacksmiths, butchers, and tanners, the shops that flank the bridge have mostly sold gold and silver since the reign of the Medici. Sunset is the ideal time to cross. 🕐 *15 min. Bus: C3 or D.*

The view of Florence from Piazzale Michelangiolo.

Florence in Two Days

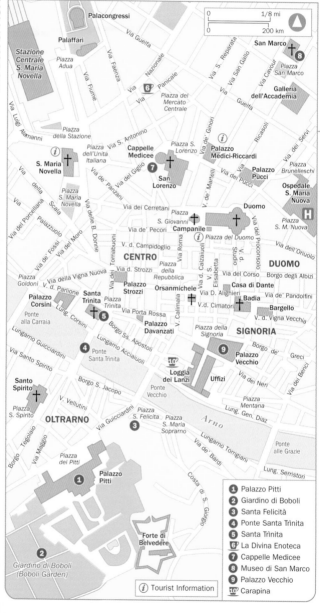

Palacongressi

Via Guelfa

Palaffari

Via Guelfa

Stazione Centrale S. Maria Novella

Piazza Adua

Via Faenza

Via Fiume

Via Nazionale

Via Panicale

San Marco

Piazza San Marco

Galleria dell'Accademia

Via S. Reparata

Via S. Gallo

Via Cavour

Via Luigi Alamanni

Piazza della Stazione

Via S. Antonino

Piazza del Mercato Centrale

Piazza S. Lorenzo

Palazzo Medici-Riccardi

Palazzo Pucci

Via de' Ginori

Via de' Martelli

Via dei Pucci

Ricasoli

Via dei Servi

Piazza Brunelleschi

Ospedale S. Maria Nuova

Via dell'Oriuolo

Piazza S. M. Nuova

Ospedale H

S. Maria Novella

Piazza dell'Unità Italiana

Cappelle Medicee

San Lorenzo

Via de' Panzani

Via del Giglio

Piazza S. Giovanni

Campanile

Duomo

Piazza del Duomo

Via della Scala

Via de' Fossi

Via del Moro

Piazza S. Maria Novella

Via dei Cerretani

S. Giovanni

Via de' Pecori

Via de' Campidoglio

CENTRO

Via de' Tornabuoni

Via d. Strozzi

Palazzo Strozzi

Piazza della Repubblica

Orsanmichele

Via d. Calzaioli

Via Roma

Via dello Studio

V. d. Proconsolo

DUOMO

Via del Corso

Borgo degli Albizi

Casa di Dante

Via D. Alighieri

V.d. Cimatori

Badia

Bargello

Via de' Pandolfini

V. d. Vigna Vecchia

Piazza Goldoni

Via della Vigna Nuova

V. d. Parlione

Palazzo Corsini

Ponte alla Carraia

Santa Trinita

Piazza Trinita

Via Porta Rossa

Palazzo Davanzati

Lungarno Corsini

Borgo Ss. Apostoli

Lungarno Acciaiuoli

Ponte Santa Trinita

Piazza della Signoria

SIGNORIA

Palazzo Vecchio

Borgo de' Greci

Via dei Benci

Borgo S. Jacopo

Loggia dei Lanzi

Uffizi

Via dei Neri

Santo Spirito

Piazza S. Spirito

V. Vellutini

OLTRARNO

Ponte Vecchio

Via Guicciardini

Piazza S. Felicita

Piazza S. Maria Soprarno

Arno

Piazza Mentana

Lung. Gen. Diaz

Lungarno Torrigiani

Via de' Bardi

Ponte alle Grazie

Lung. Serristori

Via Santo Spirito

Via Maggio

Borgo Tegolaio

Piazza dei Pitti

Palazzo Pitti

Forte di Belvedere

Costa di S. Giorgio

Giardino di Boboli (Boboli Garden)

0   1/8 mi
0   200 km

Tourist Information

1 Palazzo Pitti
2 Giardino di Boboli
3 Santa Felicità
4 Ponte Santa Trìnita
5 Santa Trìnita
6 La Divina Enoteca
7 Cappelle Medicee
8 Museo di San Marco
9 Palazzo Vecchio
🍦 Carapina

On your second day in Florence, spend the morning wandering the Oltrarno, the district on the left bank of the Arno. The set-piece attraction here is the Palazzo Pitti and adjacent Giardino di Boboli. Even if you take all morning, you will see only a part of the Pitti Palace's great collection of art, which encompasses not only Renaissance works, but painting and sculpture by later European masters. Stroll through the Boboli Garden before heading back to the Centro Storico for the Medici Chapels (with Michelangelo's sculptures), the artistic delights of Fra' Angelico at San Marco, and Florence's Gothic town hall, the Palazzo Vecchio. START: **Bus C3 or D to Piazza de' Pitti.**

1 ★★ **Palazzo Pitti.** This vast 15th-century Medici palace on the south side of the Arno is second only to the Uffizi in its wealth of artwork. The **Galleria Palatina** on the second floor is reason enough to come to Florence; visit for the Raphaels alone. And the Palatina also has a decent supporting cast if you have a little more time on your hands: the city's most extensive coterie of museums—including exhibitions of costume, modern art, and even the Medici's private digs. ⏱ *2 hr. See p 38,* **13**.

The Galleria Palatina at Palazzo Pitti.

Medici Skywalk. After Cosimo I moved to the Pitti Palace, he commissioned Giorgio Vasari to build a private, aboveground tunnel to the Uffizi and Palazzo Vecchio. The Corridoio Vasariano, built in just 5 months in 1565, runs from the Pitti Palace past the Boboli and above Santa Felicità to the Ponte Vecchio, crosses the river above the bridge's shops, then continues on to the museum that once served as the Medici offices. Lined with paintings, it's open for prebooked visits only—but is regularly shut for restoration, so call ahead. *Reservations (required) and information* ☎ 055-294883. *Guided tours also conducted by Context Travel (*☎ 06-97625204; www.contexttravel.com).

2 ★ **kids Giardino di Boboli.** Laid out between 1549 and 1656, this is the grandest Renaissance garden of Italy. Before departing, take a stroll down the Viottolone, a stunning avenue of pines and cypresses, to the Isolotto, a complex of water and statuary laid out in 1612. ⏱ *45 min. See p 38,* **12**.

3 ★★ **Santa Felicità.** The star works in this tiny Oltrarno church are in the first chapel on your right, paintings by Mannerist master Pontormo (1525–27). A *Deposition* and frescoed *Annunciation* are rife with

The Boboli Gardens (see p 17).

his garish color palette of oranges, pinks, golds, lime greens, and sky blues, and exhibit his trademark surreal sense of figure. ⏱ *15 min. Piazza Santa Felicità.* ☎ *055-213018. Free admission. Daily 8am–noon and 3:30–6:30pm. Bus: C3 or D.*

④ ★★ Ponte Santa Trinita. Cross the Arno by way of Florence's most elegant bridge (but certainly not its most famous one). Built in 1567 by Ammannati, it was destroyed by retreating Germans in 1944 and rebuilt using 16th-century tools and methods in 1957. It is guarded at both ends by statues

representing the seasons. ⏱ *10 min. Bus: C3, D, 11, 36, or 37.*

⑤ ★★ Santa Trinita. There aren't many corners of Florence where you can admire the finest works of the Quattrocento (1400s) in peace, but the historic church of Santa Trinita is one of them. The frescoed chapels are by Lorenzo Monaco (1370–1425) and Domenico Ghirlandaio (1449–94), Michelangelo's first teacher. The marble tomb of Benozzo Federighi was sculpted in 1454 by Luca Della Robbia. ⏱ *20 min. See p 47,* ⑨.

Browse your way north along Florence's upscale shopping street (see p 63), Via de' Tornabuoni, then through San Lorenzo street market to:

⑥ La Divina Enoteca. Stop in for a *panino tartufato* (truffled sandwich) or anything from a long, filling menu that employs only the best ingredients. There's a long wines-by-the-glass list, too. *Via Panicale 19R.* ☎ *055-292723. www.ladivina enoteca.it. $.*

⑦ ★★ Cappelle Medicee. The key sights here are the celebrated

The domes of the Medici Chapels flanked by San Lorenzo.

The Palazzo Vecchio.

Medici tombs by Michelangelo—two of his grandest creations that alas honored scurrilous members of the clan. Nevertheless, the great artist portrayed them as idealized princes of the Renaissance. Allegorical figures representing *Night* and *Day*, and *Dawn* and *Dusk*, face each other across his perfectly proportioned Renaissance sacristy. ⏱ *1 hr. See p 45,* ❷.

❽ ★★★ kids **Museo di San Marco.** This Dominican convent has been converted to a unique museum honoring Florence's gentlest painter of the "international Gothic" style, Fra' Angelico (1395–1455). Angelico's art is touched with a pacifying power, especially his iconic *Annunciation,* as are the walls of the 44 friars' cells upstairs, which he frescoed with scenes (and plenty of Dominican saints) to foster meditation. Don't leave without stopping in at the Pilgrim's Hospice, now a mini-museum to Angelico, centered on his beatific, weightless *Deposition.* ⏱ *1hr. Piazza San Marco 3.* ☎ *055-2388608. Admission 4€. Mon–Fri 8:15am–1:20pm; Sat–Sun 8:15am–4:20pm; closed 1st, 3rd, and 5th Sun and 2nd and 4th Mon of month. Bus: C1, 1, 6, 7, 10, 11, 14, 17, 20, 23, 25, 31, 32, or 33.*

❾ ★ kids **Palazzo Vecchio.** The civic heart of Florence, this crenellated 13th-century palace is still the city hall. The highlight inside is the **Salone dei Cinquecento,** or "Hall of the 500," where the great council met. It's decorated with gaudy Vasari frescoes, but houses Michelangelo's *Genius of Victory,* originally intended for the tomb of Pope Julius II. ⏱ *1 hr. See p 29,* ❹.

🔟 ★★★ **Carapina.** The strictly seasonal fruit flavors at this back-street gelateria are sensational. *Via Lambertesca 18R.* ☎ *055-291128. $.*

The back streets of the Oltrarno.

Florence in Three Days

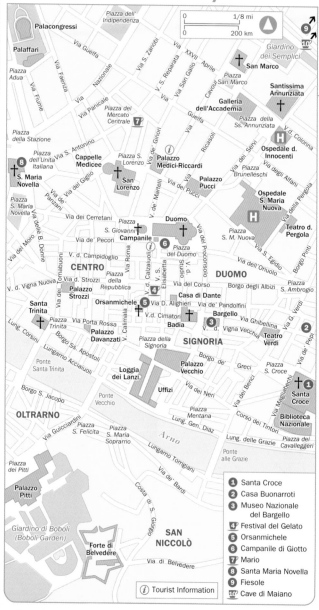

Palacongressi

Palaffari

Piazza Adua

Piazza della Stazione

Piazza dell'Unità Italiana

S. Maria Novella

Piazza S. Maria Novella

Piazza dell' Indipendenza

Via Guelfa

Via Nazionale

Via Faenza

Via Flume

Via Panicale

Via S. Antonino

Cappelle Medicee

Via del Giglio

Via de' Panzani

San Lorenzo

Piazza del Mercato Centrale

Piazza S. Lorenzo

Palazzo Medici-Riccardi

Palazzo Pucci

Via dei Pucci

Via de' Martelli

Via dei Cerretani

Piazza S. Giovanni

Campanile

Via de' Pecori

Via d. Campidoglio

CENTRO

Piazza della Repubblica

Palazzo Strozzi

V. d. Vigna Nuova

Via d. Strozzi

Santa Trinita

Piazza Trinita

Palazzo Davanzati

Via Porta Rossa

Via de' Tornabuoni

Borgo Ss. Apostoli

Via delle B. Donne

Via del Moro

Lung. Corsini

Ponte Santa Trinita

Borgo S. Jacopo

OLTRARNO

Via Guicciardini

Piazza dei Pitti

Palazzo Pitti

Giardino di Boboli (Boboli Garden)

Piazza S. Felicita

Piazza S. Maria Soprarno

Ponte Vecchio

Via de' Ginori

Via Cavour

Galleria dell'Accademia

Via Ricasoli

Via S. Zanobi

Via S. Reparata

Via XXVII Aprile

V. S. Gallo

Via San Gallo

San Marco

Piazza San Marco

Santissima Annunziata

Piazza della Ss. Annunziata

V. d. Colonna

Via dei Servi

V. d. degli Alfani

Ospedale d. Innocenti

Piazza Brunelleschi

Ospedale S. Maria Nuova

Via della Pergola

Teatro d. Pergola

Borgo Pinti

Duomo

Piazza del Duomo

Piazza S. M. Nuova

Via dell'Oriuolo

Via S. Egidio

DUOMO

Via del Corso

Borgo degli Albizi

Piazza S. Ambrogio

Via de' Calzaiuoli

Via de' Cimatori

Orsanmichele

Casa di Dante

Via D. Alighieri

Badia

Bargello

Via de' Pandolfini

Via Ghibellina

Via G. Verdi

Via d. Vigna Vecchia

Teatro Verdi

Via de' Pepi

Piazza della Signoria

SIGNORIA

Palazzo Vecchio

Loggia dei Lanzi

Uffizi

Borgo de' Greci

Via dei Neri

Via dei Benci

Piazza S. Croce

Santa Croce

Via Maglabecchi

Biblioteca Nazionale

Piazza Mentana

Lung. Gen. Diaz

Corso dei Tintori

Lung. delle Grazie

Piazza dei Cavalleggeri

Ponte alle Grazie

Arno

Lungarno Acciaiuoli

Lungarno Torrigiani

Via de' Bardi

Costa di S. Giorgio

SAN NICCOLÒ

Forte di Belvedere

Via di Belvedere

Giardino de' Semplici

0   1/8 mi
0   200 km

① Santa Croce
② Casa Buonarroti
③ Museo Nazionale del Bargello
④ Festival del Gelato
⑤ Orsanmichele
⑥ Campanile di Giotto
⑦ Mario
⑧ Santa Maria Novella
⑨ Fiesole
⑩ Cave di Maiano

ⓘ Tourist Information

A third day in Florence yields another glimpse of the city's treasures. The Bargello is the world's greatest museum of Renaissance sculpture. Combine it with the city headquarters of the Dominicans and Franciscans, respectively, Santa Maria Novella and Santa Croce, to form the cultural core of your day. (Michelangelo and Galileo, among others, are buried in the latter.) As dusk approaches, head for the hills for a stroll and a romantic dinner in the Etruscan hill-town of Fiesole. START: **Bus C3 or 23 to Piazza Santa Croce.**

① ★★ kids Santa Croce. Victorian critic John Ruskin had the right idea: "Wait then for an entirely light morning: rise with the sun and go to Santa Croce, with a good opera glass in your pocket." Travelers call it "the Westminster Abbey of Tuscany," because this 14th-century church contains the tombs of the Renaissance's brightest lights—notably Michelangelo and Galileo. The great Giotto di Bondone (ca. 1267–1337) frescoed two tiny, time-worn chapels in the right transept, but is almost outshone by better preserved works by his own student, Taddeo Gaddi, who frescoed *Scenes from the Life of the Virgin* between 1332 and 1338, including the first night scene ever painted. ⏲ *1 hr. Piazza Santa Croce.* ☎ *055-2466105. www.santacroceopera.it. Admission 5€; 8€ with Casa Buonarroti (see ②, below). Mon–Sat 9:30am–5:30pm, Sun 1–5:30pm. Bus: C3 or 23.*

② Casa Buonarroti. The house inhabited by Michelangelo's nephew Lionardo is preserved as a shrine to the master. Michelangelo's earliest sculptures are upstairs: the Donatello-esque *Madonna of the Steps,* carved before 1492 when he was a teenage student in the Medici school. A few months later, the prodigy carved another marble, a confused, almost Pisano-like tangle of bodies known as the *Battle of the Centaurs and Lapiths.* ⏲ *45 min. Via Ghibellina 70.* ☎ *055-241752. www.casabuonarroti.it. Admission 6.50€; 8€ with Santa Croce (see ①, above). Wed–Mon 9:30am–2pm. Bus: C2, C3, or 14.*

③ ★★ Museo Nazionale del Bargello. This Gothic fortress is now a vast repository holding some of the finest sculpture created during the Renaissance and later,

Santa Croce.

Some of the many gelato flavors you'll find at Festival del Gelato.

including Donatello's *St. George*, originally sculpted for Orsanmichele, and his own bronze *David*. The Bargello also houses, along with countless other works, another Michelangelo *David*—created 3 decades after the version in the Accademia. ⏱ *1½ hr. See p 30,* ⑥.

4 Festival del Gelato. You better have your decisive hat on if you stop for an ice cream here. I lost count of the fantastical, neon-lit flavors at 70. *Via del Corso 75R. No phone. $.*

5 ★★ Orsanmichele. Although the museum is now usually closed, a circuit round the outside of this

St. Mark, in one of the niches that surround Orsanmichele.

grain warehouse turned church is the perfect accompaniment to your gelato. Each of the sculpted niches was commissioned by one of Florence's great trade guilds, including the powerful Arte della Lana (wool manufacturers). After you've toured the outside, take a quick look inside. ⏱ *15 min. See p 43,* ⑩.

6 ★★ kids Campanile di Giotto. An ideal counterpoint to Brunelleschi's dome, this Gothic bell tower was completed at the end of the 14th century, long after Giotto, its designer, had died. Walk 414 steps to the top of the campanile for a panoramic view of the dome and all central Florence. Queues here are usually much shorter than those for the Duomo. ⏱ *30 min. See p 31,* ⑧.

7 ★ Mario. A tiny trattoria that has become a lunchtime institution: Expect uncompromising Florentine food, communal tables, keen prices, and a smiling crush of local workers, tourists, and market traders. *Via Rosina 2R (at Piazza del Mercato Centrale).* ☎ *055-218550. www.trattoria-mario.com. $–$$.*

8 ★★ Santa Maria Novella. The Dominicans began construction on this church in 1246, and it is filled with some of Tuscany's most important frescoes, notably Masaccio's epoch-defining 1427 *Trinity*. The *Scenes from the Lives of the Virgin Mary and St. John the Baptist* (1485–90) in the apse were painted by Michelangelo's teacher, Domenico Ghirlandaio. Twelve years later, Filippino Lippi, illegitimate son of Filippo and nun Lucrezia Buti, decorated the **Cappella Filippo Strozzi** with scenes from the life of his patron's name-saint, St. Philip. Other treasures include a carved *Crucifix* by Filippo Brunelleschi. ⏱ *45 min. See p 43,* ⓫.

⑨ ★ kids **Fiesole.** As well as its slightly overpriced archaeological (mostly Roman) attractions, the ancient hilltop settlement of Fiesole supplies a welcome change of pace, and an escape from the oppressive heat and crowds of Florence. The little town was here long before its neighbor down in the valley: It was already an important Etruscan settlement in the 8th century B.C. The best thing to do is stroll: A route along Via Marini, Via delle Mura Etrusche, then uphill on Via Giovanni and Via del Cimitero, skirts the Roman ruins, takes in the splendid little Franciscan convent, and ends up at the most spectacular balcony above Florence. ⏱ *1½ hr. www. museidifiesole.it. Bus: 7 (20 min. from Santa Maria Novella).*

The Duomo in Fiesole.

Santa Maria Novella.

⑩ ★ **Cave di Maiano.** For a final goodbye to the city, take the short ride to this converted farmhouse. Expect hearty regional cuisine, such as chicken roasted under a brick with peppers, and succulent pastas, like green tortellini. Adventurous diners might like to walk the entire 8km (5 miles) back to Florence, with the city lights, twinkling in the distance, to lead the way. You can stop at any point along the way and board bus #7 back to the center. *Via delle Cave 16, Maiano.* ☎ *055-59133. www.trattoriacavedimaiano. it. $$–$$$.*

The Best of the **Uffizi**

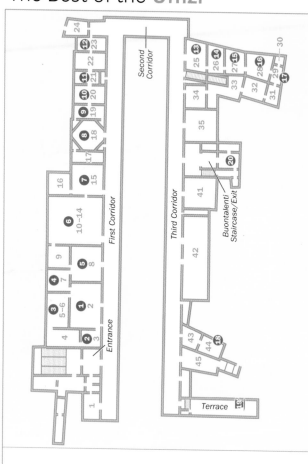

1 Cimabue, Duccio, and Giotto
2 14th-century Siena
3 International Gothic
4 Masaccio and Uccello
5 Filippo Lippi and
   Piero della Francesca
6 Botticelli
7 Verrocchio and Leonardo
8 *La Tribuna*
9 Perugino and Signorelli
10 Dürer and Cranach
11 15th-century Venice
12 Mantegna and Correggio
13 Michelangelo
14 Raphael and del Sarto
15 Florentine Mannerism
16 Titian
17 Parmigianino
18 Rembrandt
19 Uffizi café
20 Caravaggio and Gentileschi

Once the Medici business offices, the Galleria degli Uffizi is now the world's finest museum of Renaissance painting. If you don't have a Firenze Card (see p 29), reserving tickets is essential: Without reservations, expect to queue for up to 6 hours during peak periods. **Firenze Musei** takes reservations in advance, in English over the phone and online (☎ **055-294883**; www.firenzemusei.it), and also at their office opposite the main gallery entrance. START: **Bus C1 to Piazza dei Giudici. Trip length: 3 hr. Admission: 6.50€–11€ plus booking fee 4€. Opening hours: Tues–Sun 8:15am–6:50pm (sometimes Tues until 10pm in summer).**

❶ ★★★ **Room 2.** This opening gallery introduces a trio of great Madonnas. Though still with its roots in Byzantine artistic conventions, Cimabue's *Santa Trinita Maestà* (1280) takes tentative steps towards realistic painting. Duccio di Buoninsegna's *Rucellai Madonna* (1285) influenced a generation of Sienese art. Three decades later, Giotto (1276–1337) painted the most solid *Maestà* (Virgin in majesty) of them all, the *Ognissanti Madonna*.

❷ ★★★ **Room 3.** This room gives a taste of 14th-century Sienese painting—none finer than Simone Martini's ethereal *Annunciation* (1313), showing a horrified Mary learning of her Immaculate Conception. The Lorenzetti brothers, Pietro and Ambrogio, also created masterpieces displayed here, before the Black Death of 1348 claimed their lives; the most sophisticated (and much emulated) work is Ambrogio's *Presentation at the Temple* (1342).

❸ ★★ **Room 5–6.** The hyper-decorative style known as "international Gothic" is showcased here. Lorenzo Monaco (1370–1425), Fra' Angelico (1395–1455), and Gentile da Fabriano (1370–1427) were its main Florentine exponents. The latter's 1423 *Procession of the Magi* is the iconic work of the genre.

❹ ★★ **Room 7.** Renaissance innovations in painting were possible in part because of Masaccio (1401–28)

The Loggia dei Lanzi's ancient and Renaissance statues are located right outside the Uffizi.

and Paolo Uccello (1397–1475) and their revolutionary use of perspective. Look at the characteristically chaotic foreshortening in Uccello's *Battle of San Romano* (1456), depicting a Florentine victory over the Sienese army. A rare piece by Masaccio (he was dead at 27) is his *Madonna and Child with St. Anne* (1424).

❺ ★★ **Room 8.** Numerous paintings by Fra' Filippo Lippi (1406–69) are displayed in this early Renaissance room. His *Madonna and Child with Two Young Angels* is an overtly romantic portrait of the amorous monk's mistress. Piero della Francesca's *Portrait of Federico da*

Botticelli's Allegory of Spring.

Montefeltro and Battista Sforza (1470) is as famed for the perspective Tuscan landscape as for the profiles of the duke and duchess of Urbino.

⑥ ★★★ Rooms 10–14. Sandro Botticelli (1445–1510) authored perhaps the most visited paintings in Florence: his *Birth of Venus* and the enigmatic *Primavera (Allegory of Spring)*. *Primavera's* varied cast includes (from the left) Mercury, the Three Graces, Venus, and Flora—the goddess of spring who was known as Chloris, before her rape by Zephyr (the West Wind), the scene on the right of the panel.

⑦ ★★ Room 15. Leonardo da Vinci (1452–1519) is the main man here, not least for an unfinished *Adoration of the Magi*. His *Annunciation* (1480) is known for its tricky use of a vanishing point (look at it from the lower-right corner). The *Baptism of Christ* is by his teacher, Andrea del Verrocchio (1435–88).

⑧ ★★ Room 18. Octagonal *La Tribuna* is the most lavish salon in the Uffizi, decorated with lapis lazuli for air, red walls for fire, green *pietre dure* for earth, and mother-of-pearl for water. Its focus is the *Medici Venus*, a medieval copy of a Greek original whose pose was copied by Botticelli. Baroque artist Agnolo Bronzino (1503–72) painted the portrait of Eleonora of Toledo, wife of

Cosimo I. When the Medici tombs were opened in 1857, her body was discovered buried in the same satin dress she wore in the painting. Although you are no longer allowed to walk through the room, you can also just about make out Raphael's *St. John the Baptist in the Desert* (1518) through the gloom.

⑨ Room 19. Perugino's (1446–1523) stern *Portrait of Francesco delle Opere* shines brightest here. Cortonese Luca Signorelli (1445–1523), whose style influenced Michelangelo's Sistine Chapel ceiling, is also represented.

⑩ ★ Room 20. This gallery exhibits paintings by Germans who worked in Florence. Albrecht Dürer (1471–1528) was the undisputed master of the German Renaissance. Contrast his *Adam and Eve* with one by Lucas Cranach (1472–1553). Dürer's work is a study of the body; Cranach's shows a more erotic bent.

⑪ Room 21. Venetian masters of the 15th and 16th centuries shine in this *sala*—especially Giovanni Bellini (1430–1516). His complex *Sacra Allegoria* is the most memorable, showing an advanced understanding of perspective.

⑫ ★ Room 23. This gallery is a showcase for Andrea Mantegna's triptych of the *Adoration of the Magi, Circumcision,* and *Ascension*

painted between 1463 and 1470. There are also noted works by Antonio da Correggio (1489–1534).

⑬ ★★ Room 25. Michelangelo's only painting in Florence—a tondo (round painting) of the *Holy Family*, was commissioned by the Doni family, and so nicknamed the *Doni Tondo* (1506–08). Perfectionist Michelangelo even designed the frame. The family's muscular forms and contorted poses suggest Michelangelo's preference for sculpture.

⑭ ★ Room 26. This salon of High Renaissance compositions is dominated by Raphael's restored *Madonna del Cardellino*, in which his usual triangular, hierarchical layout is enlivened by a goldfinch. Also here is the *Madonna of the Harpies* by Andrea del Sarto (1486–1530), a pioneer of Florentine Mannerism.

⑮ ★ Room 27. Florentine Mannerism reaches fever pitch in this room dedicated to Rosso Fiorentino (1485–1541), Del Sarto's pupil. Fiorentino is best appreciated in his *Moses Defends the Daughters of Jethro* (1523), which owes a heavy debt to Michelangelo. Del Sarto's other renowned pupil, Jacopo Pontormo (1494–1557), is represented by *Supper at Emmaus*.

⑯ ★★ Room 28. This *sala* is dedicated to Venetian visionary and master colorist, Titian (1488–1566).

The highlight is his 1538 *Venus of Urbino,* lounging nude on her bed.

⑰ Room 29. The late Mannerist painter Parmigianino (1505–40) dominates this gallery. His *Madonna and Child* is more usually known as the *Madonna with the Long Neck*, for obvious reasons.

⑱ ★ Room 44. Compare the two self-portraits by Dutch great Rembrandt van Rijn—one in his prime (1634), the other, more melancholic, as a senior citizen in the year of his death (1669).

⑲ The Uffizi café, a bar with a view atop the loggia, serves cold drinks, snacks, and coffee at prices not so out of line with central Florence. *Piazzale degli Uffizi.* ☎ *055-23885.* $–$$.

⑳ ★ 1st Floor. Bad boy of the Baroque, Caravaggio (1571–1610) is the star of these refurbished rooms. His screeching circular *Medusa* (1599), mounted on a circular shield, is a typically deranged self-portrait. His fondness for extreme *chiaroscuro* (light and shade) shaped art for a generation. Artemisia Gentileschi's violent *Judith Slaying Holofernes* (1621) shows that she, among all who copied Caravaggio, was his true heir.

Leonardo da Vinci's Annunciation.

The Heart of the Centro Storico

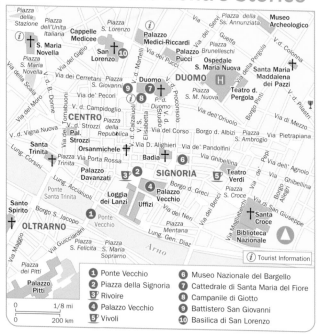

1 Ponte Vecchio
2 Piazza della Signoria
3 Rivoire
4 Palazzo Vecchio
5 Vivoli
6 Museo Nazionale del Bargello
7 Cattedrale di Santa Maria del Fiore
8 Campanile di Giotto
9 Battistero San Giovanni
10 Basilica di San Lorenzo

I n Florence's flat, compact historic core, you can wander stone streets that remain essentially the same as they were when Michelangelo, Leonardo da Vinci, and Galileo trod them. The few blocks that make up this Centro Storico tell the history of the city itself, and of its art and architecture above all. This is a demanding full-day itinerary, so wear comfortable shoes and bring water. If you're traveling in July or August, be aware that walking the hot, crowded streets can be a draining experience. START: **Bus C3 to Ponte Vecchio.**

1 ★ kids **Ponte Vecchio.** Built in 1345 across the Arno's narrowest stretch, the Ponte Vecchio was the only bridge spared destruction by the retreating Nazi army in 1944. Florence's greatest goldsmith, Benvenuto Cellini, ran his business in the middle of the bridge—one of many jewelers to have replaced the medieval butchers and tanners who originally traded here. ⏱ 10 min. Bus: C3 or D.

2 ★★ **Piazza della Signoria.** The center of civic life in Florence for centuries, this landmark square in the shadow of Arnolfo di Cambio's massive Palazzo Vecchio was the site of Savonarola's "Bonfire of the Vanities" in 1497, and then the Dominican zealot's own pyre a year later on

Rowers on the Arno, passing under the Ponte Vecchio.

(What beautiful marble you've ruined!)" ⏱ *30 min. Bus: C1 or C2.*

3 **Rivoire.** If you can (just this once) bear the inflated prices, pause for a coffee and a snack at this landmark cafe—the best positioned in Florence for taking in the glories of the piazza. *Piazza della Signoria.* ☎ *055-212412. $–$$$.*

4 ★ kids **Palazzo Vecchio.** Florence's "Old Palace" became home to Cosimo I and the Medici in 1540, but it dates to the 13th century, when it was built by Gothic master builder Arnolfo di Cambio. (Di Cambio's 92m/308-ft. landmark tower, which still graces the skyline, was an engineering feat in its day.) The highlight of the interior is the "Hall of the 500" *(Salone dei Cinquecento)*, frescoed by Giorgio Vasari and his assistants in the 16th century. Wax-pigment frescoes by Leonardo melted when braziers were brought in to speed up the drying process (their remains are still being hunted to this day).

the same spot (now marked with a small plaque). Away from the crowd-pulling blockbusters, less celebrated statuary includes Giambologna's equestrian *Cosimo I* and Bartolomeo Ammannati's controversial *Fountain of Neptune* that inspired a 16th-century chant: "*Ammannato, Ammannato, che bel marmo hai rovinato!*

Discount Sightseeing Passes

The **Firenze Card** (www.firenzecard.it) is valid for 72 hours, includes bus transport, costs 50€, and includes entrance to around 25 sites, including the Uffizi, Accademia, Cappella Brancacci, Palazzo Pitti, and San Marco. It also gets you into shorter lines, making pre-booking tickets unnecessary. Any E.U. citizen 17 and under enters free with a cardholder. **Amici degli Uffizi membership** (www.amici degliuffizi.it) costs 60€ for adults, 40€ anyone 25 and under, 100€ for a family, and is valid for a calendar year. It secures admission (without queuing) into 15 or so state museums, including the Uffizi, Accademia, San Marco, Cappelle Medicee, and Palazzo Pitti. Two children go free with a family ticket, and membership permits multiple visits (useful for the Uffizi). Join Tuesday through Saturday inside Uffizi entrance #2; take identification. The **Opera del Duomo** sells a number of *cumulativi*, including one that covers Brunelleschi's cupola and the Museo dell'Opera for 11€. Enquire at the ticket office.

The Fountain of Neptune (see p 29).

Michelangelo's sculpture *Genius of Victory* survives, thankfully, along with Donatello's bronze group upstairs, *Judith Slaying Holofernes*, cast in 1455. You can also visit the private apartments of Eleanor of Toledo, the Spanish wife of Cosimo I,

Cafe Rivoire (see p 29).

and the chamber where religious zealot Girolamo Savonarola endured a dozen torture sessions, including "twists" on the rack. ⏱ 1½ hr. *Piazza della Signoria.* ☎ *055-2768224. Admission 6€. Mon–Wed and Fri–Sat 9am–7:30pm; Thurs 9am–2pm; Sun 10am–6pm. Ticket office closes 1 hr. before palace. Bus: C1 or C2.*

5 ★★★ **Vivoli.** Detour into the warren of alleys behind the Palazzo Vecchio to this unassuming cafe-cum-gelateria, which serves the city's most celebrated ice cream. Choose your exquisite flavor: fig, melon, chocolate-orange, or even rice. *Via Isola delle Stinche 7R (at Via della Vigna Vecchia).* ☎ *055-292334. $.*

6 ★★ **Museo Nazionale del Bargello.** This grim Gothic fortress—once a site of public executions—centers on a courtyard with a vaulted loggia and portico. Its sculpture collection is the Renaissance's finest, including Donatello's *David* (the first free-standing nude since the Roman era), and side-by-side bronze reliefs depicting the

The Palazzo Vecchio (see p 29).

Sacrifice of Isaac by Brunelleschi and Ghiberti. They were judged in a 1401 competition to decide who should get the commission for the north doors of the Baptistery; Ghiberti won. Downstairs, the 1500s room features works by Giambologna and Cellini, and another *David* by Michelangelo. ⏲ *1½ hr. Via del Proconsolo 4 (at Via Ghibellina).* ☎ *055-2388606. www.firenzemusei.it/bargello. Admission 4€. Daily 8:15am–1:50pm (sometimes until 4:20pm in summer). Closed 2nd and 4th Mon and 1st, 3rd, and 5th Sun of month. Bus: C1 or C2.*

⑦ ★★ kids Cattedrale di Santa Maria del Fiore. From 1294 to 1436, builders labored to construct what was (in its day) the largest cathedral on the planet, but the flamboyant neo-Gothic facade wasn't added until the 19th century. It's a polychrome jumble of marble stripes in sugar-cane colors, but few fault the dome Brunelleschi imposed over it, 105m (351 ft.) off

the ground; climbing it is one of the joys of Florence. You mount 463 spiraling steps to the ribbed dome for a sublime panoramic view. Afterward, you needn't spend too much time inside; much of the art, frescoes, votive offerings, pews, and memorials were swept away or have been moved elsewhere for safekeeping. The most noted is Paolo Uccello's 1436 frescoed "statue" of English mercenary Sir John Hawkwood, on the wall of the left aisle. ⏲ *45 min. Piazza del Duomo. www.opera duomo.firenze.it. Free admission to cathedral; 8€ dome (Piazza del Duomo combination tickets available). Cathedral Mon–Wed, Fri 10am–5pm; Thurs 10am–4:30pm; Sat 10am–4:45pm; Sun 1:30–4:45pm. Dome Mon–Fri 8:30am–6:20pm; Sat 8:30am–5pm. Bus: C1 or C2.*

⑧ ★★ kids Campanile di Giotto. Giotto, Andrea Pisano, and Francesco Talenti collaborated to build this 81m (269-ft.) *tricolore* marble bell tower next to the Duomo. The tower's bells inside are called *Grossa, Beona, Completa, Cheirica,* and *Squilla* (or Big, Tipsy, Finished, Priestling, and Shrieker). Climb the tower's 414 steps for a panoramic

Campanile di Giotto.

Ghiberti's Baptistery doors.

view of Florence and a unique perspective on Brunelleschi's dome. When others are queuing around the block waiting to scale the dome, there's often no one waiting here. ⏱ *30 min. Piazza del Duomo (at Via dei Calzaiuoli).* ☎ *055-2302885.*

Admission 6€ (Piazza del Duomo combination tickets available). Daily 8:30am–6:50pm. Bus: C2.

❾ ★★★ Battistero San Giovanni. This 11th- and 12th-century octagonal baptistery, named

The Medici

One family, originally pharmacists from the Mugello, has come to symbolize Florence's Renaissance: the **Medici.** Excluding a brief republican interlude, they controlled Florence (often as brutal despots) for 3 centuries. The first to rise to public prominence was **Cosimo "il Vecchio"** (1389–1464), papal banker and patron of Donatello, Fra' Angelico, and Filippo Lippi. His grandson **Lorenzo "The Magnificent"** (1449–92), who survived an assassination attempt at Easter Mass (the Pazzi Conspiracy), knew Botticelli and Michelangelo, dabbled in poetry, and funded a Platonic academy. His death signaled the end of Florence's golden age—the baton passed to Rome. **Cosimo I** (1519–74), the first Grand Duke of Tuscany, built the Uffizi and bought the Pitti Palace. The family also spawned three popes, including **Leo X** and his nephew **Clement VII**—nepotism was the other great family business. Long years of dissolute decline ended with the death of drunkard Giangastone in 1737, and Medici treasures passed to Tuscany.

after San Giovanni (St. John the Baptist, patron of the city), is visited mainly for the gilded bronze doors on three of its eight sides. The doors are copies hung in 1990; originals are exhibited in the Museo dell'Opera del Duomo (p 42, **7**). The most photographed are Lorenzo Ghiberti's east doors, facing the Duomo, which the typically critical Michelangelo dubbed "The Gates of Paradise." The panels illustrate scenes from the Old Testament. Ghiberti also cast the north doors, beating Brunelleschi in a 1401 competition for the commission; the job took him 21 years. Andrea Pisano made the Gothic south doors in 1336. Dominated by a figure of Christ, and packed with imaginative detail, the 13th-century mosaics inside are very much worth a look. ⏱ *15 min. Piazza San Giovanni.* ☎ *055-2302885. Admission 4€ (Piazza del Duomo combination tickets available). Mon–Sat 12:15–6:30pm; Sun and 1st Sat of month 8:30am–1:30pm; June–Oct Thurs–Sat 12:15–10.30pm. Bus: C2.*

10 ★ **San Lorenzo.** The overall effect of this basilica, which houses the tombs of many a Medici, is almost Byzantine; one Bulgarian critic called it "a Florentine Hagia Sophia looming over a souk" (a reference to the tourist-oriented Mercato di San Lorenzo, which fills the surrounding streets). The Medici shelled out big bags of gold for it, however. The taller of the two domes at the chancel shelters the **Cappella dei Principi,** the shallower cupola covering Michelangelo's **New Sacristy** (p 45, **2**). Commissioned in 1516, Michelangelo's model for the facade was deemed unacceptable to the Medici, who went to Brunelleschi, to design the **Old Sacristy** at the end of the north transept. Donatello created two pulpits with dramatic bronze panels in the nave. ⏱ *30 min. Piazza San Lorenzo.* ☎ *055-214012. Admission 3.50€. Mon–Sat 10am–5pm; Mar–Oct also Sun 1:30–5pm. Bus: C1.*

San Lorenzo market.

Oltrarno

1 San Miniato al Monte
2 Piazzale Michelangiolo
3 Giardino delle Rose
4 Casa Siviero
5 Via dell'Olmo
6 Santa Felicità
7 Santo Spirito
8 Borgo Antico
9 Cappella Brancacci
10 La Carraia
11 La Specola
12 Giardino di Boboli
13 Palazzo Pitti

ⓘ Tourist Information

Oltrarno, Florence's "other side of the Arno," was once the artisan heart of the city. You'll see signs that tradition dies hard in the crafts and antique shops lining Borgo San Jacopo and Via Maggio. But workshops and studios aren't all the neighborhood has to offer. This tour starts with one of the finest views over Florence, before taking in the very peaks of Renaissance art and architecture, and quiet corners of a district that still has a real, working feel. START: Bus 12 or 13 to Viale Galileo Galilei.

1 ★★★ **San Miniato al Monte.** This most spiritual of Florentine churches is one of the city's truly ancient places. Built from 1018 in the Pisan-Romanesque style, inside and out, it takes its name from Florence's first Christian martyr. St. Minias apparently picked up his severed head and carried it to this spot in 250 A.D. The nave and aisles are decorated with Taddeo Gaddi's fading frescoes (from 1341) of the Gospel witnesses, and topped with a soaring, intricate inlaid wooden ceiling. Upstairs, off the raised choir, the Gothic sacristy was frescoed in 1387 with *Stories of the Legend of St. Benedict* by Spinello Aretino, a follower of Giotto. 🕐 *45 min. Viale Galileo.* ☎ *055-2342731. Free admission (1€ sacristy). Daily 8am–12:30pm and 3–5:30pm. Bus: 12 or 13.*

2 ★ kids Piazzale Michelangiolo. Tacky, perhaps; touristy, certainly, but this grand balcony over the city is *the* essential photo stop on any tour of Florence's Left Bank. From where (another) *David* looks out over his city, right at the Palazzo Vecchio that was his first home, you can do the same. 🕐 *15 min. Bus: 12 or 13.*

3 Giardino delle Rose. This little oasis of peace, planted with over 1,000 varieties of roses, makes a perfect pause half-way down the hill from Piazzale Michelangelo. There's also a little Japanese garden donated to Florence by the city of Kyoto. 🕐 *15 min. Viale Poggi 2. No phone. Free admission. May–June daily 8am–8pm. Bus: 12 or 13.*

4 ★ Casa Siviero. Inside a colonial villa right on the Arno is the private collection of resistance fighter and art historian Rodolfo Siviero (1911–83). The bulk of the paintings are minor works, ancient and modern. Of particular interest is a set of medallions Siviero commissioned after World War II to honor those who helped liberate his city, including Winston Churchill and Dwight D. Eisenhower. 🕐 *30 min. Lungarno*

Piazzale Michelangiolo.

Serristori 1–3 (at Piazza Poggi).
☎ 055-2345219. www.museocasa siviero.it. Free admission. Sat 10am–2pm and 3–7pm (Sept–June 10am–6pm); Sun–Mon 10am–1pm. Bus: D, 12, 13, or 23.

5 Via dell'Olmo. High on a wall on the western side of this tiny street is a sign that reads: *"Qui arriva la piena del Arno il 4 Novembre 1966."* That's the height the flood waters reached in November

San Miniato al Monte.

1966 before they began to subside that evening. Countless of the city's treasures were damaged, most famously Cimabue's *Crucifixion* in Santa Croce, and more than 100 Florentines lost their lives. ⏱ *5 min. Bus: D, 12, 13, or 23.*

6 ★★ **Santa Felicità.** The 2nd-century Greek sailors who lived in this neighborhood brought Christianity to Florence, and this little church was probably the second to be established in the city, the first edition of it rising in the late 4th century. The current version was built in the 1730s. Stop by to view paintings by Mannerist Pontormo (1525–27), particularly his emotive *Deposition.* ⏱ *15 min. See p 17,* **3**. *Bus: C3 or D.*

7 ★ **Santo Spirito.** This outwardly plain church is where Brunelleschi's ordered architectural style reached its apotheosis. The nave and transept are supported by an unbroken chain of columns, and supplemented with 38 peripheral chapels. The whole effect is of a space filled with light and grandeur, that's only partly spoiled by a Baroque canopy above the altar. The sacristy houses a carved wooden *Crucifixion* attributed to Michelangelo ⏱ *30 min. Piazza Santo Spirito.* ☎ *055-210030. Free admission. Church Thurs–Tues 10am–12:30pm and 4–5:30pm. Bus: D, 6, 11, 36, or 37.*

8 ★ **Borgo Antico.** Stop in for a hearty salad in this most Florentine of squares. Our favorite is made with shrimp, avocado, and buffalo mozzarella. Pizzas and pasta are great if you're hungrier. *Piazza Santo Spirito 6R.* ☎ *055-210437. www.borgoanticofirenze.com. $–$$. Bus: D, 6, 11, 36, or 37.*

9 ★★★ **Cappella Brancacci.** The frescoes in the right transept chapel of Florence's Carmelite church stand on the brink of what we now call "the Renaissance." Originally painted by Masaccio and

Piazza Santo Spirito.

The frescoes of the Cappella Brancacci.

Masolino between 1424 and 1427, the *Scenes from the Life of St. Peter* were finished off by Filippino Lippi in the 1480s (spot the stylistic differences). It was Masaccio's vivid realism and mastery of linear perspective, especially in his *Expulsion from Eden* and *Tribute Money*, that artists were still coming to study a century later. It's a miracle any of this is still here: Almost the entire remainder of the church was destroyed by fire in 1771. Outside peak season, despite what it says on the door, you may not need a reservation; otherwise, book a slot by phone. ⏱ *30 min. Piazza del Carmine.* ☎ *055-2768224. Admission 4€. Mon, Wed–Sat 10am–4:30pm; Sun 1–4:30pm. Bus: D.*

10 ★★ **La Carraia.** The left bank's best gelateria is rightly popular with locals, all day and late into the evening. *Piazza N. Sauro 25R.* ☎ *055-280695. $. Bus: C3, D, 6, 11, 36, or 37.*

11 ★ **kids La Specola.** This former headquarters of Oltrarno's World War II resistance now houses the Museo di Storia Naturale's zoology exhibits. In addition to the thousands of stuffed and pickled beasts, there's a touch of gore

that's perhaps suited to older kids only. The **Cere Anatomiche** are lifelike waxworks of the human body spliced and diced 500 different ways, used to teach anatomy in the 18th century. Grislier still are Giulio Zumbo's 17th century models of Florence during the plague, showing the dead and decomposing strewn

Giardino di Boboli (see p 17).

across the city streets. ⏱ *1 hr. Via Romana 17.* ☎ *055-2288251. www. msn.unifi.it. Admission 6€. Tues–Sun 10:30am–5:30pm (9:30am–4:30pm in winter). Bus: C3, D, 11, 36, or 37.*

⑫ ★ kids **Giardino di Boboli.** Court architect and artist, Niccolò Tribolo (1500–50), laid out these Renaissance gardens, through which the Medici romped, in the mid–16th century. Since opening to the public in 1776, the Boboli has become the most dazzling (and busy) garden in Tuscany, with splashing fountains and elegant statuary such as *Venus* by Giambologna inside the Buontalenti grotto. The nearby, much-photographed fountain—an obese *Bacchus* astride a turtle—is a copy of a statue depicting Pietro Barbino, Cosimo I's court jester. Your ticket also includes entrance to the adjacent **Giardino Bardini.** ⏱ *30 min. Piazza de' Pitti.* ☎ *055-2388791. Admission 9€ including entrance to Museo degli Argenti, Museo delle Porcellane, and Galleria del Costume. June–Aug daily 8:15am–7:30pm; Apr–May and Sept–Oct daily 8:15am–6:30pm; Mar daily 8:15am–5.30pm; Nov–Feb daily 8:15am–4:30pm. Closed 1st and last Mon of each month. Bus: D, 11, 36, or 37.*

⑬ ★★ **Palazzo Pitti.** Luca Pitti, a wealthy importer of French fabrics, wanted a palace to outclass the Medici—and he got his wish. Niccolò Macchiavelli hailed the **palazzo** as "grander than any other erected in Florence by a private citizen." When the Pittis sold up, the Medici moved in, transforming it into the most opulent palace in Europe until Louis XIV built Versailles outside Paris. In the 19th century, the Pitti sheltered the Italian royal family, when Florence was briefly the country's capital. Victor Emmanuel III gave it to the state in 1919, which turned it into a series of museums.

Palazzo Pitti.

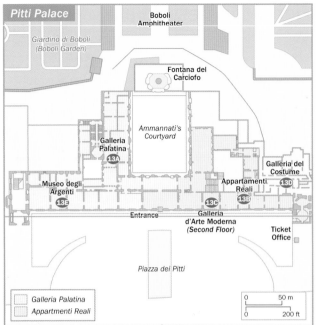

Pitti Palace

Giardino di Boboli
(Boboli Garden)

Boboli
Amphitheater

Fontana del
Carciofo

Ammannati's
Courtyard

Galleria
Palatina
13A

Galleria del
Costume
13D

Museo degli
Argenti
13E

Appartamenti
Reali
13B

13C

Entrance

Galleria
d'Arte Moderna
(Second Floor)

Ticket
Office

Piazza dei Pitti

Galleria Palatina

Appartamenti Reali

0   50 m

0   200 ft

After climbing 140 steps, you enter the **A ★★★ Galleria Palatina.** Head here if you have to skip everything else. It's filled with masterpieces from the High Renaissance and later eras, collected by the Medici and later the ruling dukes of Lorraine. Perhaps the most famous resident in the collection is Raphael, whose *Madonna of the Chair* graces the Sala di Saturno and *La Velata* the Sala di Giove. Raphael is accompanied by several works by Venetian Titian and Flemish Peter Paul Rubens, whose giant *Consequences of War* dominates the Sala di Marte. Baroque sumptuousness defines the **B Appartmenti Reali,** former home to the Kings of Savoy, the first rulers of a united Italy. Note Caravaggio's *Portrait of a Knight of Malta,* painted before his expulsion from the island in 1608. In the shadow of the Renaissance rooms, the **C ★ Galleria d'Arte Moderna** showcases the Macchiaioli, the 19th-century Tuscan school of pre-Impressionist painters who revolted against academicism. The movement's key figure was Livornese Giovanni Fattori. The **D Galleria del Costume** is filled with 18th- to 20th-century clothing, including historic wardrobes such as Eleanor of Toledo's burial dress. The ground floor, **E Museo degli Argenti** is a camp glorification of the Medici household wares, with treasures in ivory and silver, among other metals. It's ostentatious but fun.

Florence's Best Small Museums

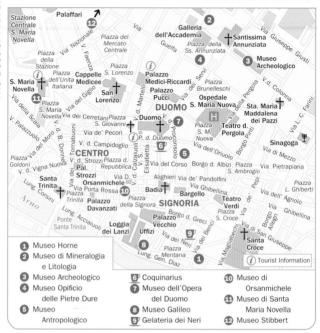

1. Museo Horne
2. Museo di Mineralogia e Litologia
3. Museo Archeologico
4. Museo Opificio delle Pietre Dure
5. Museo Antropologico
6. Coquinarius
7. Museo dell'Opera del Duomo
8. Museo Galileo
9. Gelateria dei Neri
10. Museo di Orsanmichele
11. Museo di Santa Maria Novella
12. Museo Stibbert

ⓘ Tourist Information

Cast into shadow by the marvels of the Uffizi and Palazzo Pitti, the small museums of Florence are often overlooked. But the city has even more to offer than its vast repositories of great art: Away from the tourist-trodden paths are one of Italy's most intriguing archaeological collections, offbeat museums of science, and private museums housing lesser-known Renaissance masterpieces. Because many of these collections are open mornings only, plan an intensive viewing session before lunch. START: **Bus C3 to Via dei Benci.**

1 ★ **Museo Horne.** English-born Herbert Horne, an art historian, immortalized himself by building the nucleus of this collection, including minor masterpieces by some top-rank artists. Works are displayed in his preserved Renaissance home, around a porticoed courtyard. Horne's greatest acquisitions were Giotto's *St. Stephen*, dating from the early 14th century, and a small 1320s diptych by Simone Martini depicting the *Man of Sorrows*. ⏱ *45 min. Via dei Benci 6 (at Corso dei Tintori).* ☎ *055-244661. www. museohorne.it. Admission 6€. Mon–Sat 9am–1pm. Bus: C3, 12, 13, or 23.*

Take bus #23 to Piazza San Marco.

2 kids **Museo di Mineralogia e Litologia.** This outpost of Florence's multicenter Museo di Storia

Naturale (Natural History Museum) is a treasure-trove for aspiring (or actual) gemologists and geologists. Hundreds of curious, colorful rocks from all corners of the planet are displayed in detailed, illuminated cross section; kids are free to touch and handle some of them. ⏱ *30 min. Via La Pira 4.* ☎ *055-234-6760. www.msn.unifi.it. Admission 6€; 8€ with Museo Antropologico (❺, below). June–Sept Sun–Tues and Thurs–Fri 10am–1pm, Sat 10am–6pm; Oct–May Mon–Tues and Thurs–Fri 9am–1pm, Sat–Sun 10am–5pm. Bus: C1, 1, 7, 20, or 25.*

❸ ★ **Museo Archeologico.** A marvelous *palazzo* is home to one of Italy's best (if slightly haphazard) collections of Egyptian and Etruscan artifacts, much of it gathered by the Medici and later Leopold II of Lorraine, in the 1830s. The collection is regularly rearranged, but the highlights are usually upstairs, including eerie Egyptian sarcophagi. The 4th-century *Arezzo Chimera* (a bronze lion with a serpent for a tail) is the prize exhibit. Look out, too, for a couple of precious bronzes: the Roman *Idolino*, whose provenance is a little mysterious, and the Etruscan *Arringatore*, found near Perugia in Umbria. ⏱ *1 hr. Via della Colonna 38 (at Piazza della SS. Annunziata).* ☎ *055-23575. Admission 4€. Tues–Fri 8:30am–7pm; Sat–Sun 8:30am–2pm. Bus: 6, 31, or 32.*

❹ **Museo Opificio delle Pietre Dure.** This unique collection grew out of the Medici's passion for *pietre dure,* a type of mosaic work made from semiprecious stones and marble, popular in the 16th century. (The craft is sometimes called "Florentine Mosaic.") Since 1796 this workshop has been dedicated to restoring *pietre dure* works. Attached is a small museum with some examples of the art form, including intricate Tuscan landscapes. ⏱ *30 min. Via degli Alfani*

Catching a Show at the Strozzi

The two spaces inside the Renaissance Palazzo Strozzi, Piazza Strozzi (☎ **055-2645155**; www.palazzostrozzi.org)—known as the Piano Nobile and the basement Strozzina—are Florence's major spaces for temporary and contemporary art shows, and have been experiencing a 21st-century renaissance of their own under energetic directorship. Hits of recent years have included 2011's "Picasso, Miró, Dalí." There's always lots going on around the shows, too, including talks, late-night events, and discovery trails aimed at 5- to 9-year-olds. Check the website.

One of the rotating pieces of art at the Palazzo Strozzi.

78 (at Via Ricasoli). ☎ 055-218709. Admission 4€. Mon–Sat 8:15am–2pm. Bus: C1.

5 Museo Antropologico.
Extend your timeout from the Renaissance at this fascinating little anthropological enclave of the University of Florence. Inuit canoes, Japanese *kabuki* masks, Sumatran spears, and Inca mummies from Cuzco, Peru, were all collected during the heyday of European imperialism in the 19th century. Displays are in Italian, but a guide in English is available at the ticket office. ⏱ *45 min. Via del Proconsolo 12.* ☎ *055-2396449. www. msn.unifi.it. Admission 6€; 8€ with Museo di Mineralogia e Litologia (2, above). Same hours as Museo di Mineralogia e Litologia. Bus: C1 or C2.*

6 ★ Coquinarius.
Enjoy a plate of mixed crostini or something tasty from a lengthy bruschetta list at this traditional brick-walled enoteca. *Via delle Oche 15R.* ☎ *055-2302153. www.coquinarius.it. $–$$.*

7 ★ Museo dell'Opera del Duomo.
The former workshop where Michelangelo carved his iconic *David* is now a repository for the loot from the Duomo and Baptistery, and all the external sculptures from Giotto's Campanile. Undisputed stars of the collection are Ghiberti's freshly restored and reassembled "Gates of Paradise," from the Baptistery. There's also a couple of Michelangelos, including his *Pietà,* originally intended for the artist's tomb. Upstairs are joyous 1430s *cantorie* (singing galleries)—one by Donatello, the other by Luca della Robbia—and Donatello's *Mary Magdalene,* one of his most celebrated penitent works, from 1455. ⏱ *1 hr. Piazza del Duomo 9.* ☎ *055-2302885. Admission 6€ (combined Piazza del Duomo tickets*

available). Mon–Sat 9am–6:50pm; Sun 9am–1pm. Bus: C1, C2, 14, or 23.

8 ★ kids Museo Galileo.
The city's renamed and revamped Museo di Storia della Scienza (History of Science Museum) houses such treasures as the lens Galileo used to discover the four moons of Jupiter and the great scientist's right-hand middle finger, stolen before his burial at Santa Croce. The collection was started by the science-minded later Medici dukes, but a hands-on multimedia approach (including a superb website) really appeals to older kids. ⏱ *1 hr. Piazza dei Guidici 1.* ☎ *055-265311. www. museogalileo.it. Admission 8€. Wed–Mon 9:30am–5pm; Tues 9:30am–1pm. Bus: C1.*

9 ★ Gelateria dei Neri.
Plenty of locals think this, rather than the more famous names, is the best ice-cream stop in town. *Via dei Neri 20–22R.* ☎ *055-210034. $.*

Santa Maria Novella.

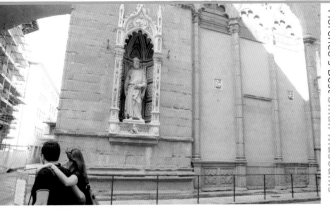

The gothic exterior of Orsanmichele.

⑩ ★ Museo di Orsanmichele. The former granary rooms above Orsanmichele now house the statues that once surrounded the Gothic church's exterior—though sadly, it's usually open just 1 day per week. Many of the original sculptures are here, well labeled, including Donatello's marble *St. Mark* (1411–13); Ghiberti's bronze *St. John the Baptist* (1413–16), the first life-size bronze of the Renaissance; and Verrocchio's *Incredulity of St. Thomas* (1473–83). ⏱ *20 min. Via dell'Arte della Lana.* ☎ *055-210305. Free admission. Mon 10am–5pm. Bus: C2.*

⑪ ★★ Museo di Santa Maria Novella. Attached to the Basilica di Santa Maria Novella (p 44, ①) is the **Chiostro Verde** (Green Cloisters), open to the public as a museum. Paolo Uccello's 15th-century frescoes were almost destroyed in the 1966 flood, which given their subject matter (Biblical inundation) is perhaps appropriate. Uccello's *Universal Deluge* lunette exhibits his trademark crazy use of perspective. The better preserved

Spanish Chapel was frescoed earlier (ca. 1365) by Andrea di Bonaiuto. It tells a complex story that places the Dominicans at the center of spreading the word of Christ. ⏱ *45 min. Piazza Santa Maria Novella.* ☎ *055-282187. Admission 2.70€. Fri–Mon 10am–4pm. Bus: C2, 4, 11, 22, 36, or 37.*

Friday through Sunday, make the short walk north to Piazza dell'Unità Italiana to catch bus #4. Alight on Via Vittorio Emanuele II and make for the last time-slot of the day (5pm) at:

⑫ kids Museo Stibbert. Frederick Stibbert (1838–1906), half-Italian, half-Scot, was an eclectic collector, as the 50,000 *objets d'art* (tapestries, antiques, porcelain, paintings) in these 57 rooms testify. As you'll see, Stibbert also had a fetish about war and weaponry: Expect lances, swords, and suits of Japanese, European, and Middle Eastern armor. ⏱ *45 min. Via Stibbert 26.* ☎ *055-475520. www.museostibbert.it. Admission 6€. Mon–Wed 10am–1pm; Fri–Sun 10am–5pm. Bus: 4.*

Florence's Masters of the Renaissance

1 Basilica di Santa Maria Novella
2 Cappelle Medicee
3 Cenacolo di Sant'Appolonia
4 Santissima Annunziata
5 Pugi
6 Palazzo Medici-Riccardi
7 Orsanmichele
8 Palazzo Rucellai
9 Santa Trinita
10 Galleria degli Uffizi

(i) Tourist Information

For over a century, Florence was the center of the world. The period we now call the Renaissance ("the rebirth") is often dated from Lorenzo Ghiberti's commission for the North Doors of the Baptistery, in 1401, until Michelangelo's final departure for Rome, in the 1530s. This remarkable period of artistic and architectural development, initially led by such figures as Masaccio, Donatello, and Brunelleschi, created the city we see today. On this tour, I'll take you to the best works left behind by the sculptors, painters, and architects who changed art forever. START: **Piazza Santa Maria Novella.**

1 ★★ **Basilica di Santa Maria Novella.** This basilica's iconic green and white marble facade was completed in 1470 by the Renaissance's key architectural theorist, L. B. Alberti, while the interior dates to the 13th century. (Writer Boccaccio used it for scenes in his *Decameron*.) Of the many interior frescoes, Masaccio's *Trinity* is the most significant in the history of art, and astonished onlookers when it was unveiled in 1427: they'd never seen such realistic perspective painted onto a flat

wall. Domenico Ghirlandaio's sumptuous frescoes adorning the **Cappella Tornabuoni** ostensibly depict *Scenes from the Lives of the Virgin and St. John the Baptist*, but they're also a unique snapshot of wealthy society in 1490 Florence. Multitalented Brunelleschi carved the *Crucifix* in the **Cappella Gondi.** By the 1800s, Santa Maria Novella had become Florence's "church for foreigners," attracting expatriate literati, including Percy Bysshe Shelley. ⏱ *45 min. Piazza Santa Maria Novella.* ☎ *055-219257. Admission 3.50€. Mon–Thurs 9am–5:30pm; Fri 11am–5:30pm; Sat 9am–5pm; Sun noon–5pm. Bus: C2, 1, 4, 6, 11, 14, 17, 22, 23, 36, or 37.*

② ★★ **Cappelle Medicee (Medici Chapels).** Make a fast trek to the **Sagrestia Nuova (New Sacristy),** Michelangelo's first realized architectural work—begun in 1520, but left unfinished until 1534. As an architectural space, it echoes Brunelleschi's Pazzi Chapel in Santa Croce. From the door, on the left, the tomb of Lorenzo, Duke of Urbino, bears the artist's reclining figures representing *Dawn* and *Dusk.* On the right, the tomb of Giuliano, Duke of Nemours (and youngest son of Lorenzo the Magnificent), features Michelangelo's allegorical figures of *Day* and *Night.* Shrewd observers will note that Michelangelo obviously hadn't seen many naked female bodies. The artist never completed two other tombs commissioned to him, but in 1521 he did finish a moving *Madonna and Child,* for the tomb of Lorenzo "The Magnificent." ⏱ *40 min. Piazza Madonna degli Aldobrandini 6 (behind San Lorenzo).* ☎ *055-2388602. Admission 6€. Daily 8:15am–4:20pm. Closed 2nd and 4th Sun and 1st, 3rd, and 5th Mon of month. Bus: C1, C2, 4, 11, 22, 36, or 37.*

Basilica di Santa Maria Novella.

③ ★ **Cenacolo di Sant'Appolonia.** Andrea del Castagno (1421–57) first rose to prominence when he was employed to paint the faces of condemned men on the walls of the Bargello. He went on to become, alongside Piero della Francesca (1412–92), one of the great perspective painters of the mid-Quattrocento (1400s). Here, in what remains of the Benedictine convent of Sant'Appolonia, he gives his intense, rather dark take on the *Last Supper* (1447). No prizes for naming the only diner without his halo. ⏱ *15 min. Via XX Aprile 1.* ☎ *055-2388607. Free admission. Daily 8:15am–1:50pm. Closed 1st, 3rd, 5th Sun and 2nd, 4th Mon of month. Bus: 1, 6, 11, 14, 17, or 23.*

④ ★ **Santissima Annunziata.** As the artistic style we now call "Renaissance" waned, Florence hosted its last great artistic

The domes of the Cappelle Medicee, flanked by the San Lorenzo market stalls.

movement before the action moved south to Rome: Mannerism. Behind this church's Michelozzo-designed portico, the **Chiostro dei Voti (Votive Cloister)** has some of the city's finest Mannerist frescoes. Rosso Fiorentino provided an *Assumption* (1513) and Pontormo a *Visitation* (1515) just to the right of the door, but the highlights are by their master, Andrea del Sarto. His *Birth of the Virgin* (1513), in the far right corner, is one of his finest works, and his *Coming of the Magi* (1514) includes a self-portrait at the far right, looking out at us from under his blue hat. ⏱ *20 min. Piazza SS Annunziata.* ☎ *055-266181. Free admission. Daily 7:30am–12:30pm and 4–6:30pm. Bus: C1, 6, 14, 23, 31, or 32.*

5 ★ **Pugi.** Choose your topping, and your portion size, of freshly baked *schiacciata* (flatbread) and munch it in the square across the street. Closed Sundays. *Piazza San Marco 9.* ☎ *055-280981. www. focacceria-pugi.it.* $.

6 ★ kids **Palazzo Medici-Riccardi.** The onset of the Florentine Renaissance didn't totally kill off the decorative style of painting known as "international Gothic," as this tiny chapel frescoed in 1459 by Benozzo Gozzoli shows. Gozzoli's *Procession of the Magi* includes a pageant of Medici friends and family, accompanied by a beautifully rendered menagerie of creatures. Downstairs in this Michelozzo-designed palace (1444), a giant interactive multimedia display relates to the fresco. ⏱ *30 min. Via Cavour 3.* ☎ *055-2760340. www. palazzo-medici.it. Admission 7€. Thurs–Tues 9am–7pm. Bus: C1.*

7 ★ **Orsanmichele.** This 1337 Gothic grain warehouse was converted into a church in medieval times. The external niches were adorned with statuary commissioned by Florence's trade guilds. (Most of the originals are now inside the rarely-open Museo di Orsanmichele; see p 43, **10**.) The sculptors chosen included such luminaries of the early Renaissance as Lorenzo Ghiberti, Nanni di Banco, and Donatello, whose path-breaking *St George* is now in the Bargello. Inside is Andrea Orcagna's elaborate Gothic Tabernacle (1349–59), housing a *Virgin and Child* (1346) by Giotto's student,

Bernardo Daddi. ⏱ *30 min. Via dell'Arte della Lana 1.* ☎ *055-210305. Free admission. Tues–Sun 10am–5pm. Bus: C2.*

8 Palazzo Rucellai. Although it stands somewhat uncelebrated on a quiet side street, this was perhaps the most influential *palazzo* ever built in Florence. Harmoniously designed by Alberti and built by Bernardo Rossellino (who more famously worked in Pienza; see p 147), it was the first Renaissance building to feature classical pilasters on its facade. ⏱ *5 min. Via della Vigna Nuova. Bus: C3 or 6.*

9 ★★ Santa Trinita. This oft-missed church, founded in the 11th century, was the original home of Gentile da Fabriano's Gothic icon, *Procession of the Magi*, now in the Uffizi. Lorenzo Monaco frescoed the **Cappella Bartolini Salimbeni** in the 1420s with *Scenes from the Life of the Virgin*; Domenico Ghirlandaio, in uncharacteristically pious mood,

frescoed the **Cappella Sassetti** in the 1480s with a *Life of St Francis*. Comparing them side by side paints a picture of progress made in the depiction of space during the early Renaissance. Opposite the church, across the tiny piazza, is Baccio d'Agnolo's 1523 **Palazzo Bartolini Salimbeni,** one of the city's most handsome late Renaissance palaces. ⏱ *40 min. Piazza di Santa Trinita.* ☎ *055-216912. Free admission. Mon–Sat 8am-noon and 4–6pm; Sun 4–6pm. Bus: C3 or 6.*

10 ★★★ Galleria degli Uffizi. If you've still got energy for more Renaissance, finish your day at the planet's greatest repository of 13th, 14th, and 15th century painting. Here you'll find influential works by such important Renaissance figures as Leonardo da Vinci, Paolo Uccello, Raphael, and Piero della Francesca. One weeknight in summer you'll usually find it open until 10pm. (Exact days change.) *See p 25. Bus: C1.*

The Galleria degli Uffizi.

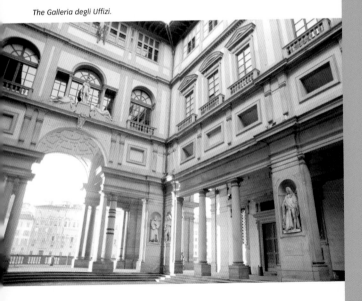

The Best Dining in Florence

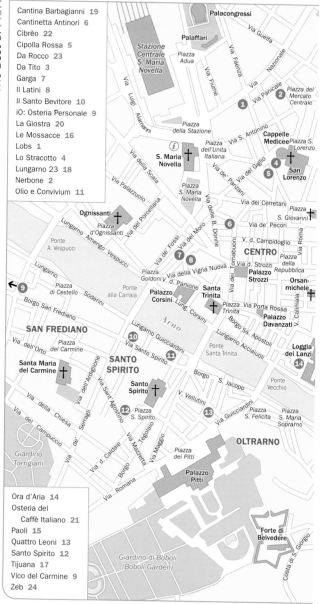

Cantina Barbagianni 19
Cantinetta Antinori 6
Cibrèo 22
Cipolla Rossa 5
Da Rocco 23
Da Tito 3
Garga 7
Il Latini 8
Il Santo Bevitore 10
iO: Osteria Personale 9
La Giostra 20
Le Mossacce 16
Lobs 1
Lo Stracotto 4
Lungarno 23 18
Nerbone 2
Olio e Convivium 11

Ora d'Aria 14
Osteria del
  Caffè Italiano 21
Paoli 15
Quattro Leoni 13
Santo Spirito 12
Tijuana 17
Vico del Carmine 9
Zeb 24

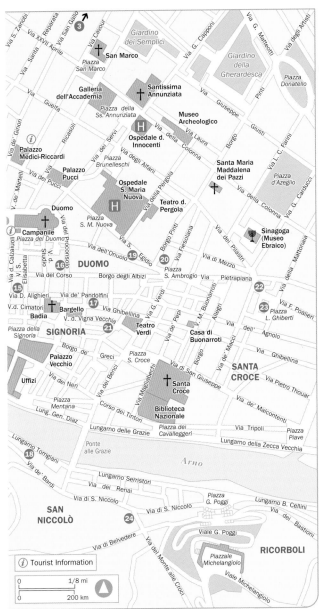

Via S. Zanobi
Via S. Gallo
Via XXVII Aprile
Via Santa Reparata
3
Via Cavour
Giardino dei Semplici
Via G. Capponi
Via G. Matteotti
Via degli Artisti

San Marco
Piazza San Marco
Giardino della Gherardesca
Piazza Donatello

Via Santa
Via Guelfa
Via de' Ginori
Galleria dell'Accademia
Piazza della Ss. Annunziata
Santissima Annunziata
Via Giuseppe
Pinti
Giusti

Via Ricasoli
Museo Archeologico
Via della Colonna
Via Laura
Borgo
Via L. C. Farini
Piazza d'Azeglio

(i)
Palazzo Medici-Riccardi
Via de' Servi
Ospedale d. Innocenti
Via degli Alfani
Santa Maria Maddalena dei Pazzi
Via della Colonna
Via G. Carducci

Via de' Martelli
Palazzo Pucci
Via dei Pucci
Piazza Brunelleschi
Ospedale S. Maria Nuova
Via della Pergola
Teatro d. Pergola

V. de' Pucci
Duomo
Piazza S. M. Nuova
Via S. Egidio
Sinagoga (Museo Ebraico)
Via della Mattonaia

(i)
Campanile
Piazza del Duomo
Via del Proconsolo
Via Studio
V. S. Elisabetta
Via d. Calzaiuoli
16
DUOMO
Via dell'Oriuolo
19
Borgo Pinti
Via Fiesolana
Via dei Pilastri
Via di Mezzo

Via del Corso
Borgo degli Albizi
20
Piazza S. Ambrogio
Via Pietrapiana
22
Via F. Poalieri

Via D. Alighieri
Via de' Pandolfini
17
Via G. Verdi
Via
dell'
Agnolo
23
Piazza L. Ghiberti

V.d. Cimatori
Bargello
Via Ghibellina
Via de' Pepi
Via V. M. Buonarroti
Allegri
Via Ghibellina

Badia
V. d. Vigna Vecchia
21
Teatro Verdi
Casa di Buonarroti
Via de' Macci
SANTA CROCE
Via Pietro Thouar

Piazza della Signoria
SIGNORIA
Borgo de'
Greci
Piazza S. Croce
Via di San Giuseppe
Bongo
Via de' Macci

Palazzo Vecchio
Via dei Neri
Via de' Benci
Santa Croce
Via de' Malcontenti

Uffizi
Piazza Mentana
Lung. Gen. Diaz
Corso dei Tintori
Via Magliabechi
Biblioteca Nazionale
Piazza dei Cavalleggeri
Via Tripoli
Piazza Piave

18
Lungarno Torrigiani
Lungarno delle Grazie
Lungarno della Zecca Vecchia
Ponte alle Grazie
Arno

Via de' Bardi
Lungarno Serristori
Via dei Renai
Piazza G. Poggi
Lungarno B. Cellini
Via dei Bastioni

SAN NICCOLÒ
Via di S. Niccolo
24
Via di S. Niccolo
Viale G. Poggi
RICORBOLI

Via di Belvedere
Via del Monte alle Croci
Piazzale Michelangiolo
Viale Michelangiolo

(i) Tourist Information

0   1/8 mi
0   200 km

Dining Best Bets

Best for a Romantic Evening
★★ Cantina Barbagianni $$–$$$
Via Sant'Egidio 13R (p 51)

Best for a Budget Dinner Close
to the Duomo
★ Le Mossacce $–$$ *Via del
Proconsolo 55R (p 52)*

Best for Affordable Seafood
★ Lobs $$–$$$ *Via Faenza 75
(p 52)*

Best Steaks
★★ Cipolla Rossa $$$ *Via dei Conti
53R (p 51)*

Best for Family Dining
★ Quattro Leoni $$–$$$ *Via dei
Vellutini 1R (p 53)*

Best Pizza
★ Vico del Carmine $$ *Via Pisana
40R (p 53)*

Best Sandwich
★ Nerbone $ *Mercato Centrale
(p 52)*

Most Atmospheric Dining
Room
★★ Il Santo Bevitore $$$ *Via Santo
Spirito 66R (p 52)*

Best for a Filling Budget Lunch
★ Da Rocco $ *Mercato di
Sant'Ambrogio (p 51)*

Most Creative Contemporary
Cooking
★★★ Ora d'Aria $$$$$ *Via dei
Georgofili 11R (p 53)*; and ★★★ iO:
Osteria Personale $$$ *Borgo San
Frediano 167R (p 52)*

Best for Traditional Florentine
Ambience
Paoli $$–$$$ *Via dei Tavolini 12R
(p 53)*

*Steak—bistecca—is a Florentine
specialty.*

Most Refined Deli Dining
★★ Zeb $$ *Via San Miniato 2R
(p 53)*; and ★★ Olio e Convivium
$$$–$$$$ *Via Santo Spirito 4
(p 53)*

Best for a Business Lunch
★ Cantinetta Antinori $$$$ *Piazza
Antinori 3 (p 51)*

Best Gelato
★★★ Carapina $ *Via Lambertesca
18R (p 19)*

Best for Enthusiastic, Friendly
Service
★ Da Tito $–$$ *Via San Gallo 112R
(p 51)*

★★ Cantina Barbagianni SANTA CROCE *MODERN TUSCAN* A romantic spot that successfully combines the traditional and the contemporary in mood and food. Seasonal Tuscan dishes like *filetto di manzo ai mirtilli* (beef filet with blueberries) are given a light, inventive interpretation. *Via Sant'Egidio 13R.* ☎ *055-2480508. www.cantinabarbagianni.it. Entrees 12€–22€. AE, DC, MC, V. Lunch Mon–Fri; dinner daily. Bus: C1, C2, 14, or 23.*

★ Cantinetta Antinori CENTRO STORICO *TUSCAN* For 600 years, the Antinori family has dazzled with ingredients and wines from their own farms and vineyards, served in a 15th-century *palazzo*. *Palazzo Antinori, Piazza Antinori 3.* ☎ *055-292234. www.cantinetta-antinori. com. Entrees 24€–30€. AE, DC, MC, V. Lunch, dinner Mon–Fri. Closed Aug. Bus: 6, 11, 22, 36, or 37.*

★★ Cibrèo SANT'AMBROGIO *MEDITERRANEAN* Fabio Picchi's innovative restaurant remains one of Florence's finest. Simple soups share the menu with ventures like fricasseed roosters' combs and innards in an egg. *Via Verrocchio 8R.* ☎ *055-2341100. Entrees 36€. AE, DC, MC, V. Lunch, dinner Tues–Sat. Closed Aug. Bus: C2, C3, or 14.*

★★ Cipolla Rossa SAN LORENZO *MODERN TUSCAN/GRILL* A modern-rustic dining room with a honed, contemporary take on combining Tuscan ingredients. Beef (*Chianina*) and pork (*Cinta Senese*) steaks are the kings. *Via dei Conti 53R.* ☎ *055-214210. www.osteriacipollarossa. com. Entrees 16€–25€. MC, V. Lunch, dinner Wed–Mon. Bus: C1, 4, 11, 22, 36, or 37.*

★ kids Da Rocco SANT'AMBROGIO *ITALIAN* Simple, market-fresh plates served to hungry local workers.

Expect the likes of lasagna or roasted rabbit. *Inside Mercato di Sant'Ambrogio. No phone. Entrees 5€. No credit cards. Lunch Mon–Sat. Bus: C2, C3, or 14.*

★ Da Tito SAN MARCO *TUSCAN* A beloved (and busy) century-old trattoria where the staff is as warm and welcoming as the food, which sticks to well-executed Tuscan classics like *lombatina di vitella* (thick veal cutlet). *Via San Gallo 112R.* ☎ *055-472475. www.trattoriadatito.it. Entrees 9€–16€. MC, V. Lunch, dinner Mon–Sat. Bus: C1, 1, 7, 20, or 25.*

★ Garga SANTA MARIA NOVELLA *MODERN TUSCAN* Long frequented by the foodie crowd, which gathers for dishes such as angel-hair pasta with prawn and citrus sauce. *Via del Moro 48R.* ☎ *055-2398898. www.garga.it. Entrees 20€–25€. AE, MC, V. Dinner Tues–Sun. Bus: C3, 6, 11, 36, or 37.*

★ kids Il Latini CENTRO STORICO *TUSCAN* At this buzzing dive, diners feast at communal tables on dishes such as *arrosto misto*—slabs of assorted meats cooked on the grill.

The well-stocked bar at Cibrèo.

Intimate dining at La Giostra.

Via del Palchetti 6R. ☎ *055-210916. www.illatini.com. Entrees 14€–22€. AE, DC, MC, V. Lunch, dinner Tues– Sun. Closed 2 weeks in Aug. Bus: C3,6, 11, 36, or 37.*

★★ Il Santo Bevitore SAN FREDI-ANO *MODERN ITALIAN* Savvy food-ies patronize the candle-lit interior of this new-generation Florentine eatery. Flavors originate from across Italy. *Via Santo Spirito 66R.* ☎ *055-211264. www.ilsantobevitore.com. Entrees 16€–24€. MC, V. Lunch Mon–Sat, dinner daily. Bus: C3, D, 6, 11, 36, or 37.*

★★★ iO: Osteria Personale SAN FREDIANO *MODERN TUSCAN* The best Tuscan ingredients cooked creatively on a modular menu with meat, fish, and vegetarian choices (no pasta). Fresh, friendly, and fash-ionable. *Borgo San Frediano 167R.* ☎ *055-9331341. www.io-osteria personale.it. Entrees 13€–20€. AE, DC, MC, V. Dinner Mon–Sat. Closed Aug and 10 days in Jan. Bus: D or 6.*

★ La Giostra SANTA CROCE *TUS-CAN* A Habsburg prince with Medici blood welcomes guests to this inti-mate restaurant, with some dishes based on noble family recipes. *Borgo Pinti 12R.* ☎ *055-241341. www. ristorantelagiostra.com. Entrees 16€–24€. AE, DC, MC, V. Lunch, dinner daily. Bus: C1, 14, or 23.*

★ Le Mossacce CENTRO STORICO *FLORENTINE* This noisy, traditional

workers' trattoria has a short menu that features Tuscan basics like *ribollita* (mixed veg soup-stew) and *spezzatino* (veal stew). *Via del Pro-consolo 55R.* ☎ *055-294361. www. trattorialemossacce.it. Entrees 9€–11€. AE, MC, V. Lunch, dinner Mon–Fri. Closed Aug. Bus: C1 or C2.*

★ Lo Stracotto SAN LORENZO *TUSCAN* Traditional dishes are exe-cuted a notch better here than in surrounding San Lorenzo trattorias. Go for classics like *pappa al pomo-doro* (thick tomato and bread soup) or *peposo* (peppery beef stew). *Piazza Madonna degli Aldobrandini 17.* ☎ *055-2302062. www.trattoria lostracotto.it. Entrees 8€–12€. MC, V. Lunch, dinner daily. Bus: C1, 4, 11, 22, 36, or 37.*

★ Lobs SAN LORENZO *SEAFOOD* This shack-styled Mediterranean seafood trattoria serves up the city's most reliable fish dishes. Pasta dishes like *orecchiete con pesce persico* (with perch) are a great value. *Via Faenza 75.* ☎ *055-212478. www.lobsrestaurant.com. Entrees 12€–20€. AE, DC, MC, V. Lunch, dinner daily (closed Sun lunch in Aug). Bus: 1, 6, 11, 14, 17, or 23.*

★ Lungarno 23 OLTRARNO *AMERICAN* It's like the hamburger got dressed by Gucci at this trendy eatery, where they use only Chi-anina beef from a single farm on their short menu of grills, tartare, and carpaccio. *Lungarno Torrigiani 23.* ☎ *055-2345957. www.lungarno 23.it. Entrees 14€–25€. MC, V. Lunch, dinner Mon–Sat. Bus: C3 or D.*

★ Nerbone SAN LORENZO *FLO-RENTINE* Hasten to this 1872 five-table market dive for the *bagnato* (a boiled beef sandwich dipped in meat juices). *Mercato Centrale (at Via dell'Ariento, stand #292).* ☎ *055-219949. Entrees 4€–7€. No credit cards. Lunch Mon–Sat. Closed 2 weeks in Aug. Bus: C1.*

★★ Olio e Convivium OLTRARNO *MODERN ITALIAN* Upscale deli dining with a classical soundtrack. Creative pasta dishes are good, but even better are the "gastronomy tasting plates" made up from the best of what's on the counter out front. *Via Santo Spirito 4.* ☎ *055-2658198. www.conviviumfirenze.it. Entrees 14€–28€. MC, V. Lunch Mon–Sat; dinner Tues–Sat. Closed 3 weeks in Aug. Bus: C3, D, 11, 36, or 37.*

★★★ Ora d'Aria CENTRO STORICO *MODERN TUSCAN* Florence's most creative chef Marco Stabile has worked in Sonoma and France, but the flavors in his design-savvy restaurant are staunchly Tuscan and always seasonal. *Via dei Georgofili 11R.* ☎ *055-2001699. www.oradariaristorante.com. Entrees 32€–34€. AE, MC, V. Lunch Tues–Sat; dinner Mon–Sat. Bus: C1.*

★ Osteria del Caffè Italiano SANTA CROCE *TUSCAN* In a 13th-century *palazzo,* this lively enoteca-restaurant has some of the city's best Tuscan dishes like *galletto al mattone* (brick-roasted cockerel). *Via Isola delle Stinche 11–13R.* ☎ *055-289368. Entrees 16€–24€. MC, V. Lunch, dinner Tues–Sun. Bus: C1, C2, or C3.*

A mixed antipasti plate is a classic appetizer in Florence's restaurants.

Paoli CENTRO STORICO *TRADITIONAL ITALIAN* In an alley almost opposite Orsanmichele, this 1824 restaurant in 13th-century digs is touristy, but the Italian cuisine is well done. *Via dei Tavolini 12R.* ☎ *055-216215. www.casatrattoria. com. Entrees 12€–22€. AE, DC, MC, V. Lunch, dinner daily. Bus: C2.*

★ kids Quattro Leoni OLTRARNO *TUSCAN* A mixed local and tourist crowd pack this Left Bank trattoria for well-executed regional dishes. *Via dei Vellutini 1R.* ☎ *055-218562. www. 4leoni.com. Entrees 10€–25€. MC, V. Lunch, dinner daily. Bus: C3 or D.*

Santo Spirito OLTRARNO *ITALIAN/FLORENTINE* Local specialties like salt cod with leeks share menu space with grills and large bowls of pasta at this smart little *osteria.* Be patient because everything's cooked from scratch. *Piazza Santo Spirito 16R.* ☎ *055-2382383. Entrees 12€–25€. AE, MC, V. Lunch, dinner daily. Bus: D.*

kids Tijuana SANTA CROCE *MEXICAN* Fajitas, burritos, nachos, and cerveza, and plenty of chili, just like it tastes south of the border. (Well, almost.) *Via Ghibellina 156R.* ☎ *055-2341330. www.tijuanaristorante.it. Entrees 8€–14€. AE, MC, V. Dinner daily. Bus: C1, C2, or C3.*

★ kids Vico del Carmine SAN FREDIANO *PIZZA* The city's best pizzeria, tricked out in Neapolitan style with only Neapolitan ingredients. *Via Pisana 40R.* ☎ *055-2336862. Pizzas 6€–12€. MC, V. Dinner Tues–Sun. Closed Aug. Bus: 6.*

★★ Zeb SAN NICCOLO *MODERN ITALIAN* Intimate dining right at the deli counter, with an all-chalkboard menu using the finest ingredients. No reservations. *Via San Miniato 2R.* ☎ *055-2342864. www.zeb gastronomia.com. Entrees 8€–15€. MC, V. Lunch Thurs–Tues; dinner Thurs–Sat. Bus: D, 12, or 13.*

The Best Lodging in Florence

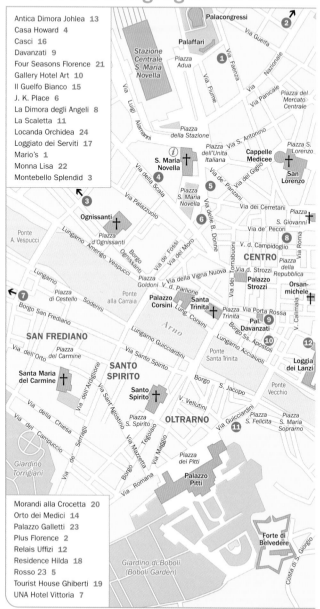

Antica Dimora Johlea 13
Casa Howard 4
Casci 16
Davanzati 9
Four Seasons Florence 21
Gallery Hotel Art 10
Il Guelfo Bianco 15
J. K. Place 6
La Dimora degli Angeli 8
La Scaletta 11
Locanda Orchidea 24
Loggiato dei Servriti 17
Mario's 1
Monna Lisa 22
Montebello Splendid 3

Morandi alla Crocetta 20
Orto dei Medici 14
Palazzo Galletti 23
Plus Florence 2
Relais Uffizi 12
Residence Hilda 18
Rosso 23 5
Tourist House Ghiberti 19
UNA Hotel Vittoria 7

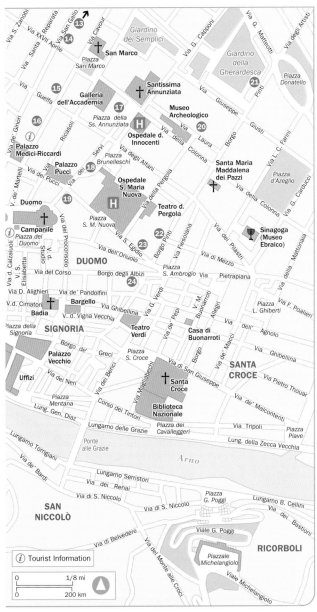

Via S. Zanobi
Via XXVII Aprile
Via Santa Reparata
Via S. Gallo
Via Cavour
Via G. Capponi
Via G. Matteotti
Via degli Artisti

13
14

Giardino dei Semplici

Giardino della Gherardesca

Piazza Donatello

San Marco
Piazza San Marco

Via

Via Guelfa

15 Galleria dell'Accademia

17

Santissima Annunziata

Via Giuseppe

21
Pinti

Piazza SS. Annunziata

Museo Archeologico

Via della Laura

20

Via Giusti

Via L. C. Farini

16

Via de' Ginori

Via Ricasoli

Palazzo Medici-Riccardi

Via de' Martelli

Ospedale d. Innocenti H

Santa Maria Maddalena dei Pazzi

Piazza d'Azeglio

Via G. La Carducci

Via dei Servi

18 Palazzo Pucci

Via de' Pucci

Piazza Brunelleschi

Via degli Alfani

Via della Colonna

Borgo

Duomo

19

Ospedale S. Maria Nuova H

Via della Pergola

Via della Colonna

Campanile
Piazza del Duomo

Via del Proconsolo

Piazza S. M. Nuova

Teatro d. Pergola

Via Fiesolana

Sinagoga (Museo Ebraico)

Via d. Calzaiuoli
Via d. Studio

Via S. Egidio

Via dei Pilastri

Via della Mattonaia

Via dell'Oriuolo

22
23

Borgo Pinti

Via di Mezzo

DUOMO

Via del Corso

Borgo degli Albizi

Piazza S. Ambrogio

Via Pietrapiana

Via D. Alighieri

Via de' Pandolfini

24

Via G. Verdi

Via

dell'

Agnolo

V.d. Cimatori

Bargello

Via Ghibellina

V. M. Buonarroti

Piazza L. Ghiberti

Via F. Poalieri

Badia

V. d. Vigna Vecchia

Casa di Buonarroti

Via de' Macci

Piazza della Signoria

SIGNORIA

Teatro Verdi

Via Ghibellina

Borgo de' Greci

Piazza S. Croce

Via de' Pepi

SANTA CROCE

Palazzo Vecchio

Via dei Neri

Via dei Benci

Via di San Giuseppe

Borgo

Via Pietro Thouar

Uffizi

Piazza Mentana

Corso dei Tintori

Via Maffalechi

Santa Croce

Via de' Malcontenti

Lung. Gen. Diaz

Biblioteca Nazionale

Via Tripoli

Piazza Piave

Lungarno delle Grazie

Piazza dei Cavalleggeri

Lung. della Zecca Vecchia

Lungarno Torrigiani

Ponte alle Grazie

Arno

Via de' Bardi

Lungarno Serristori

Via dei Renai

SAN NICCOLÒ

Via di S. Niccolò

Piazza G. Poggi

Lungarno B. Cellini

Via di S. Niccolò

Via dei Bastioni

Viale G. Poggi

RICORBOLI

Via di Belvedere

Via del Monte alle Croci

Piazzale Michelangiolo

Viale Michelangiolo

ⓘ Tourist Information

0 — 1/8 mi
0 — 200 km

Hotel Best Bets

Best for Families
★★ Residence Hilda $$$$ *Via dei Servi 40 (p 59)*

Best Budget-Friendly Boutique Hotel
★ Rosso 23 $$ *Piazza Santa Maria Novella 23 (p 59)*

Most Luxurious Address
★★★ Four Seasons Florence $$$$$ *Borgo Pinti 99 (p 57)*

Best Central Cheap Sleep
★ Locanda Orchidea $ *Borgo degli Albizi 11 (p 58)*

Best for a Quiet Night
★★ Montebello Splendid $$$$-$$$$$ *Via Garibaldi 14 (p 58)*; and ★ Orto dei Medici $$-$$$ *Via San Gallo 30 (p 59)*

Best Flashpacking Hostel
Plus Florence $ *Via Santa Caterina d'Alessandria 15 (p 59)*

Best for Bohemian Chic
★★ Antica Dimora Johlea $$-$$$ *Via San Gallo 80 (p 57)*

Best Piazza Location
★ Loggiato dei Serviti $$-$$$ *Piazza Santissima Annunziata 3 (p 58)*

Best for Affordable Contemporary Design
★★ Casa Howard $$$ *Via della Scala 18 (p 57)*

Most Stylish Rooms
★★★ J. K. Place $$$$$ *Piazza Santa Maria Novella 7 (p 59)*

Best B&B in the Center
★★ La Dimora degli Angeli $$ *Via Brunelleschi 4 (p 58)*

Best for Great Service
★★ Davanzati $$$ *Via Porta Rossa 5 (p 57)*; and ★★ Il Guelfo Bianco $$-$$$ *Via Cavour 29 (p 59)*

Most Elegant *Palazzo* Accommodations at a Reasonable Price
★★ Palazzo Galletti $$ *Via Sant'Egidio 12 (p 59)*

A suite at the Four Seasons.

Florence Hotels A to Z

Simple decor in the always-friendly Davanzati.

★★ **Antica Dimora Johlea** SAN MARCO A regal Florentine *dimora* whose cozy, small-ish rooms are tricked out in decor that draws inspiration from East and West. The best roof terrace in the city in this price bracket is a knockout extra. *Via San Gallo 80.* ☎ *055-4633292. www.johanna.it. 6 units. Doubles 100€–170€ w/breakfast. No credit cards. Bus: C1, 1, 7, 20, or 25.*

★★ **Casa Howard** SANTA MARIA NOVELLA Quirky, plush, individual rooms in this *palazzo* turned chic guesthouse come with self-explanatory, stylized themes, from "Black and White" to "Oriental." *Via della Scala 18.* ☎ *0669-924555. www.casa howard.com. 13 units. Doubles 120€–240€. AE, MC, V. Bus: 11, 36, or 37.*

★ kids **Casci** SAN LORENZO Antonio Rossini *(Barber of Seville)* once lived in this old hostelry near the Duomo. Renovations have upgraded it without destroying the old charm. Family suites sleep four or five. *Via Cavour 13.* ☎ *055-211686. www. hotelcasci.com. 25 units. Doubles 80€–150€ w/breakfast. AE, DC, MC, V. Bus: C1, 14, or 23.*

★★ kids **Davanzati** CENTRO STORICO From laptops and PlayStations in each of the tasteful rooms to complimentary drinks with the family proprietors each evening, they've thought of it all at this most welcoming of *palazzo* hotels. *Via Porta Rossa 5 (at Piazza Davanzati).* ☎ *055-286666. www.hoteldavanzati. it. 21 units. Doubles 120€–188€ w/ breakfast. AE, DC, MC, V. Bus: C2.*

★★★ **Four Seasons Florence** NORTH OF CENTER Should the Medici miraculously return to the city, they would surely lodge here. The best address in Florence comes with frescoes, gardens, a spa, luxurious appointments—and a price tag to match. *Borgo Pinti 99.* ☎ *055-2626250. www.fourseasons. com/florence. 116 units. Doubles 550€–850€. AE, DC, MC, V. Bus: 8.*

★★ **Gallery Hotel Art** CENTRO STORICO Florence's original boutique hotel, opened by the Ferragamo fashion family, is still a bastion of designer comfort. *Vicolo dell'Oro 5.* ☎ *055-27263. www. lungarnohotels.com. 74 units. Doubles 300€–560€. AE, DC, MC, V. Bus: C3.*

★★ **Il Guelfo Bianco** SAN LORENZO Each room in this sympathetically converted 16th-century *palazzo* is different, but the friendly welcome is universal. Deluxe units have a separate seating area. *Via Cavour 29.* ☎ *055-288330. www. ilguelfobianco.it. 40 units. Doubles 99€–250€ w/breakfast. AE, DC, MC, V. Bus: C1, 14, or 23.*

★★★ **J. K. Place** SANTA MARIA NOVELLA This architectural gem, blending contemporary and Liberty styles, has elegant rooms with four-poster beds and fireplaces, a glass-covered courtyard, a rooftop

The lounge at J. K. Place.

terrace, and a splendid library. *Piazza Santa Maria Novella 7.* ☎ *055-2645181. www.jkplace.com. 20 units. Doubles 350€–550€ w/breakfast. AE, MC, V. Bus: 11, 36, or 37.*

★★ La Dimora degli Angeli
CENTRO STORICO A blend of contemporary and 19th-century styles in midsize rooms creates a romantic atmosphere at this B&B wedged between the Duomo and Florence's upscale shopping district. *Via Brunelleschi 4.* ☎ *055-288478. www.ladimoradegliangeli.it. 6 units. Doubles 110€—155€ w/breakfast. Closed Jan 20–Feb 14. MC, V. Bus: C2.*

La Scaletta OLTRARNO If you like vintage charm, check into this aging *palazzo* across the Arno and hang out on its flower-decked terrace, with a view down into the Boboli Garden. *Via Guicciardini 13.* ☎ *055-283028. www. hotellascaletta.it. 17 units. Doubles 75€–140€. AE, MC, V. Bus: C3 or D.*

★ Locanda Orchidea SANTA
CROCE If you need to flop on a tight budget but don't want to compromise on location, there's nowhere cleaner and friendlier at the price. *Borgo degli Albizi 11.* ☎ *055-2480346. www.hotelorchideaflorence.it. 7 units. Doubles 50€–80€. No credit cards. Bus: C1, C2, 14, or 23.*

★ Loggiato dei Serviti SAN
MARCO A monastery in 1527, this comfortably elegant hotel has beamed or vaulted ceilings and terra-cotta floors on an iconic Brunelleschi square. *Piazza SS. Annunziata 3.* ☎ *055-289592. www.loggiatodei servitihotel.it. 38 units. Doubles 120€–205€ w/breakfast. AE, DC, MC, V. Bus: 6, 14, 23, 31, or 32.*

★★ Mario's SAN LORENZO This
spotless, friendly, home-style city inn has small to midsize bedrooms stylishly decorated and furnished for comfort. *Via Faenza 89.* ☎ *055-216801. www.hotelmarios.com. 16 units. Doubles 80€–150€ w/breakfast. AE, DC, MC, V. Bus: 1, 2, 12, 13, 28, 29, 30, 35, or 57.*

★ Monna Lisa SANTA CROCE
Behind a severe facade, this sculpture-filled 14th-century *palazzo* is reminiscent of an English country manor. Superior units have Jacuzzi tubs, and outbuildings overlook a tranquil garden. *Borgo Pinti 27.* ☎ *055-2479755. www.monnalisa.it. 45 units. Doubles 139€–289€ w/ breakfast. AE, DC, MC, V. Bus: C1, C2, 14, or 23.*

★★ Montebello Splendid WEST
OF CENTER A citadel of refinement that is a 10-minute walk outside the center, this elegant hideaway offers the most realistically-priced luxury rooms in the city. *Via Garibaldi 14.* ☎ *055-27471. www.montebello splendid.com. 60 units. Doubles 199€–369€. AE, DC, MC, V. Bus: C2, C3, or D.*

Morandi alla Crocetta SAN
MARCO In a 16th-century convent, this quaint *pensione* evokes the era when Grand Tourists sought private homelike lodgings with family heirlooms. *Via Laura 50.* ☎ *055-2344747. www.hotelmorandi.it. 10 units. Doubles 100€–150€ w/breakfast. AE, DC, MC, V. Bus: 6, 14, 23, 31, or 32.*

★ **Orto dei Medici** SAN MARCO A tranquil *palazzo* with full hotel amenities. Midsize deluxe units, renovated in 2009, sport contemporary decor and terraces overlooking the peaceful courtyard garden. *Via San Gallo 30.* ☎ *055-483427. www.ortodeimedici.it. 42 units. Doubles 90€–190€ w/breakfast. AE, DC, MC, V. Bus: 1, 6, 11, 14, 17, or 23.*

★★ **Palazzo Galletti** SANTA CROCE Rooms at this converted 18th-century *palazzo* are large (for Florence), and come with high ceilings and grandeur as standard. Upgrade to a suite for restored frescoes, too. *Via Sant'Egidio 12.* ☎ *055-3905750. www.palazzo galletti.it. 11 units. Doubles 100€–160€ w/breakfast. MC, V. Bus: C1, C2, 14, or 23.*

kids **Plus Florence** NORTH OF CENTER Hotel amenities, private rooms sleeping up to three, a swimming pool, Turkish bath, and free Wi-Fi: You'd never think this was a hostel, until you saw the building (ugly) and the price (incredible value). *Via Santa Caterina d'Alessandria 15.* ☎ *055-4628934. www.plusflorence. com. 110 units. Doubles 55€–65€. MC, V. Bus: 8 or 20.*

The view from La Scaletta's roof terrace.

Relais Uffizi CENTRO STORICO Tucked down an alley behind the Loggia dei Lanzi, this hotel is a great value for its location, in a 15th-century building with homey, midsize to large rooms. *Chiasso de' Baroncelli.* ☎ *055-2676239. www.relais uffizi.it. 12 units. Doubles 120€–220€ w/breakfast. AE, MC, V. Bus: B.*

★★ kids **Residence Hilda** CENTRO STORICO These bright, modern apartments with hotel amenities come fully equipped and with a great location between the Duomo and Santissima Annunziata. No minimum stay. *Via dei Servi 40.* ☎ *055-288021. www.residencehilda.com. 12 units. Apartments 150€–450€. AE, MC, V. Bus: C1, 6, 14, 23, 31, or 32.*

★ **Rosso 23** SANTA MARIA NOVELLA Hip visitors shell out small fortunes for a room on Florence's trendiest piazza. You can secure one at a fraction of the price without sacrificing (too much) style. *Piazza Santa Maria Novella 23.* ☎ *055-277300. www.hotelrosso23. com. 42 units. Doubles 82€–160€ w/ breakfast. MC, V. Bus: 11, 36, or 37.*

★ **Tourist House Ghiberti** CENTRO STORICO Large rooms with clean lines but a traditional Florentine flavor characterize this modern B&B near the Duomo. There's a shared guest Jacuzzi for tired feet and a computer in every room. *Via Bufalini 1.* ☎ *055-284858. www. touristhouseghiberti.com. 5 units. Doubles 79€–150€ w/breakfast. AE, MC, V. Bus: C1, 14, or 23.*

★ **UNA Hotel Vittoria** SAN FREDIANO The Florence outpost of boutique chain UNA offers bold, affordable designer rooms loaded with modern amenities. A dependable business choice with a stylish kick. *Via Pisana 59.* ☎ *055-22771. www.unahotels.it. 84 units. Doubles 109€–306€ w/breakfast. MC, V. Bus: 6.*

The Best Shopping in Florence

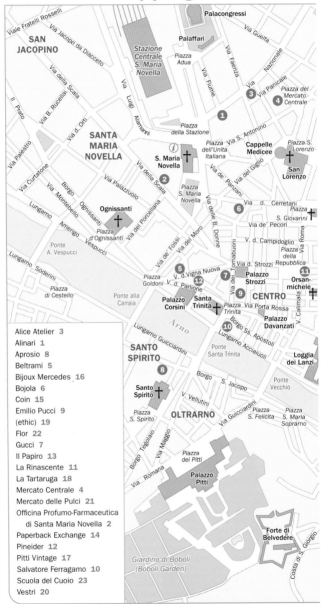

Alice Atelier 3
Alinari 1
Aprosio 8
Beltrami 5
Bijoux Mercedes 16
Bojola 6
Coin 15
Emilio Pucci 9
(ethic) 19
Flor 22
Gucci 7
Il Papiro 13
La Rinascente 11
La Tartaruga 18
Mercato Centrale 4
Mercato delle Pulci 21
Officina Profumo-Farmaceutica
    di Santa Maria Novella 2
Paperback Exchange 14
Pineider 12
Pitti Vintage 17
Salvatore Ferragamo 10
Scuola del Cuoio 23
Vestri 20

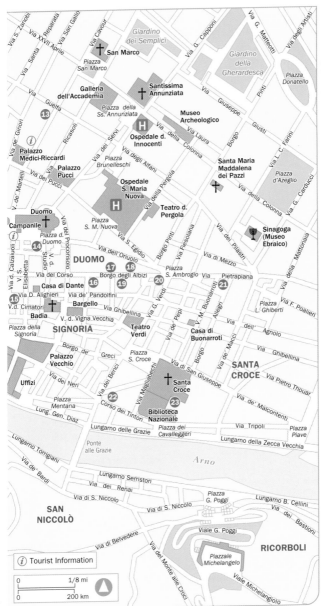

Via S. Zanobi
Via XXVII Aprile
Via San Gallo
Via S. Reparata
Via Caviour
San Marco
Piazza
San Marco
Giardino
dei Semplici
Via G. Capponi
Via G. Marteoti
Via degli Artisti
Giardino
della
Gherardesca
Piazza
Donatello
Via Santa
Via Guelfa
Galleria
dell'Accademia
Santissima
Annunziata
Piazza della
Ss. Annunziata
Museo
Archeologico
Via Giuseppe
Giusti
Via G. Pinti
Piazza
d'Azeglio
Via L. C. Farini
Via della Mattonaia
Via della Colonna
Via G. Carducci
13
Via de' Ginori
Via Ricasoli
Via de' Servi
Via degli Alfani
Via della Colonna
Ospedale d.
Innocenti
H
Via della Laura
Borgo
Pinti
Palazzo
Medici-Riccardi
Palazzo
Pucci
Via dei Pucci
Piazza
Brunelleschi
Santa Maria
Maddalena
dei Pazzi
V. de' Martelli
Ospedale
S. Maria
Nuova
H
Piazza
S. M. Nuova
Teatro d.
Pergola
Via della Pergola
Sinagoga
(Museo
Ebraico)
Duomo
Campanile
Piazza d.
Duomo
Via del Proconsolo
Via S. Egidio
Via de' Pilastri
Via d. Calzaiuoli
V. d. Studio
V. S. Elisabetta
14
Via dell'Oriuolo
DUOMO
17
18
Piazza
S. Ambrogio
Via Pietrapiana
Via di Mezzo
Via del Corso
Borgo degli Albizi
Borgo Pinti
Via Fiesolana
Via
Via F. Poalieri
Casa di Dante
16
19
Via de' Pandolfini
20
Via G. Verdi
Piazza
L. Ghiberti
Via Allegri
21
Bargello
Via Ghibellina
Via de' Pepi
Via V. M. Buonarroti
15
V.d. Cimatori
Badia
V. d. Vigna Vecchia
SIGNORIA
Teatro
Verdi
Piazza
S. Croce
Casa di
Buonarroti
Via de' Macci
Via dell' Agnolo
SANTA
CROCE
Via Ghibellina
Piazza della
Signoria
Borgo de'
Greci
Via di San Giuseppe
Via Pietro Thouar
Palazzo
Vecchio
Via Magliabechi
Santa
Croce
Via de' Malcontenti
Uffizi
Via dei Neri
Via de' Benci
22
Corso dei Tintori
23
Biblioteca
Nazionale
Via Tripoli
Piazza
Piave
Piazza
Mentana
Lung. Gen. Diaz
Piazza dei
Cavalleggeri
Lungarno della Zecca Vecchia
Lungarno delle Grazie
Ponte
alle Grazie
Arno
Lungarno Torrigiani
Via de' Bardi
Lungarno Serristori
Via dei Renai
Via di S. Niccolò
Piazza
G. Poggi
Lungarno B. Cellini
Via dei Bastioni
SAN
NICCOLÒ
Via di S. Niccolò
Viale G. Poggi
RICORBOLI
Via di Belvedere
Via del Monte alle Croci
Piazzale
Michelangelo
Viale Michelangiolo

(i) Tourist Information

0   1/8 mi
0   200 km

Shopping Best Bets

Handmade stationery makes a great Florentine gift.

Best for Affordable Jewelry
★★ Bijoux Mercedes, *Borgo degli Albizi 45R (p 63)*

Best for Florentine High Fashion
★★★ Gucci, *Via de' Tornabuoni 73R (p 64)*

Best for Leather Goods
★★ Scuola del Cuoio, *Piazza Santa Croce 16 (p 65)*

Best Food Market
★★ Mercato Centrale, *Piazza del Mercato Centrale (p 65)*

Best for Vintage Clothes
★★ Pitti Vintage, *Borgo degli Albizi 72R (p 64)*

Best for Paper Goods
★★ Pineider, *Piazza Rucellai (p 65)*

Best Beauty Products
★★★ Officina Profumo-Farmaceutica di Santa Maria Novella, *Via della Scala 16 (p 63)*

Best for Souvenir Prints
★ Alinari, *Largo Alinari 15 (p 65)*

Best Street for Haute Couture Labels
Via de' Tornabuoni

Best Street for Browsing Small Indie Stores
Borgo degli Albizi

Best Department Store
Coin, *Via dei Calzaiuoli 56R (p 64)*

Best Shoes for Men and Women
★★ Salvatore Ferragamo, *Via de' Tornabuoni 14R (p 65)*

Best for Bric-a-Brac Browsing
★ Mercato delle Pulci, *Piazza de' Ciompi (p 65)*

Best Local Craftsmanship
★★ Alice Atelier, *Via Faenza 72R (p 64)*

Florence Shopping A to Z

Florence is known for its showrooms of famous designers and for its artisan workshops, turning out jewelry and leather of the highest quality. The most fashionable shops—and the most expensive—are clustered along **Via de' Tornabuoni.** There you'll find big international names like **Prada** (51R; ☎ 055-283439), **Giorgio Armani** (48R; ☎ 055-219041), **Celine** (26R; ☎ 055-2645521), **MaxMara** (68–70R; ☎ 055-214133), and **Roberto Cavalli** (83R; ☎ 055-2396226). **Via della Vigna Nuova** and **Via degli Strozzi** also pack a high style quotient. **Borgo degli Albizi** is the street to hit for independent fashion and affordable stylish jewelry.

Accessories

★ **Aprosio** OLTRARNO Glass and crystal jewelry without equal in the city are sold at this temple to upscale creativity. *Via Santo Spirito 11.* ☎ *055-290534. www.aprosio.it. MC, V. Bus: C3, D, 6, 11, 36, or 37.*

★★ **Bijoux Mercedes** SANTA CROCE Handmade jewelry for fashion-conscious women of all ages. Gold, silver, bronze, semiprecious stones, and acrylic are fashioned right in the store. *Borgo degli Albizi 45R.* ☎ *055-2342226. MC, V. Bus: C1 or C2.*

Beauty Products

★★ **Flor** SANTA CROCE Handcrafted fragrances, soaps, and creams sold from the elegant surrounds of a former *deposito. Borgo Santa Croce 6.* ☎ *055-2343471. MC, V. Bus: C3, 13, or 23.*

★★★ **Officina Profumo-Farmaceutica di Santa Maria Novella** CENTRO STORICO Herbal secrets used by the Medici are still sold here in a wonderfully antique atmosphere—potpourris, perfumes, scented soaps, and more. *Via della Scala 16.* ☎ *055-216276. www. smnovella.it. AE, MC, V. Bus: 11, 36, or 37.*

Books

kids Paperback Exchange CENTRO STORICO New and used titles, all in English. *Via delle Oche 4R.* ☎ *055-293460. www.papex.it. AE, DC, MC, V. Bus: C1 or C2.*

VAT Refund

Visitors from non-European Union countries who spend 155€ or more at any one shop are entitled to a value-added tax (VAT) refund worth 4% to 20% of the total. To get a refund, pick up a tax-free form from the retailer. Present your unused purchases and their receipt for inspection at the Customs Office (Dogana) at your point of departure. An inspector will stamp your form, enabling you to pick up a refund (minus commission) from a refunds agent on the spot.

Florence's flagship department stores, Coin and La Rinascente, are great places to shop for housewares.

Chocolate
★ **kids Vestri** SANTA CROCE There's no mistaking the aroma . . . cocoa, made into all shapes and sizes, including gelato, granita, and cold drinking chocolate, at this artisan chocolatier. *Borgo degli Albizi 11R.* ☎ *055-2340374. www.vestri.it. MC, V. Bus: C1, C2, 14, or 23.*

Crafts
★★ **kids Alice Atelier** SAN LORENZO Handmade theatrical masks in Venetian *Carnevale* and *Commedia dell'arte* styles. *Via Faenza 72R.* ☎ *055-287370. www.alicemasks.com. AE, MC, V. Bus: 2, 12, 13, 28, 29, 30, 35, or 57.*

Department Stores
kids Coin CENTRO STORICO This department store in a 16th-century *palazzo* sells everything from affordable clothing for men, women, and children, to Italian-designed kitchenware, to cosmetics. *Via dei Calzaiuoli 56R.* ☎ *055-280531. www.coin.it. AE, DC, MC, V. Bus: C2.*

La Rinascente CENTRO STORICO This six-story emporium sells top Italian designerwear at affordable prices. *Piazza della Repubblica 1. www.rinascente.it.* ☎ *055-219113. AE, DC, MC, V. Bus: C2.*

Fashion
★★ **Emilio Pucci** CENTRO STORICO Marilyn Monroe left a request to be buried in her favorite Pucci dress, and their bright, busy patterns are in fashion again. *Via de' Tornabuoni 20–22R.* ☎ *055-2658082. www.pucci.com. AE, DC, MC, V. Bus: 6, 11, 22, 36, or 37.*

kids (ethic) SANTA CROCE Edgy high-street styles for women and girls. They also carry the latest CDs, soaps, fashion magazines, and more. *Borgo degli Albizi 37R.* ☎ *055-2260065. MC, V. Bus: C1 or C2.*

★★★ **Gucci** CENTRO STORICO Unforgettable luxury leather goods and high fashion in the city Gucci calls home. *Via de' Tornabuoni 73R.* ☎ *055-264011. www.gucci.com. AE, DC, MC, V. Bus: 6, 11, 22, 36, or 37.*

★★ **Pitti Vintage** SANTA CROCE Vintage heaven: classic threads, stylish men's shirts, and accessories for women such as silk scarves, 1980s bags, and haute couture dresses. *Borgo degli Albizi 72R.* ☎ *055-2344115. www.pittivintage.com. MC, V. Bus: C1 or C2.*

Leather
★★ **Beltrami** CENTRO STORICO This world-famous, Florence-based leathermaker offers stunning footwear, handbags, belts, briefcases, and luggage at fair prices. *Via della Vigna Nuova 70R.* ☎ *055-287779. AE, DC, MC, V. Bus: C3, 6, 11, 36, or 37.*

★ **Bojola** CENTRO STORICO A leading retailer of traditional Florentine leather goods. The store pioneered the 1960s trend of combining leather and cotton fabric. *Via dei Rondinelli 25R.* ☎ *055-211155. www.bojola.it. AE, DC, MC, V. Bus: C2, 4, 6, 11, 22, 36, or 37.*

★★ Scuola del Cuoio SANTA CROCE The sales outlet for genuine handcrafted leather goods made at Florence's world-famous leather school. *Piazza Santa Croce 16 (entrance behind church in Via San Giuseppe).* ☎ *055-244534. AE, DC, MC, V. Bus: C3 or 23.*

Markets

★★ Mercato Centrale SAN LORENZO Wine, olive oil, porcini mushrooms, and pecorino cheese— it's all on sale on two floors of Europe's largest covered food hall. *Piazza del Mercato Centrale. No phone. Bus: C1.*

★ Mercato delle Pulci SANTA CROCE Florence's daily flea market specializes in a bit of everything: costume jewelry, ornaments, vintage buttons, silver, antique bric-a-brac, and yesteryear postcards. *Piazza de' Ciompi. No phone. Bus: C1, C2, C3, or 14.*

Paper & Stationery

★ Il Papiro CENTRO STORICO Sumptuous stationery, photo frames, and more at this boutique chain. *Via Cavour 49R.* ☎ *055-215262. www.ilpapirofirenze.it. AE, MC, V. Bus: C1, 14, or 23.*

★★ Pineider CENTRO STORICO Since 1774 customers from

Produce at the Mercato Centrale.

Napoléon to Elizabeth Taylor have ordered personal stationery, greeting cards, and handcrafted diaries here. *Piazza Rucellai 4–7R.* ☎ *055-284655. www.pineider.com. AE, DC, MC, V. Bus: C3, 6, 11, 36, or 37.*

Prints

★ Alinari SAN LORENZO Black-and-white prints of old Florence courtesy of the world's oldest photo archive. Prices from 30€. *Largo Alinari 15 (inside courtyard at Via Nazionale).* ☎ *055-23951. www.alinari.it. MC, V. Bus: 2, 12, 13, 28, 29, 30, 35, or 57.*

Shoes

★★ Salvatore Ferragamo CENTRO STORICO Shoes (and bags) are big news here, with some world-class fashionwear and accessories for men and women. *Via de' Tornabuoni 2.* ☎ *055-292123. www.salvatoreferragamo.it. AE, DC, MC, V. Bus: C3, 6, 11, 36, or 37.*

Toys

★ kids La Tartaruga SANTA CROCE An enchanting, old-fashioned toy store packed with handmade wooden toys, stuffed dolls, and wrapping paper. *Borgo degli Albizi 60R.* ☎ *055-2340845. MC, V. Bus: C1 or C2.*

Shoes and bags are the stars at Salvatore Ferragamo.

The Best Nightlife/A&E in Florence

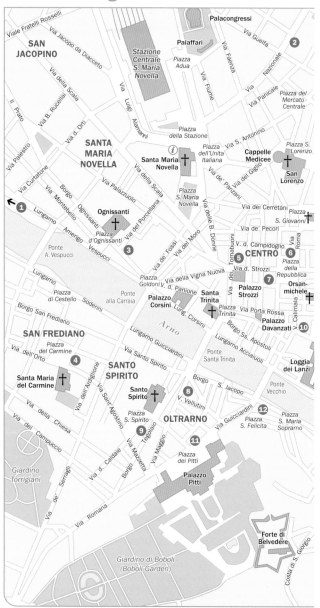

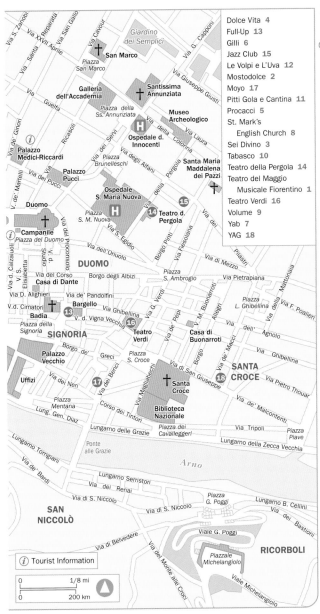

Dolce Vita 4
Full-Up 13
Gilli 6
Jazz Club 15
Le Volpi e L'Uva 12
Mostodolce 2
Moyo 17
Pitti Gola e Cantina 11
Procacci 5
St. Mark's
  English Church 8
Sei Divino 3
Tabasco 10
Teatro della Pergola 14
Teatro del Maggio
  Musicale Fiorentino 1
Teatro Verdi 16
Volume 9
Yab 7
YAG 18

Nightlife/A&E Best Bets

Best Wine Bar
★★ Le Volpi e l'Uva, *Piazza de' Rossi 1 (p 69)*

Best Cafe
★★ Procacci, *Via de' Tornabuoni 64R (p 69)*

Best Aperitivo Hour
★ Moyo, *Via de' Benci 23R (p 69)*

Best Gay Club
★ Tabasco, *Piazza Santa Cecilia 3 (p 70)*

Best for Jazz & Blues
★ Jazz Club, *Via Nuova de' Caccini 3 (p 70)*

Best Theater
★★ Teatro della Pergola, *Via della Pergola 12–32 (p 70)*

Best Opera & Ballet
★★ Teatro del Maggio Musicale Fiorentino, *Corso Italia 16 (p 70)*

Outdoor summer music events are a staple of the Tuscan festival calendar.

Best Bar for Twentysomething Hipsters
★★ Volume, *Piazza Santo Spirito 5R (p 69)*

Club & Concert Tips

Italian clubs are cliquey—people usually go in groups to hang out and dance with one another. Plenty of flesh is on display, but single travelers hoping to find dance partners may be disappointed. If you're clubbing at the cutting edge, pick up a copy of the latest *Firenze Spettacolo* at newsstands (2€) or check the website for **Zero** (http://firenze.zero.eu).

Florence is wanting for the grand opera houses of Milan and Rome, but the city has two symphony orchestras and Fiesole's fine music school. Florence's theaters are respectable, and most major touring companies stop in town on their way through Italy. **St. Mark's English Church** (☎ 340-8119192; www.concertoclassico.info), in Oltrarno, also stages regular opera and classical music concerts. Each summer **Opera Festival** (☎ 055-5978309; www.festivalopera.it) organizes operas and musicals in atmospheric locations like the Giardino di Boboli.

Tickets for most cultural and music events are available through **Boxol** (☎ 055-210804; www.boxol.it).

Florence Nightlife/A&E A to Z

Bars & Wine Bars

★★ **Le Volpi e L'Uva** OLTRARNO Over 50 Tuscan vintages by the glass draw them in to this quirky wine bar in a tiny piazza behind Santa Felicità church. *Piazza de' Rossi 1.* ☎ *055-2398132. www. levolpieluva.com. Bus: C3 or D.*

Mostodolce SAN LORENZO A young crowd enjoys artisan beer brewed in nearby Prato, and sports (usually soccer) on the screens. *Via Nazionale 114R.* ☎ *055-2302928. www.mostodolce.it. Bus: 1, 6, 11, 14, 17, or 23.*

★ **Moyo** SANTA CROCE One of the tastiest 7pm *aperitivo* buffets in the city. Cocktails and pumping tunes flow later. *Via de' Benci 23R.* ☎ *055-2479738. Bus: C1, C3, or 23.*

★ **Pitti Gola e Cantina** OLTRARNO This refined little wine bar opposite the Pitti Palace has a carefully selected wines-by-the-glass list. *Piazza de' Pitti 16.* ☎ *055-212704. Bus: C3 or D.*

★ **Sei Divino** CENTRO STORICO Sei Divino features an abundance of artisan beers, Tuscan wines by the glass, interesting cocktails, and *aperitivo* plates piled high every night. *Borgo Ognissanti 42R.* ☎ *055-217791. Bus: C3, 11, 36, or 37.*

★★ **Volume** OLTRARNO At Volume, you'll find an artsy cafe by day, and cocktails and live acoustic music after dark. *Piazza Santo Spirito 5R.* ☎ *055-2381460. www. volume.fi.it. Bus: C3, D, 11, or 36.*

Cafes

★ **Gilli** CENTRO STORICO Dating from 1733, this is the oldest, most elegant cafe in Florence. *Risorgimento* leaders convened here in the 1850s to plot the unification of Italy. *Piazza della Repubblica 39R.* ☎ *055-213896. www.gilli.it. Bus: C2, 6, 11, 22, 36, or 37.*

★★ **Procacci** CENTRO STORICO This darling cafe/bar is beloved by *fashionistas.* Its specialty is *panini tartufati,* rolls filled with truffle paste. *Via de' Tornabuoni 64R.* ☎ *055-211656. Bus: C1, 6, 11, 36, or 37.*

Clubs & DJ Bars

★ **Dolce Vita** SAN FREDIANO Going strong after 3 decades leading Florence's nightlife scene; these days it

The terrace of Gilli cafe is an ideal spot for people-watching.

Musicians performing at the Jazz Club.

attracts fashionable 30-somethings. *Piazza del Carmine.* ☎ *055-284595. www.dolcevitaflorence.com. Bus: D or 6.*

Full-Up SANTA CROCE This old cellar with a small dance floor has DJs playing hip-hop, house, or glam depending on what night you show up (Wed through Sat). *Via della Vigna Vecchia 23–25R.* ☎ *055-293006. www.fullupclub.com. Bus: C1 or C2.*

Yab CENTRO STORICO This glamorous hall of mirrors has been a popular dance club since the 1960s. Expect 20-somethings shaking their stuff, beats, and a rope line. Closed Sunday and Tuesday. *Via Sassetti 5R.* ☎ *055-215160. www.yab.it. Bus: C2, 6, 11, 22, 36, or 37.*

Gay Bars & Clubs

YAG SANTA CROCE Pre-disco drinks with a lively gay, lesbian, bisexual, and trans crowd. *Via de' Macci 8R.* ☎ *055-2469022. www. yagbar.com. Bus: C2, C3, or 14.*

★ **Tabasco** CENTRO STORICO The oldest gay dance club in Italy lives up to its fiery name, with pumping beats, strobe lights, and Tuscan studs. *Piazza Santa Cecilia 3.* ☎ *055-213000. www. tabascogay.it. Bus: C1 or C2.*

Jazz

★ **Jazz Club** SANTA CROCE The best live jazz and blues in town, in an atmospheric basement. Closed July and August. *Via Nuova de' Caccini 3.* ☎ *055-2479700. www.jazzclub firenze.com. Membership 8€. Bus: C1.*

Theater

★★ **Teatro della Pergola** SANTA CROCE This is the major classic theater of Tuscany, but you'd better understand Italian. *Via della Pergola 12–32.* ☎ *055-22641. www. teatrodellapergola.com. Tickets 15€–30€. Bus: C1, 6, 14, 31, or 32.*

Opera & Ballet

★★ **Teatro del Maggio Musicale Fiorentino** WEST OF CENTER This is Florence's main cultural venue for opera, ballet, and classical concerts, and home of the Maggio Musicale. *Corso Italia 16.* ☎ *055-2779350. www.maggiofiorentino.it. Tickets 15€–100€. Bus: C2 or C3.*

★★ **Teatro Verdi** SANTA CROCE Expect everything from Tchaikovsky to *High School Musical* at the home of the Orchestra della Toscana. *Via Ghibellina 99.* ☎ *055-212320. www. teatroverdionline.it. Tickets 17€–50€. Bus: C1, C2, C3, or 23.* ●

3

The Best **Full-Day Tours of Tuscany**

The Best of Tuscany **in Three Days**

DAY 1
1 Pisa
DAY 2
2 San Gimignano
DAY 3
3 Siena

I f you have only 3 days to see Tuscany beyond Florence, focus on Pisa, with its gravity-defying tower; San Gimignano, known for its medieval "skyscrapers"; and Siena, a living repository of Gothic art and architecture. From Florence, you'll shoot 81km (50 miles) west to Pisa, for day 1; 92km (57 miles) southeast to San Gimignano for day 2; and 40km (24 miles) southeast again to Siena.
START: **Florence. Trip length: 283km (174 mile) loop.**

Travel Tip

The most economical way to cover the Campo dei Miracoli is with an **Opera Pisana** pass, available from ticket offices on the piazza. For 10€, you'll get into everything except the Tower. Alternatively, it's 6€ for any two monuments.

Previous page: The Leaning Tower of Pisa.

Pisa is just over an hour west of Florence by car. Follow signs for the four-lane FI–PI–LI *raccordo.*

1 ★★★ kids **Pisa.** Pisa is one of the easiest Tuscan cities to explore, both because it's flat and because nearly all the major attractions center on Piazza del Duomo (also known as the Campo dei Miracoli— "Field of Miracles"). Your half-hour in and at the **Leaning Tower,** or *Torre Pendente,* is a memorable, though

expensive, experience. You certainly shouldn't miss the **Duomo** (cathedral) or **Battistero** (baptistery), and the **Camposanto** (burial ground) provides a more contemplative contrast. The **Museo dell'Opera del Duomo** (cathedral museum) and **Museo Nazionale di San Matteo** are must-sees for anyone with a keen interest in painting and sculpture.

For dining and nightlife, head into the heart of "real" Pisa, closer to the river, where the city's produce market still thrives. After a night of Pisan fare at a local trattoria, bed down and head out the following morning to San Gimignano.

For detailed coverage of sights, hotels, restaurants, shops, and nightlife in Pisa, see p 151 of chapter 6.

From Pisa, head east along the FI–PI–LI *raccordo* until the S429 turnoff at Ponte a Elsa. Take the S429 southeast as far as Certaldo; San Gimignano is signposted on a scenic road south from here. Journey time should be approximately 1½ hr.

The pulpit inside Pisa's Battistero.

② ★★ kids **San Gimignano.** Like Pisa, San Gimignano makes for a doable day trip because its major attractions are tightly packed. Once

The Cattedrale and Baptistery on Pisa's Campo dei Miracoli.

Artwork at the Museo Civico in San Gimignano.

you've parked and dropped your bags at the hotel, you can easily get around the town, with its ancient streets and medieval towers, in a day. The *centro storico* centers around the magnificent twin squares of Piazza del Duomo and Piazza della Cisterna.

Undoubtedly, the art highlight is the frescoed interior of the **Collegiata,** no longer a proper "cathedral" because it doesn't have a bishop's seat. **Sant'Agostino** and the **Museo Civico,** as well as the ascent of the **Torre Grossa,** are all within a few minutes' walk. You should have time left for a real-life horror show at the **Museo della Tortura.** Teens will love it, although little ones may prefer the enchanting reproduction that is **San Gimignano 1300.**

The first essential culinary pause is for an unforgettable ice cream at **Gelateria "di Piazza."** If you're planning a dose of slow food heaven at **Dorandó,** be sure to

book ahead. After dinner, stroll the historic core: With the day-trippers gone, and just you left in town, it's a place of unparalleled magic.

For detailed coverage of sights, hotels, restaurants, shops, and nightlife in San Gimignano, see p 161 of chapter 6.

Siena is 40km (24 miles) southeast of San Gimignano. Head east on the S324 to meet the Firenze–Siena *raccordo* at Poggibonsi, then south to Siena. Enter town via the "Siena Ovest" exit. You should be out of your car and on the way to the Campo within 45 min.

❸ ★★★ **Siena.** Seeing Siena in a day is the biggest challenge of your trip. Begin at the functional and spiritual heart of town, scallop-shaped **Piazza del Campo.** The Lorenzetti and Martini frescoes at the **Museo Civico** (inside the Palazzo Pubblico) should be your first stop. Serious Sienese art fans should then detour to the **Pinacoteca Nazionale,** Siena's picture gallery, for a more in-depth crash course in Sienese art.

Siena's Piazza del Campo.

The richly embellished facade of Siena's cathedral.

After lunch, head for the cathedral complex centered around Piazza del Duomo. You can easily spend 3 hours seeing the **Duomo,** the **Museo dell'Opera Metropolitana** (home of Duccio's *Maestà*), and the **Battistero.** The former hospital of **Santa Maria della Scala,** opposite the Duomo, is a great spot to end your day. (If you have little ones in tow, it's here you'll also find **Bambimus,** the children's art museum.)

If time remains, squeeze in some shopping and cafe time. Siena is renowned for both craftsmanship and bakery products.

With just 1 night in Siena, sleep close to the center to maximize your time. Depending on your budget, the **Antica Residenza Cicogna** or nearby **Campo Regio Relais** will suit, and could hardly be more central. Take your pick between dinner at **Da Divo** (refined Sienese cuisine) or **L'Osteria** (my favorite neighborhood eatery).

For detailed coverage of sights, hotels, restaurants, shops, and nightlife in Siena, see p 168 of chapter 6.

To return to Florence, where you began this whirlwind tour, take the Firenze–Siena *raccordo* north. Total distance is 70km (43 miles). Journey time is around an hour, depending on Florence traffic.

Travel Tip

For detailed information on sights and recommended hotels and restaurants in this chapter, see the individual sections on Arezzo, Cortona, Lucca, Montepulciano, Pienza, Pisa, San Gimignano, Siena, and Volterra in chapter 6, "Charming Tuscan Towns & Villages." For details of tourist offices in all of Tuscany's major destinations, see p 182.

The Best of Tuscany **in One Week**

DAY 1
1. Lucca

DAY 2
2. Pisa

DAY 3
3. Volterra

DAY 4
4. San Gimignano

DAY 5
5. Siena

DAY 6
6. Pienza

DAY 7
7. Montepulciano

8. Arezzo

An extra **4 days in Tuscany means you can experience four** more towns, because driving distances in the region are short and manageable. This weeklong itinerary expands on the 3-day tour to include Lucca, with its Roman street plan ensconced behind mighty ramparts; Pienza, the "ideal Renaissance city" commissioned by Pope Pius II in the 15th century; Montepulciano, which yields one of the world's best wines, Vino Nobile; and Arezzo, home of Tuscany's greatest fresco cycle. START: **Florence. Trip length: 407km (282 mile) loop.**

From Florence, Lucca is 72km (45 miles) west on the A11.

1 ★★ kids **Lucca.** At one time, Lucca was the unofficial capital of Tuscany, and a Roman colony known to Caesar and Pompey. Today, it's celebrated for the most complete Renaissance ramparts in Europe. I recommend you start by circumnavigating them on a bicycle.

After your ride, you can see the highlights of Lucca from closer up: although it is light on truly first-class museums, the town shelters some of Tuscany's loveliest churches. Try to visit the **Cattedrale di San Martino, San Frediano,** and **San Michele in Foro,** if only to check out their Pisan-Romanesque facades. Leave yourselves time for one of Lucca's great pleasures:

wandering the main pedestrian shopping street, **Via Fillungo.**

There are plenty of trattorias where you can dine on Lucchese fare that evening, before bedding down for the night. Lodge inside the walls for more atmosphere.

For detailed coverage of sights, hotels, restaurants, shops, and nightlife in Lucca, see p 133 of chapter 6.

Leave early and drive 22km (14 miles) southwest on the S12r to:

❷ ★★★ kids **Pisa.** For detailed suggestions on how to make the most of Pisa in a day, see "The Best of Tuscany in Three Days," p 72, ❶.

For detailed coverage of sights, hotels, restaurants, shops, and nightlife in Pisa, see p 151 of chapter 6.

From Pisa, head southeast along the FI–PI–LI *raccordo* to the S439 turnoff at Ponsacco. Take the S439, following signs for Capannoli then for Volterra. Total journey time for the 69km (43-mile) trip is around 1¼ hr.

❸ ★★ **Volterra.** If you arrive in the morning, you can cover Volterra's attractions in a day. Take in the **Duomo;** a major Etruscan treasure-trove in the **Museo Guarnacci;** the frescoed chapel inside **San Francesco;** and best of all, the town's

Biking is an ideal way to tour Lucca.

Volterra's Duomo.

Pinacoteca, home of Rosso Fiorentino's iconic *Deposition.*

For detailed coverage of sights, hotels, restaurants, shops, and nightlife in Volterra, see p 176 of chapter 6.

Head east on the S68 as far as Castelsangimignano, then turn north. The journey from Volterra to San Gimignano is 30km (18½ miles).

❹ ★★ kids **San Gimignano.** Arrive in San Gimignano in the morning and set about exploring the town, with its once-fortified medieval towers. For guidance, see "The Best of Tuscany in Three Days," p 73, ❷.

For detailed coverage of sights, hotels, restaurants, shops, and nightlife in San Gimignano, see p 161 of chapter 6.

Siena is 40km (24 miles) southeast of San Gimignano. Head east on the S324 to meet the Firenze–Siena *raccordo* at Poggibonsi, then south to Siena. Enter via the "Siena Ovest" exit.

❺ ★★★ **Siena.** There's no Gothic city like it anywhere in the world—follow the outline in "The Best of Tuscany in Three Days," p 72, to see the best of it in a day. Siena's center is more alluring on a summer evening than even Florence, so round off your evening with a gelato at my favorite place in town, **Kopa Kabana.**

For detailed coverage of sights, hotels, restaurants, shops, and nightlife in Siena, see p 168 of chapter 6.

Travel Tip

This itinerary does not leave you much time to relax at your stops. If you prefer to move more slowly, consider sacrificing one of the stops to spend an extra day in Siena: See Siena, in "The Best of Tuscany in Ten Days," p 80, for suggestions on how to spend that day.

Leave Siena early, the morning of your sixth day, and drive southeast 55km (33 miles) on the S2 then S146 to:

⑥ ★ **Pienza.** You can see all of Pienza's major attractions in about 3 hours, before heading out for your next stopover. The highlights of this

model Renaissance town are all in **Piazza Pio II,** chiefly the **Duomo, Museo Diocesano,** and **Palazzo Piccolomini.** Wine collectors shouldn't depart without at least looking in at the **Enoteca di Ghino.** Grab a *porchetta* sandwich from **Nannetti e Bernardini** and make for your next stop.

For detailed coverage of sights, hotels, restaurants, shops, and nightlife in Pienza, see p 146 of chapter 6.

Montepulciano is 14km (8¾ miles) east, on the S146.

⑦ ★★ **Montepulciano.** After the morning in Pienza, strike out for an afternoon in Montepulciano. Plan to arrive right after lunch, so you can see Montepulciano's attractions before nightfall. The unmissable sights here are the **Cattedrale,** the **Tempio di San Biagio** (just outside the gates), and the **Palazzo Nobili-Tarugi.** Leave time for tasting some Vino Nobile: **Gattavecchi** is my favorite cellar in town. End your day with one of the best steaks you're ever going to eat, at **Acquacheta.**

For detailed coverage of sights, hotels, restaurants, shops, and nightlife in Montepulciano, see p 142 of chapter 6.

The medieval towers of San Gimignano.

The interior of Pienza's Duomo.

Leave Montepulciano first thing, driving 53km (33 miles) north to Arezzo. Head northeast on the S327 to the Firenze–Roma autostrada, then north until you reach the signposted exit.

8 ★★ **Arezzo.** For your final look at Tuscany, Arezzo won't disappoint; it's the major reason to visit the northeastern part of the region. Its steep medieval streets were made for walking (in sensible shoes), but the chief attraction is painted inside the **Basilica di San Francesco:** Piero della Francesca's *Legend of the True Cross.* Book your timed entrance slot as soon as you hit town. If you're rushed, you can skip the **Duomo,** but don't miss the **Pieve di Santa Maria,** crazy-sloping **Piazza Grande,** or a trip to the **Casa di Vasari,** native-son Giorgio's old digs. The city goes very quiet during the afternoon *riposo* (Italian *siesta*), so I try to make lunch at **Gastronomia Il Cervo** stretch through the middle part of the day. If you're not due back in Florence until the following day, Arezzo has a couple of stylish, central boutique accommodations at very fair prices.

For detailed coverage of sights, hotels, restaurants, shops, and nightlife in Arezzo, see p 124 of chapter 6.

Arezzo is only 81km (50 miles) southeast of Florence, an easy drive up the A1.

The steep streets of Montepulciano.

The Best of Tuscany **in Ten Days**

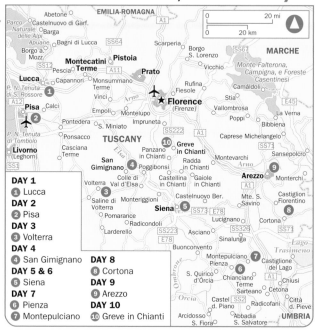

DAY 1
1 Lucca
DAY 2
2 Pisa
DAY 3
3 Volterra
DAY 4
4 San Gimignano
DAY 5 & 6
5 Siena
DAY 7
6 Pienza
7 Montepulciano

DAY 8
8 Cortona
DAY 9
9 Arezzo
DAY 10
10 Greve in Chianti

This tour is similar to Tuscany in 1 week, with the extra days allowing a few additional stops, notably in Cortona, a steeply pitched throwback to the Middle Ages with two fine museums; and in Chianti Country, where you should have time to visit a vineyard or two before your return to Florence. Those extra days also allow you to take things a little slower. START: **Florence. Trip length: 510km (305 miles) round-trip.**

From Florence, Lucca is 72km (45 miles) west on the A11.

1 ★★ kids **Lucca.** Head west from Florence for a 1-day visit to Lucca, where you can circumnavigate its intact Renaissance walls by bike. A 1-day itinerary is detailed in "The Best of Tuscany in One Week," p 76.

For detailed coverage of sights, hotels, restaurants, shops, and night-life in Lucca, see p 133 of chapter 6.

Leave Lucca early and drive 22km (14 miles) southwest on the S12r to:

2 ★★★ kids **Pisa.** If you arrive early enough, you can see Pisa's sights before twilight, and then spend the night on the town. See Pisa, in "The Best of Tuscany in Three Days," p 72.

For detailed coverage of sights, hotels, restaurants, shops, and night-life in Pisa, see p 151 in chapter 6.

From Pisa, head east toward Florence on the FI-PI-LI and take the turn south at Ponsacco signposted for Volterra. Total distance is 65km (40 miles).

❸ ★★ **Volterra.** If you arrive in the morning, you can cover Volterra's attractions in a day, including the town's **Pinacoteca,** home of Rosso Fiorentino's iconic *Deposition*. See Volterra, in "The Best of Tuscany in One Week," p 176.

For detailed coverage of sights, hotels, restaurants, shops, and nightlife in Volterra, see p 176 of chapter 6.

Head east 17km (11 miles) along the S68 as far as Castelsangimignano, then follow signs 13km (8 miles) north to:

❹ ★★ kids **San Gimignano.** Get here early to do San Gimignano in a day. For the 1-day tour, see "The Best of Tuscany in Three Days," p 73, ❷.

For detailed coverage of sights, hotels, restaurants, shops, and nightlife, see p 161 of chapter 6.

Siena is 40km (24 miles) southeast of San Gimignano. Head east on the S324 to meet the Firenze–Siena *raccordo* at Poggibonsi, then south to Siena. Enter via the "Siena Ovest" exit.

Pisa's Duomo and Leaning Tower.

The pulpit inside Siena's Duomo.

❺ ★★★ **Siena.** As a Tuscan destination, Siena is rivaled only by Florence. Because there is so much to see and do, schedule a 2-night stopover. See "The Best of Tuscany in Three Days," p 72, for the best 1-day itinerary—although you can afford to move a little more slowly, leaving a sight or two for your second day.

Start that second day with the **Archivio di Stato,** and you shouldn't miss the **Torre del Mangia,** if you haven't climbed it already. Then visit

the **Casa di Santa Caterina,** with mementos of Italy's patron saint, and **San Domenico,** a church also linked with St. Catherine, where you can see her preserved head.

For detailed coverage of sights, hotels, restaurants, shops, and nightlife in Siena, see p 168 of chapter 6.

Leave Siena early, the morning of your seventh day, and drive southeast on the S2 and S146 for 55km (33 miles) to:

6 ★ **Pienza.** The Renaissance town is compact enough to cover in a morning. See Pienza, in "The Best of Tuscany in One Week," p 78. After lunch, continue to Montepulciano for the afternoon and night.

For detailed coverage of sights, hotels, restaurants, shops, and nightlife in Pienza, see p 146 of chapter 6.

From Pienza, take the S146 east for 13km (8 miles) to:

7 ★★ **Montepulciano.** For a half-day itinerary in Montepulciano, see Montepulciano in "The Best of Tuscany in One Week," p 78. Spend the night here and head onward in the morning.

For detailed coverage of sights, hotels, restaurants, shops, and nightlife in Montepulciano, see p 142 of chapter 6.

Sangiovese grapes hanging from vines in Greve.

From Montepulciano, head for Cortona, a distance of 45km (28 miles), via Bettolle and the Siena–Perugia *raccordo.*

8 ★★ **kids Cortona.** This medieval hilltown is major-league steep, but you can still do it in a day. The chief sights are a revamped **Museo dell'Accademia Etrusca e della Città (MAEC)** and sublime panels by Signorelli and Fra' Angelico at the **Museo Diocesano.** If you're fit, take a hike and finish your day with the views from high up on the **Fortezza Medicea.**

For complete coverage of Cortona, see p 128 in chapter 6.

From Cortona, drive north 34km (22 miles) on the S71 to:

9 ★★ **Arezzo.** Build your day here around the Piero della Francesca frescoes. For a 1-day itinerary, see Arezzo in "The Best of Tuscany in One Week."

For detailed coverage of Arezzo, see p 124 in chapter 6.

Drive northwest, following signs to Firenze. Take the autostrada northwest toward Florence, to the exit for Figline Valdarno. Follow a signposted route west to:

10 ★ **Greve in Chianti.** On your way back to Florence, make a detour for some good living in Chianti Country. Centered around Piazza Matteotti, **Greve** is riddled with wine shops *(enoteches),* and you'll have time to visit a winery or two in the surrounding hills. Our local favorite is **Vignamaggio,** just south of Greve. Divert 7km (4 miles) south to Panzano for tasting and an entertaining wine education at Chianti's best enoteca, the **Accademia del Buon Gusto.**

For more coverage of Chianti Country, see the dedicated tour on p 112 of chapter 5.

Florence is 27km (17 miles) north of Greve on the S222. ●

Tuscany for **Art & Architecture Lovers**

1 Lucca
2 Prato
3 Pistoia
4 Pisa
5 Volterra
6 San Gimignano
7 Siena
8 Monte Oliveto Maggiore
9 Pienza
10 Montepulciano
11 Arezzo
12 Sansepolcro
13 Museo "Madonna del Parto"

During the Middle Ages and Renaissance, painters and sculptors who wanted to make a living went to Florence, Pisa, or Siena, where the churches, guilds, and wealthy patrons were. For the most part, the art stayed where it was created. This doesn't mean you won't find great art elsewhere in Tuscany; Arezzo has the region's finest wall paintings. Architecture buffs have a broader playing field: Where the *palazzi* and city plans of Montepulciano and Pienza attracted the stars of the Renaissance, provincial towns such as Lucca mix medieval and Liberty styles. START: **Lucca is 72km (45 miles) west of Florence on the A11. Trip length: 9 days.**

Travel Tip

For recommended hotels and restaurants, see Lucca, Pisa, San Gimignano, Volterra, Montepulciano, Pienza, Arezzo, and Siena in chapter 6, "Charming Tuscan Towns & Villages."

1 ★ **Lucca.** While light on the art front, for architecture buffs Lucca is one of the most rewarding stops in Tuscany. The facades of the town's many churches exemplify the

Previous page: Grapes on the vine in Tuscany.

Pisan-Romanesque style, richly embroidered with polychrome marble insets and relief carvings, often by visiting Lombard and Pisan sculptors. The finest two are the **Cattedrale di San Martino,** with its green and white marble facade by Guidetto da Como; and the exceptionally tall **San Michele in Foro**— another stellar example of Luccan influence on the Pisan-Romanesque style, with its twisted columns and arcades.

The more restrained "Luccan-Romanesque" style of **San Frediano** is graced with white marble plundered from Lucca's Roman amphitheater and embellished with a giant Byzantine-style gold mosaic by Berlinghieri.

For more on Lucca, see p 132 of chapter 6.

Lodge 2 nights in Lucca, visiting both Prato and Pistoia on your second day by train.

2 ★★ **Prato.** One of central Italy's outstanding fresco cycles, the apse paintings of Prato's **Duomo** were executed between 1452 and 1466 by Fra' Filippo Lippi, a Dominican monk. The frescoes were reopened to the public, after a dazzling restoration, in 2007. The cathedral's

Prato's Duomo.

Assunta Chapel also has incomplete frescoes by Florentine pioneer of perspective, Paolo Uccello (painted 1435–36). Designed by Giuliano da Sangallo, **Santa Maria delle Carceri** was the first centrally planned temple-like church of the High Renaissance.

See also p 98, **1**.

3 ★★ **Pistoia.** The greatest of the four Gothic pulpits carved by father-and-son team Nicola and Giovanni Pisano (see **4**, below) is inside the little Romanesque church of **Sant'Andrea.** Elsewhere in the

The Ospedale del Ceppo in Pistoia.

One of the narrow entrances to Siena's Campo.

compact center, visit Giovanni della Robbia's terra-cotta frieze on the **Ospedale del Ceppo** and the 1372 frescoes of the **Cappella del Tau.**

For more on Pistoia, see p 156 of chapter 6.

From Lucca, take the S12r south 21km (13 miles), following signs for:

④ ★★★ **Pisa.** With its **Duomo** and **Leaning Tower,** Pisa introduced the world to the Arab-influenced "Pisan-Romanesque" style of architecture—which flourished from the 11th to the 13th centuries, when the Pisan Republic was a powerful maritime city-state. Gothic sculpture flourished here as well, in the hands of sculptor Nicola Pisano (1220–84) and his son, Giovanni Pisano (1250–1315).

Touring Pisa is easy; its major monuments center around Piazza del Duomo (also known as the **Campo dei Miracoli,** or "Field of Miracles"). Here you'll also find the **Battistero,** with its unusual Gothic dome and Pisano pulpit; and the **Museo dell'Opera del Duomo,** a repository of Gothic sculpture in marble and bronze.

The **Museo Nazionale di San Matteo,** a short trek across town, houses the city's best paintings, notably works by Masaccio (1401–28) and Simone Martini (1284–1344).

For more on Pisa, see p 151 of chapter 6.

On your fourth morning, head east toward Florence on the *FI-PI-LI* and take the turn south at Ponsacco signposted for Volterra. Total distance is 65km (40 miles).

⑤ ★ **Volterra.** Don't pass by this Etruscan hilltown without stopping in at its picture gallery, the **Pinacoteca.** On the first floor you'll find the exemplar of early Florentine Mannerism, in the form of Rosso Fiorentino's 1521 *Deposition*. It was one of Tuscany's first works of truly "modern" art. Architecture buffs should see the **Palazzo dei Priori,** the oldest Gothic town hall in Tuscany. It was the template for Florence's Palazzo Vecchio.

For more on Volterra, see p 176 of chapter 6.

Start your fifth day by heading east 17km (11 miles) along the S68 as far as Castelsangimignano, then following signs 13km (8 miles) north to:

⑥ ★★ **San Gimignano.** Although Italy's best-preserved medieval town is today unique in appearance, in the Middle Ages towns throughout central Italy were much like it. Visit **San Gimignano 1300** to see how it once looked.

Thirteen of 70+ original towers are left standing from that heyday in the decades before the devastating Black Death. More than defensive strongholds, the towers stood as symbols of a family's prestige and worth. Art outposts not to miss include Benozzo Gozzoli's frescoes inside **Sant'-Agostino,** and

Domenico Ghirlandaio's *Legend of Santa Fina* frescoes inside the **Collegiata**.

For more on San Gimignano, see p 161 of chapter 6.

Siena is 40km (24 miles) southeast of San Gimignano—set out early to make the most of just 1 day there. Head east on the S324 to Poggibonsi and take the Firenze–Siena *raccordo* south to the "Siena Ovest" exit.

⑦ ★★★ Siena. In the Middle Ages, Siena rivaled, even outshone, Florence as an art center. Duccio di Buoninsegna and Simone Martini were pioneers in bringing greater realism to the schematic, static Byzantine style, adding flowing lines and expressive human features. Duccio's *Maestà*, inside the **Museo dell'Opera Metropolitana,** is the most important work of this (or any) period in Siena. The Lorenzettis, Pietro and Ambrogio, worked for patrons across Tuscany—and Ambrogio left the greatest work of

civic art in Italy on the walls of the **Palazzo Pubblico,** his *Allegories.*

The Black Death of 1348, which decimated Siena's population, also dealt a crippling blow to its artistic aspirations. Florence rose to prominence. But the vitality of Renaissance Siena is evident inside the **Duomo.** The marble intarsia floor, built over centuries, is joined by Pinturicchio's frescoed Libreria Piccolominea as must-sees for any Tuscan art tourist.

The other place to see where Sienese art went with the onset of what we now call "the Renaissance" is the **Pinacoteca Nazionale:** Look out for works by Francesco di Giorgio Martini, Matteo di Giovanni, and Domenico Beccafumi.

For more on Siena, see p 168 in chapter 6.

Travel Tip

Alongside Florence, the Gothic alleyways of Siena hold more pleasures for art and architecture lovers than any other Tuscan stop. If you have an extra day to allocate, spend it there.

San Biagio, just outside Montepulciano's walls (see p 144).

Your seventh day is spent touring south of Siena before lodging overnight in Montepulciano. Monte Oliveto Maggiore is best reached by the spectacular S438 then S451 via Asciano, at 38km (23½ miles) one of Tuscany's great drives. Afterward head to the S2, then 22km (13 miles) southeast to San Quirico d'Orcia, where you'll turn east on the S146 for 10km (6 miles) to Pienza. Montepulciano is a farther 13km (8 miles) to the east.

⑧ ★★ Monte Oliveto Maggiore. The open-air frescoes of the **Chiostro Grande** ("Great Cloister") at this most bucolic of rural monasteries were started between 1495 and 1508 by Cortonese painter Luca Signorelli, then completed by Antonio Bazzi, known as Sodoma. (He included a self-portrait, with his pet badger, in panel 3.) They recount *Scenes from the Life of St. Benedict,* based on the biographical *Dialogues* of Gregory the Great. 🕐 *1 hr.* ☎ *0577-707611. Free admission. Daily 9am–noon and 3:15–6pm (until 5pm Oct–Mar).*

⑨ ★★ Pienza. This village owes its grandiose look to Pope Pius II, who was born here of Sienese stock in 1405. He set out to transform his modest birthplace of Corsignano into a model Renaissance town: Bernardo Rossellino (1409–64), protégé of the Florentine theorist Leon Battista Alberti, carried out the pope's mandate, creating a **Duomo** with a classicized facade, the adjacent **Palazzo Piccolomini,** and a square, **Piazza Pio II,** that remains a miniature Renaissance jewel. Fifty thousand gold florins poorer, but delighted with the job, Pius renamed the village after himself, hence "Pi-enza."

For more on Pienza, see p 146 of chapter 6.

⑩ ★ Montepulciano. First on your agenda in this famous wine town should be a parade of the Renaissance *palazzi* flanking its steep main street, known locally as "Il Corso." The meandering climb ends at **Piazza Grande,** where you'll find Michelozzo's **Palazzo Comunale,** Sangallo's **Palazzo Nobili-Tarugi,** and, inside the **Duomo,** Taddeo di Bartolo's giant *Assumption* altarpiece. Architecture fans mustn't leave town without a short trek outside the gates to the **Tempio di San Biagio,** an architectural masterpiece of the High Renaissance.

For more on Montepulciano, see p 146 of chapter 6.

On day 8, drive east to the autostrada, taking it north toward Firenze for 53km (33 miles) until the Arezzo turnoff.

⑪ ★★★ Arezzo. This prosperous little jewelry town is home to the greatest fresco cycle in Tuscany, justly mentioned in the same breath as Michelangelo's Sistine Chapel and Giotto's Cappella Scrovegni in Padua: Piero della Francesca's *Legend of the True Cross* (1452–66), on the apse walls of **San Francesco.**

Piero was a visionary who imbued his art with an ethereal quality. A pioneering master

The meeting of Solomon and the Queen of Sheba, from Piero's Legend of the True Cross.

Via Matteotti in Sansepolcro.

of perspective, he created human figures that seem to have souls that survive centuries after his death, in the year Columbus reached the Americas. He also painted a small fresco in Arezzo's **Duomo**.

For more on Arezzo, see p 124 of chapter 6.

On the final morning, head east on the S73 for 39km (24 miles) to Sansepolcro. On the road back, take the turnoff for Monterchi after 13km (8 miles).

⑫ ★★ **Sansepolcro.** There's hardly a Tuscan town more interwoven with art than Sansepolcro. Sienese School painter Matteo di Giovanni was born here, and the **Cattedrale di San Giovanni Evangelista,** Via Matteotti 4 (☎ 0575-742078), has a Perugino *Ascension* (1495). But it's the local boy and Early Renaissance master Piero della Francesca (1420–92) that draws the art-lovers.

Head for the **Museo Civico,** Via Aggiunti 65 (☎ 0575-732218), to see his masterpieces. During World War II, the British officer commanding the heights over the town remembered he'd read an essay by Aldous Huxley—entitled "The

Greatest Picture"—which accorded that status to Piero's 1468 *Resurrection of Christ,* still in the same building. He ordered shelling to cease lest a masterpiece be lost, maybe saving Sansepolcro in the process. Also here is Piero's earlier *Polyptych of the Misericordia* (1445–62). Admission 6€. Daily June 15–Sept 15 9:30am–1:30pm and 2:30–7pm; Sept 16–June 14 9:30am–1pm and 2:30–6pm.

For more on Sansepolcro, see p 93, ⑤.

⑬ **Museo "Madonna del Parto."** Art lovers detour to the village of Monterchi for one reason: to see Piero's *Madonna del Parto*. It's almost unique in Italian art in that it depicts the Virgin Mary heavily pregnant—and if you're pregnant, admission to the museum is free. It was painted sometime after 1459 (dating Piero is notoriously tricky). ⏱ *45 min. Via Reglia 1.* ☎ *0575-70713. Admission 3.50€. Apr–Oct daily 9am–1pm and 2–7pm (Sat–Sun 9am–7pm); Nov–Mar daily 9am–1pm and 2–5pm.*

Follow the S73 back to Arezzo (or continue to Florence) for your final night.

Tuscany for **Food & Wine Lovers**

1. Siena
2. Chianti Country
3. Montalcino
4. Montepulciano
5. Sansepolcro
6. Prato

Gastronomes celebrate the fertile, sunbaked countryside of Tuscany for its olive groves and the extra-virgin oil they yield; for its Chianina cattle, acclaimed for producing the most succulent beef in Italy; and for its sangiovese grapes, which give forth chianti, in a region easily explored along the Chiantigiana (the "Chianti Road"). With such a bounty of locally available ingredients, it's only right that Tuscan food be a simply prepared, rural cuisine, known as *cucina povera*. This moveable feast was designed to help you experience the region at its most delicious. START: **Siena (65km/40 miles south of Florence), where you should stay at least 1 night. Trip length: 7 days.**

Travel Tip

For detailed information on sights and recommended hotels and restaurants, see Montepulciano and Siena in chapter 6, "Charming Tuscan Towns & Villages," p 142 and 166.

1 ★★ **Siena.** The Sienese are supposedly "cursed with the sweetest teeth in Tuscany." Since the 13th century, locals have been known for their candied fruit-and-almond cakes and other delicious bakery treats.

Panforte and *panpepato* are the two most famous Sienese cakes, baked to ancient recipes. *Panpepato* is a flat, honey-sweetened cake filled with candied fruits and nuts and flavored with spices; the finishing touch is a dusting of ground pepper, cinnamon, and allspice. *Panforte* is dusted with sugar instead. *Ricciarelli* are lozenge-shaped cakes made from almond, sugar, and honey. Originally a jawbreaker dipped in wine at Christmas, *cavallucci* are made with honey-coated, aniseed-flavored walnuts; for modern tastes, they have been softened.

All are available at family-run bakeries throughout town: **Nannini–Conca d'Oro,** Banchi di Sopra 24 (☎ 0577-41591), is the upscale favorite.

Other Sienese goodies like hung hams, *Cinta Senese* salami (made from a local breed of pig), and

Tuscan wines are available from the city's most extravagant deli: **Pizzicheria de' Miccoli,** Via di Città 95 (☎ 0577-289164).

The town is also home to one of my favorite gelaterie in Tuscany. Far too many ice creams later, I still haven't found a flavor I like better than the *panpepato* at **Kopa Kabana,** Via de' Rossi 52 (☎ 0577-223744).

From Siena, head north on the S222 toward Greve in Chianti, a distance of 42km (26 miles). Stay over a couple of nights to tour the area.

2 ★★ **Chianti Country.** Against a quintessential Tuscan landscape—of medieval wine castles and silver-green olive groves—Chianti Country south of Florence is home to some

The white grape harvest at a vineyard in Tuscany.

Pouring the chianti at Castello di Verrazzano.

of Italy's finest food producers, restaurants, and markets. And then there's the wine: First codified by Cosimo III in 1716, and with a history that stretches back at least to the 7th century A.D., chianti is one of the world's iconic reds. A good base for touring the area is its unofficial capital, **Greve in Chianti.** The town is busiest in September when it hosts the annual Rassegna del Chianti Classico wine fair. You'll find the best local reds at **Vignamaggio,** 5km (3 miles) southeast of town.

Don't leave the Chianti without calling in on one of the region's classic butchers: **Dario Cecchini,** in Panzano, and **Falorni** in Greve are my two favorites.

For more on the Chianti, see the dedicated tour on p 112 of chapter 5.

Head back to Siena then drive south down the S2 for 42km (25 miles), following signs into:

③ ★★★ **Montalcino.** The hills surrounding (largely south of) this medieval town yield **Brunello di Montalcino,** one of the greatest red wines in the world. Many wineries welcome visitors, and the town itself is filled with *enoteches* (wine shops).

The center of the town's foodstuffs, including gourmet honey and Pecorino cheese, is **Enoteca La Fortezza.** While in Montalcino, you can also sample Brunello's "younger brother," the less noble **Rosso di Montalcino** made of the same sangiovese grapes as its more famous counterpart. Aged for only a year after harvest, this is a fruity red with hints of Brunello's complex flavor at a third of the price.

My favorite nearby wine estate is **Poggio Antico** (☎ 0577-848044; www.poggioantico.com), 4km (2½ miles) south of town along the Grosseto road. Its Brunellos, especially the *riserva,* are consistently voted among the top wines in the world. Their sangiovese-cabernet "Supertuscan" Madre is elegant and velvety. *Cantina* visits are free but must be reserved at least a day in advance (more in summer). Tasting on-site costs from 2€ for the Rosso to 22€ for all five of the estate's labels.

For visits to other wineries, check with the **Consorzio del Vino Brunello di Montalcino,** Piazza Cavour 8 (☎ 0577-848246; www.consorziobrunellodimontalcino.it).

For more on Montalcino see p 117, ②.

From Montalcino, head out on your fifth morning via the S146 east 32km (23 miles) to:

④ ★★ **Montepulciano.** This ancient town of Etruscan origin, which perches like an eyrie above the Valdichiana, is celebrated for its violet-scented, ruby wine, **Vino Nobile di Montepulciano,** known since the 8th century. Although Brunello is more beefy and is considered number-one by many connoisseurs, the silkier delights of a good Vino Nobile are well worth sampling. On a tighter budget, as in nearby Montalcino, a younger and less expensive **Rosso di Montepulciano** exists. It is aged less and sold sooner. **Gattavecchi** makes an especially noble selection of wines.

The area is also known for its fine sheep's milk cheese, *pecorino di Pienza*. **Cugusi,** Via della Boccia 8 (2km/ 1¼ miles outside Montepulciano on the road to Pienza; ☎ 0578-757558; www.caseificiocugusi.it), sells directly from the farm. The vast range includes artisan pecorino at every aging stage (from *fresco* to *stagionato*) as well as cheeses wrapped in hazelnut leaves, or herbs and oil, or infused with grapes (known as *ubriaco*, or "drunk").

For a complete rundown on Montepulciano, including hotels, restaurants, and where to taste its wines, see p 146 in chapter 6.

From Montepulciano, head east to the A1 autostrada, and take it north toward Florence. Continue until the turnoff northeast for Arezzo. Continue past this city on the S73 for Sansepolcro. Total distance is 89km (55 miles).

⑤ ★ Sansepolcro. The hometown of Piero della Francesca is the gastronomic center of eastern Tuscany—as well as a normal, workaday Tuscan town, where almost everything is priced for local rather than tourist pockets.

When prepared properly, a *bistecca alla fiorentina* is among the best steaks in the world. Authentic versions hail only from the indigenous purebred Chianina cattle. **Carni Shop,** Via dei Lorena 31 (☎ 0575-742924; closed Aug), sells it ready to flamegrill. **Pasticceria Chieli,** Via Vittorio Veneto 35A (☎ 0575-742026; www.pasticceriachieli.it), is the best pastry shop for miles around. Wait until you try the pine-nut-studded ricotta tarts or the almond macaroons. Classic breads are baked daily in a 15th-century building at **Panificio La Spiga,** Via Santa Caterina 72 (☎ 0575-740522).

Stay overnight at B&B **Casa Mila** (☎ 0575-733477; www.casamila.it), in a 14th-century building with rooms overlooking quiet gardens.

For more on the town's artistic highlights, see p 89, in the "Art and Architecture Lovers" tour, earlier in this chapter.

Return to the A1 via Arezzo and continue around Florence as far as the junction for the A11, which you'll take to Prato, a 136km (84-mile) journey.

⑥ ★ Prato. *Cantuccini* (twice-baked almond cookies), that so often round out a Tuscan lunch, in fact originate from Prato. To pick up a bag of these *biscotti di Prato*, before your return to Florence, stop by the city's venerable *biscottificio* (biscuit-maker), **Antonio Mattei,** Via Ricasoli 20–22 (☎ 0574-25756; www.antoniomattei.it), which has been selling the famous *cantucci* and the *vin santo* in which to dunk them since 1858.

For more on Prato, see p 107, **②**.

Wine vats at one of Montalcino's vineyards.

Tuscany for **Families**

1 Lucca
2 Collodi
3 The Garfagnana
4 Pisa
5 Elba
6 San Gimignano
7 Siena
8 Monteriggioni

With its Renaissance art and architectural wonders, Tuscany isn't the obvious choice as a destination for the kids. Fortunately, many of the region's palaces, castles, and fortified hill-towns look like they were dreamt up by Walt Disney himself. On this tour, I've created a balance between cultural sites and outdoor activities that will thrill the entire family—and added a trip to Tuscany's most picturesque island sands. START: **Lucca, on the A12 autostrada 71km (44 miles) west of Florence, makes the best base for the first 3 nights of the tour. Trip length: 9 days.**

Travel Tip

For information on sights and recommended hotels and restaurants in Lucca, Pisa, San Gimignano, and Siena, see each town in chapter 6, "Charming Tuscan Towns & Villages." For details of all local tourist offices, turn to p 182.

1 ★★ **Lucca.** All family members will delight in walking or biking (or even rollerblading) the 5km (2¾ miles) of Renaissance walls that ring the old town. Lucca is also Italy's comic capital, so fans shouldn't miss the **Museo del Fumetto,** Piazza San Romano 4 (☎ 0583-56326; www.museoitalianodelfumetto.it), with its mixture of Italian

cult classics and familiar names like *Batman* and *Topolino* (Mickey Mouse to you and me). *Admission 4€. Tues–Sun 10am–6pm.*

For more on Lucca, see p 133 in chapter 6.

For your first, easy day trip from Lucca head east on the S435 for 15km (9 miles); just before Pescia, is the little town of:

2 Collodi. This is the hometown of Carlo Lorenzini, who wrote the *Adventures of Pinocchio* in 1881. (He later adopted the name "Carlo Collodi.") The world-famous children's story is celebrated at the **Parco di Pinocchio** (☎ 0572-429342; www.pinocchio.it/park.htm) with diversions ranging from a giant mosaic about Geppetto and his fibbing puppet to a fantastical maze and a painting corner. Try to read the book with your kids before you go (the Disney movie is significantly different). The park could do with a lick of paint, but will enchant tots with imagination. *Admission 11€. Daily 8:30am–sunset.*

For a second, fuller day trip, head into the Garfagnana, north of town via the S12 and S445. The total round-trip is 96km (60 miles).

3 ★★ The Garfagnana. This upland corner of northwestern Tuscany is riddled with chestnut forests, hiking trails, and perfect picnicking pastures tucked between the Apennines and the Apuane Alps. The prettiest town up here is **Barga,** where a climb of the steep, winding streets ends at a mountain panorama outside the 14th-century **Collegiata.** Our favorite lunch spot in town is **Scacciaguai,** Via di Mezzo 23 (☎ 0583-711368; www.scacciaguai.it).

After lunch explore the **Grotta del Vento,** or "Wind Cave," loc. Vergemoli (☎ 0583-722024; www.grottadelvento.com), 16km (10 miles) southwest of Barga. Deep under the limestone you'll encounter the most dramatic caves in Tuscany, a subterranean landscape of tunnels, stalactites, stalagmites, and surreal calcite formations. A 1-hour tour guides you and your family safely through; take warm clothing because it's always 52°F (11°C) down there. *Tour 9€. Daily on the hour (except 1pm) 10am–6pm.*

Relocate to Pisa, just 20km (12 miles) southwest of Lucca, along the S12r.

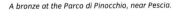

A bronze at the Parco di Pinocchio, near Pescia.

A family photo stop at the Leaning Tower.

4 ★★★ **Pisa.** At the **Campo dei Miracoli** ("Field of Miracles"), all kids will want to make the memorable climb to the top of the **Leaning Tower,** but the minimum age is 8 years old.

Budding scientists of any age can stray into the **Duomo** to follow in the footsteps of Galileo Galilei (1564–1642). He supposedly discovered the laws of pendulum motion right there, while watching the chandelier now known as the "Lamp of Galileo." (Who cares if it's a true story?)

For more on Pisa, see p 151 in chapter 6.

From Pisa, head 110km (68 miles) down the coast on the A12 then the S1 to Piombino. From there catch the car ferry (40 min.) to the island of:

5 ★★ **Elba.** The jewel in Tuscany's Mediterranean coast is this island, where French emperor Napoléon was exiled after the Treaty of Fontainebleau in 1814. It has Tuscany's best beaches, and given the detour required to reach it, you'll want to stay at least 2 nights. Affordable family apartments come with no minimum rental period (outside Aug) at **Casa Campanella Resort,** near Capoliveri (☎ 0565-915740; www.casa campanella.it).

Magical strips of sand include the perfect white crescents at **Fetovaia** and **Cavoli** and the little rock-pool-and-sand cove of **Sant'Andrea,** all on the island's west side. There are more family beachfront facilities at **Marina di Campo.**

For views right along the arc of the Tuscan coast, kids will love the ride in an open cage to the top of 1,019m (3,343-ft.) Monte Capanne. The **Cabinovia** is just outside Marciana. A round-trip costs 17€, and the cableway is open mornings and

The Medici forts guarding Portoferralo, Elba.

afternoons, daily in summer but with seasonal variations.

Elba is best avoided in packed August, when it becomes party central for young Tuscans.

Ferries are run by Moby (www. moby.it) and Toremar (www. toremar.it).

From Piombino, head north on the S1 to Cecina, then east on S68 to Castelsangimignano, from where you'll see signs to San Gimignano. It's a journey of 112km (70 miles).

⑥ ★★ San Gimignano. With its preserved medieval towers, San Gimignano is like a stage set for kids, who will love romping through its pedestrian-only historic core. The adventure begins at the **Torre Grossa,** which everyone can climb for a panoramic sweep of the bucolic countryside that surrounds this hilltown. Then decide whether to subject the children to the **Museo della Tortura**—a Tuscan chamber of horrors, with an authentic collection of instruments of torture. Most older kids find the exhibits fascinating, but little ones will prefer the enchanting re-creation of the medieval city in clay, at **San Gimignano 1300.**

For more on the town, see "San Gimignano" in chapter 6.

On your eighth morning, travel 11km (7 miles) east on the S324 to Poggibonsi, where you can hook up with the Firenze–Siena raccordo. Drive 31km (19 miles) south and exit at "Siena Ovest."

⑦ ★★ Siena. The Gothic city of Siena is a place kids will never forget. Climb the **Torre del Mangia,** the bell tower of the **Palazzo Pubblico,** for a dramatic view down into the **Campo,** site of summer pageantry and horse racing at the Palio.

The towers of Monteriggioni.

At the converted hospital of **Santa Maria della Scala,** kids have their own art on-site, too: **Bambimus,** with art exhibits by and for young children displayed at a child-friendly height.

You'll see a different side of Tuscany, and get to know football Italian-style, if you catch a match at **A.C. Siena,** Stadio A. Franchi (☎ 0577-271288; www.acsiena.it). The team usually plays in Serie A, Italy's top flight, and games are quite genteel by European standards (except those against Florence rivals Fiorentina). Ask for a seat in the "Gradinata." *Alternate Sun (occasionally Sat or midweek) Sept–May. Tickets from kiosk next to TRA.IN, below Piazza Gramsci; Sogno Siena, Via dei Termini 54 (☎ 0577-225703). Prices 20€–45€.*

For more, see "Siena" in chapter 6.

⑧ ★ Monteriggioni. For an afternoon adventure, drive your kids to Monteriggioni, 18km (11 miles) north along the Florence road. It's a tiny, perfectly preserved medieval village in its own set of fortified walls (part of which you can scramble onto). Even Walt couldn't have done it better.

See p 114, ⑥*.*

Tuscany by **Rail & Bus**

1 Prato
2 Pistoia
3 Lucca
4 Pisa
5 Siena
6 San Gimignano
7 Pienza
8 Colle di Val d'Elsa
9 Arezzo

—— Railroad

Much of this guide has been written for motorists to discover the Tuscan countryside in their own sets of wheels. But increasing numbers of visitors want to travel light and save money in the face of mounting fuel prices, or simply prefer the unique feel you get for somewhere when you arrive by rail. To explore all of Tuscany by train, you'd have to double back to Florence many times. With a few additional connections made by bus, you can easily see many of the region's highlights. I've designed this itinerary to minimize hassle, using Siena as a base for the second half of the trip. START: **Florence's Santa Maria Novella station. Trip length: 8 days.**

Travel Tip

For detailed information on sights and recommended hotels and restaurants, see the Lucca, Pisa, Pistoia, Siena, San Gimignano, Volterra, Montepulciano, and Arezzo sections of chapter 6, "Charming Tuscan Towns & Villages."

On your first day, there's time to visit both Prato and Pistoia. Lodge in the latter or take a late train back to Florence or on to Lucca.

1 ★ **Prato.** Tuscany's second city is your ideal first stop, served by two or three trains per hour and just a half-hour journey from Florence.

Alight at Prato's **Porta al Serraglio** station, and the **Duomo** is just a couple of minutes' walk down arrow-straight Via Magnolfi. A one-way ticket is 1.90€. See p 107, ❷.

❷ ★★ **Pistoia.** I love visiting this little city by rail, because my 10-minute walk from the station to Piazza del Duomo takes me through the heart of a "real," working Tuscan town. Around three trains an hour run from Prato, just 15–20 minutes away. The one-way fare is 1.90€. To find the tourist office, walk straight ahead on Via XX Settembre, past the old walls, then take the fifth right on Via degli Orafi into the main square. See p 156, in chapter 6.

Set out early for Lucca, where you'll spend your second night.

❸ ★★ **Lucca.** This lovely walled city receives trains from both Florence and Pistoia approximately every hour, beginning daily before 6am and running up until around 10:30pm. (All pass through Prato.) Trip time from Pistoia is between 45 minutes and 1 hour, and a one-way ticket is 3.80€. Trains pull into the station on **Piazza Ricasoli,** just south of the city walls; exit the station and walk right ahead to reach the center. See p 132, in chapter 6.

Either spend your next night in Pisa, or visit it as an easy day trip from Lucca.

❹ ★★★ **Pisa.** Pisa and Lucca share a convenient rail link: Trains leave Lucca every half-hour daily, from 5:40am to 9:40pm, for the 30-minute trip. If you're heading straight for the Campo dei Miracoli, do *not* get off at Pisa Centrale, at the southern end of town; you want **Pisa San Rossore,** just west of the old wall. A one-way fare is 2.50€. See p 151, in chapter 6.

> **Travel Tip**
>
> The golden rule of rail travel in Italy: Don't forget to validate your ticket by inserting it into the yellow machines you find on every platform, often marked "convalida." You may be fined if you forget. Regular tickets are valid for 6 hours from validation, so you are allowed to jump off en route (say, at Prato or Pistoia on the way to Lucca).

Head to Siena, which makes an ideal base for the next 5 days.

❺ ★★★ **Siena.** To reach Siena you have to double back from Pisa toward Florence, changing trains at Empoli. During the day, at least one train an hour makes the connection. Total journey time is 1¾ hours, and it's 7.40€ one-way. Trains arrive in Siena at **Piazza Rosselli,** 15 minutes by frequent bus north of the center. Buy your local bus ticket from the booth inside the station.

After seeing the sights of Siena, spend the rest of your time here taking a series of day trips to some of the enchanting towns of central and southern Tuscany, and return to Siena by nightfall. To do this

Prato's Campanile.

Rail Passes & Packages

Rail travel in Italy is inexpensive and easy to navigate. Trip planning is simple using the website for the national rail company, **Trenitalia** (☎ 892021; www.trenitalia.com).

If you're traveling only within Tuscany, it's very unlikely you'll ride enough to get value for any prepaid rail pass. Passes are useful, however, if you're also taking more expensive high-speed routes to Rome, Venice, or farther afield. (**Note:** All high-speed trains must be booked in advance, at a cost of 10€ per booking even if you hold a pass.) It's worth upgrading to a first-class pass only if you're using high-speed trains—many local trains don't even have a first-class carriage.

From the U.S., the **Eurail Italy Pass** offers any 3 days within 2 months for around $200 for second-class travel; additional days, up to 10 days, cost around $25 each. A **Saver** pass offers discounts to two or more people traveling together. The **Italy Rail 'n Drive** package allows you to combine train travel with car rental.

From the U.K., the **InterRail Italy** pass for Italy costs £104 for any 3 days in a month, £179 for any 6 days, second class.

Passes are available from **Rail Europe** (www.raileurope.com), **International Rail** (www.internationalrail.com), **Railpass.com,** and others. Travelers ages 25 and under get discounts on all Italy passes.

efficiently, you'll have to rely on the bus instead of the train. Bus services are operated by **TRA.IN** (☎ 0577-204111; www.trainspa.it), whose ticket office is below street level at Piazza Gramsci/Via Tozzi. Request a timetable *(un orario)*. Many buses also depart from here.

For a complete guide to Siena, see p 168, in chapter 6.

6 ★★ **San Gimignano.** This hilltop fortress town with its famous towers and medieval lanes is comfortably accessible from Siena. TRA.IN runs buses at least hourly (fewer on Sun) linking Siena with San

A farm outside Pienza.

Colle di Val d'Elsa.

Gimignano. Most require a change at Poggibonsi, so check when you buy your ticket. Total journey time—including the connection, which is usually slick—is around 1¼ hours. You can see the sights and take a bus back to Siena for dinner. *See p 161, in chapter 6.*

7 ★★ **Pienza.** A bus run by **TRA. IN** (☎ 0577-204111; www.train spa.it) is also your best bet for a day trip to this model Renaissance town. Buy your ticket, as before, from below Piazza Gramsci. Bus 112 departs from outside Porta Ovile and reaches Pienza, via Buonconvento, in 70 minutes. A few hours is enough to see the major sights of this diminutive Tuscan town.

Buses depart Siena for Pienza at the rate of around six a day. You have a choice of overnighting in Pienza (it's a delight when the day-trippers have left after dark), or returning to Siena for the night. The last bus departs Pienza just before 6pm, requiring a change to a local service at Monteroni d'Arbia. *See p 146, in chapter 6.*

8 **Colle di Val d'Elsa.** The best served by bus of all the towns within easy reach of Siena, Colle also lies a little off the regular tourist circuit, and so provides a break from high-season crowds. Lunch at the **Officina della Cucina Popolare** (p 115) is worth the visit alone. Most TRA.IN buses linking Siena with Poggibonsi or San Gimignano stop in Colle, as does the hourly "slow" bus to Florence. Services depart Siena's Piazza Gramsci, and journey time is between 30 and 40 minutes. *See p 114,* **8**.

9 ★ **Arezzo.** The art city of Piero della Francesca is comfortably tackled in a day. A TRA.IN bus links Siena and Arezzo every couple of hours, departing the bus terminal at Piazza Gramsci. Journey time is 1½ hours. Buses arrive in Arezzo just by the rail station in **Piazza della Repubblica.** As soon as you hit town, you should make the short walk uphill to book your timed slot for the Piero della Francesca frescoes at San Francesco. After a day seeing the art sights of the city, either return to Siena or hop on one of the frequent rail services back to Florence. *See p 124, in chapter 6.*

Distinctive yellow machines stamp bus tickets throughout Tuscany.

Tuscany **by Bike**

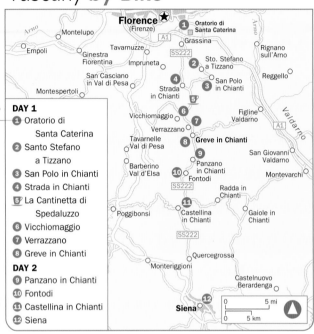

DAY 1
1. Oratorio di Santa Caterina
2. Santo Stefano a Tizzano
3. San Polo in Chianti
4. Strada in Chianti
5. La Cantinetta di Spedaluzzo
6. Vicchiomaggio
7. Verrazzano
8. Greve in Chianti

DAY 2
9. Panzano in Chianti
10. Fontodi
11. Castellina in Chianti
12. Siena

I f you're someone who feels the need to spike a visit to wineries and old churches with a dose of fresh country air, this is the tour for you. For a guided cycling expedition, or if you only have a single day to spare, you could also contact **I Bike Italy** (☎ 055-0123994; www.ibikeitaly.com). Based in Florence, I Bike Italy offers 1- or 2-day tours, with return transportation, including from Florence to Siena. START: **Florence. Trip length: 79km (49 miles)/2 days.**

Travel Tip

We suggest a well-maintained road bike, with at least 24 speeds, for this trip. My favorite roadside lunch stop is recommended below, but if you prefer to picnic, stock up on supplies in Florence; you'll find dozens of idyllic places along the route. For more on the Chianti, see the dedicated tour, starting on p 112 of chapter 5.

Cross the Ponte San Niccolò, spanning the Arno River at the eastern end of Florence, and follow signs from Piazza Ferrucci to the town of Grassina and the S222. At Ponte a Ema, 4km (2½ miles) southeast of Florence, follow the brown signs to:

1 ★ **Oratorio di Santa Caterina.** A wall fresco of this church at S. Piero a Ema traces the *Life of St. Catherine.* Spinello

Biking is one of the best ways to tour Tuscany.

Aretino completed it in 1390, just before he executed his cycle at San Miniato al Monte, in Florence. The apse displays more frescoes of St. Catherine (ca. 1360), by the "Master of Barberino" and Piero Nelli. *Call ahead at ☎ 055-6390356 to book a tour of the interior (3.50€).*

Return to the S222, then take a left at Grassina on a road marked "San Polo." It's a steady, gentle climb to:

2 Santo Stefano a Tizzano. Four kilometers (2½ miles) south, up a rutted track on the right, you'll come upon this vine-clad Romanesque church. It was built by the Buondemontis, a local ruling family, and offers a spectacular panorama back toward Florence below.

Rejoin the main road and continue to:

3 San Polo in Chianti. This little town is the center of Tuscany's iris industry—an annual Iris Festival takes place here each May. The main road continues to Strada (**4**, below), but signposted 2.5km (1½ miles) up a steep hill above San Polo, you can also visit the ancient church of **San Miniato in Robbiana.** It was consecrated in 1077 and heavily restored in 1841.

From San Polo a byroad points the way west back toward:

4 Strada in Chianti. Taking its name, Strada (street), from an old Roman road that ran through here, this town lies 14km (8½ miles) south of Florence. The byroad hits the Chiantigiana south of the center, and there's no need to go in. From this point, it's rolling countryside until lunch.

Continue south on the S222 to:

5 ★ La Cantinetta di Spedaluzzo. The terrace here, on the brow of a hill south of Strada, is a fine perch to peruse what you've cycled so far. Bowls of pasta are tasty, satisfyingly carb-loaded, and good value. *Via Mugnana 93, Loc. Spedaluzzo.* ☎ *055-0196030. $$–$$$. Closed Mon.*

Continue on the S222 to:

6 ★ Vicchiomaggio. The **Castello di Vicchiomaggio** (☎ 055-854079; www.vicchiomaggio.it) was once a 10th-century Lombard fortress. Tours of the estate (1 hr.) are staged daily March through October,

Chianti aged in oak barrels in a Tuscan cellar.

but booking is essential. You can also take part in free tastings at their roadside Cantinetta San Jacopo wine shop, on the S222 at the signposted turnoff to the castle. As well as classic Tuscan red wines, pick up a jar of their acclaimed honey.

7 ★★ **Verrazzano.** This hamlet south of Vicchiomaggio was the birthplace of Giovanni da Verrazzano, the first European colonial to sail into the bay of New York in 1524. His former home, wine estate **Castello di Verrazzano** (☎ 055-854243; www.verrazzano.com), is in a 10th-century tower surrounded by 15th- and 16th-century buildings. Tours run Monday through Friday, costing from 14€ per person. Booking at least 1 day ahead is essential. If you're more pressed for time and just want to taste their excellent estate wines, stop in at the roadside tasting room.

Continue south on the S222 for 5km (3 miles) to Greve, where you should stay overnight.

8 ★★ **Greve in Chianti.** On the banks of the Greve River stands

Wine at Castello di Verrazzano.

wine country's unofficial capital. Head for the central square, **Piazza Matteotti,** and park your bike amid 17th-century buildings, wine bars, and restaurants.

For more on Greve, see p 112, **1**.

Start day 2 with a slow climb 6km (3¾ miles) south of Greve to:

9 ★★ **Panzano in Chianti.** This ancient wine village sits on a crest above the Chianti's most famous winegrowing stretch, the Conca d'Oro, or "Golden Shell." Views over the vineyards from the saddle are among the finest in Tuscany.

For more on Panzano, see p 113, **3**.

10 ★ **Fontodi.** By the roadside just south of Panzano, this aristocratic estate—which in fact owns most of the Conca d'Oro—turns out some of the region's best organic Chianti Classico, although its flagship label, Flaccianello, is a 100% sangiovese sold with IGT status. Visits to the cellars are possible by reservation. The estate also produces sublime extra-virgin olive oil. *Via San Leolino.* ☎ *055-852005. www.fontodi.com.*

The remainder of the cycle continues south on the S222 to its end, at Siena.

11 ★ **Castellina in Chianti.** Continue straight down the Chianti Road to this fortified town in the "Sienese Chianti." *See p 113,* **5**.

12 ★★★ **Siena.** At the end of the road lies the most beautiful Gothic city in Italy.

For a complete guide to Siena, see the dedicated tour on p 168, in chapter 6.

Return to Florence by train (bikes are permitted onboard). ●

5 The Best Regional Tours of Tuscany

Northwest Tuscany

1 Lucca
2 Prato
3 Montecatini Terme
4 Pistoia
5 Pisa
6 Livorno
7 Viareggio
8 Torre del Lago
9 The Garfagnana

Northwest Tuscany, land of Puccini, is best known for the ancient maritime republic of Pisa. But beyond the city and its wonky Tower, there's Lucca, with its tree-lined Renaissance ramparts; the art and architecture of Prato and Pistoia; and the former Medici port of Livorno, with the best seafood restaurants in Tuscany. Finally, when you've had enough of old churches and want your music loud, your beach crowd raucous, and your nightlife frantic, there is Viareggio. START: **Lucca, 80km (50 miles) west of Florence on the A11. Trip Length: 7 days.**

A Note on Hotels, Restaurants, and Tourist Offices.

For hotels, restaurants, and detailed information on attractions in Lucca, see p 132; for Pisa, see p 151. I suggest you use the former as an

Previous page: A vineyard outside Montalcino.

accommodations base and visit everywhere on this tour as day trips from there. For details on all of Tuscany's local tourist offices, see p 182.

1 ★★ kids **Lucca.** The Lucchese say their city—with its 5km (2¾ miles) of stone ramparts—is more impressive than Florence, Pisa, or Siena,

rivals since the Middle Ages. It is worth at least a day of your time. Bike the walls, admire the ornate Romanesque facades of its churches, and leave time to join the evening *passeggiata* along **Via Fillungo.**

For more on Lucca, see p 132.

On day 2, you have time to visit both Prato (66km/41 miles east of Lucca) and Montecatini Terme (33km/20½ miles northeast of Lucca) by car or train. By rail, alight at Prato Porta al Serraglio for Prato and Montecatini Centro for Montecatini.

② ★★ **Prato.** Known since the 13th century for its textiles, Prato has long lived in the shadow of nearby Florence. The city's reputation for business was well established before Francesco di Marco Datini, the 14th-century "Merchant of Prato," made his money trading with the Papal entourage in Avignon, France. You can visit his former home, the **Palazzo Datini,** Via Mazzei 43 (☎ 0574-21391; www. museocasadatini.it), where much of the frescoed interior commissioned by Datini survives. *Free admission. Mon–Fri 9am–12:30pm and 3–6pm (mornings only July–Aug); Sat 9am–12:30pm.*

The modern city is home to Italy's largest Chinese community, but it's Prato's Romanesque **Duomo,** Piazza del Duomo (☎ 0574-26234), that supplies the principal reason to visit. Housed in an elaborate chapel left of the entrance is the *Sacro Cingolo* (Holy Girdle) reputedly presented to the Apostle "Doubting" Thomas during the Virgin's Assumption. More dazzling still, after a restoration completed in 2007, are the apse frescoes by Fra' Filippo Lippi. Executed between 1452 and 1466, they recount the lives and martyrdoms of St. Stephen and John the Baptist. Prato was the setting for Lippi's seduction of nun Lucrezia Buti, and

the birthplace of their son, High Renaissance painter Filippino (1457–1504). *Admission to chapels 3€. Mon–Sat 10am–5pm; Sun 1–5pm.*

The cathedral facade sports a circular pulpit by Donatello and his workshop. What you see today is a copy: The original forms the centerpiece of the **Museo dell'Opera del Duomo,** Piazza del Duomo 49 (☎ 0574-29339), next door. Michelozzo's bronze pulpit capital also returned here after restoration in 2011. The collection is an otherwise modest one, but your ticket also gets you into the 12th-century cathedral cloister and atmospheric vaults directly below the altar. *Admission 5€. Mon, Thurs–Fri 9:30am–1pm and 2:30–6:30pm; Wed 9am–1pm; Sat 10am–1pm and 2:30–6:30pm; Sun 10am–1pm.*

③ **Montecatini Terme.** Immortalized in Fellini's *8½,* this is Tuscany's most celebrated spa town. Its waters were known by the Romans for their curative powers, and popularized by Grand Duke Pietro Leopoldo I (who later became Holy Roman Emperor Leopold II) in the late 1700s.

Prato's Piazza del Duomo.

The peaceful surroundings of Terme Tettuccio, one of Montecatini's spas.

The current buildings sprang up in the early 20th century, as suggested by the eclectic, vaguely Art Nouveau style of **Viale Verdi.**

Montecatini's waters supposedly have beneficial effects for the liver, intestines, and kidneys. At the oldest and most stately of the thermal houses, **Terme Tettuccio,** Viale Verdi 71 (☎ 0572-778501; www.termemontecatini.it), clients arrive every morning to enjoy neoclassical grandeur, a live orchestra, a healthy breakfast, and the rapid laxative effects of the mineral-rich water. *Cure 14€. Daily Easter–Oct.*

Nearby **Excelsior,** Viale Verdi 61 (☎ 0572-778511), the only local spa open all year, provides a wide range of treatments including mud soaks, thermal baths, and ayurvedic massages. *Treatments 22€–115€.*

From Viale Diaz, a funicular railway ascends to the original Roman settlement, now known as **Montecatini Alto.** Enjoy the summer breezes, an espresso on the piazza, and dramatic views over the Valdinievole. ☎ *0572-766862. www.funicolare1898.it. Round-trip 7€.*

Spend day 3 in Pistoia, 45km (28 miles) northeast of Lucca. It's easy to reach by both car (via the A11) or train (40 min.–1 hr.).

④ ★★ Pistoia. Around here, if it's green and grows in straight lines, it probably started life somewhere near Pistoia, Tuscany's market garden. The area wasn't always so serene, however: For centuries the Pistoiesi were known for rudeness and bellicosity. Machiavelli described them as "brought up to slaughter and war," and the first pistols were made here in the 1540s.

The core of town, **Piazza del Duomo,** centers around the **Cattedrale di San Zeno** and octagonal **Baptistery** opposite. You'll find my favorite Gothic sculpture in all of Italy inside the Romanesque church of **Sant' Andrea.**

For more on Pistoia, including details of a 1-day tour around the center as well as the city's best restaurants, see p 156, in chapter 6.

On day 4, leave Lucca early by train (30 min.) or drive 22km (14 miles) southwest on the S12r to:

⑤ ★★★ kids Pisa. The **Duomo** and the **Leaning Tower** are triumphs of the Pisan-Romanesque style—and the city's **Campo dei**

Miracoli is rightly among Europe's top tourist magnets.

For more on Pisa, see p 150.

Spend day 5 in Livorno, 50km (31 miles) southwest of Lucca off the A12.

6 ★ **Livorno.** Called "Leghorn" by the English (a name later immortalized by a cartoon rooster), the free-port of Livorno has a long Anglophile history. Romantic poet Percy Bysshe Shelley wrote *To a Skylark* nearby and sailed to his death from the dock—also built by an Englishman, "Roberto" Dudley. The city, though, was heavily bombed in World War II, and is thus short on traditional "sights." The colonial streets and canals of ambitiously named **Vene-zia Nuova** ("New Venice") are the best part of town for a stroll, particularly in the shadow of the 18th-century merchants' palaces along **Via Borra.**

In Piazza Micheli is Livorno's sculptural treasure, the Mannerist **Monumento dei Quattro Mori** (1623–26), the contorted bronze masterpiece of Pietro Tacca, crowned by a statue of Duke Ferdinand I.

The art highlight is the **Museo Civico** in Villa Mimbelli, Via San Jacopo in Acquaviva 65

Monumento dei Quattro Mori.

Pistoia's Piazza del Duomo.

(☎ 0586-808001), with an unmatched collection of paintings by the Macchiaioli, 19th-century Tuscan forerunners to Impressionism. Native son Giovanni Fattori, who worked from the 1860s until 1908, is the star attraction. *Admission 4€. Tues–Sun 10am–1pm and 4–7pm.*

The overhaul of the waterfront and its centerpiece, the checkerboard **Terrazza Mascagni,** south of the center, had a profound effect on Livornese life. For one thing, bar action has gravitated south to take advantage of the seaside energy. It's also here you'll find the city's best

The Passeggiata Margherita, one of Italy's most elegant boardwalks.

ice cream, at **Gelateria Popolare,** Via Meyer 11 (☎ 0586-260354).

7 Fruits of the Sea. If you've made it to Livorno, don't leave without trying its seafood, Tuscany's best—and best value. The local specialty is *cacciucco*—a spicy, tomato-based seafood soup-stew. **Osteria del Mare,** Borgo Cappuccini 12 (☎ 0586-881027; closed Thurs), is my favorite napkin-and-tablecloth restaurant in the city, with a menu that changes daily based on the

freshest catch. **Cantina Senese,** Borgo Cappuccini 95 (☎ 0586-890239; www.ristorantecantina seneselivorno.com; closed Sun), is slightly blue-collar by comparison—but with an equally firm commitment to delivering the best of the seas onto your plate. It's hard to go wrong anywhere in Livorno with a *fritto misto,* a mixed fry of today's catch, likely to feature some (or all) anchovies, squid, or *totani* (baby cuttlefish). Spend your sixth day at the twin (but very different) beach resorts of Torre del Lago and Viareggio. The latter is 31km (19 miles) northwest of Lucca off the A11.

8 kids Viareggio. The "Biarritz of the Versilia," an Italian seaside resort *par excellence,* had its heyday in the late 19th century. Its promenade, the **Passeggiata Margherita,** remains one of Italy's most elegant boardwalks—against a backdrop of fashion boutiques, Art Deco bathing establishments *(stablimenti),* cafes, and overpriced seafood restaurants. Its main "sight," the Art Nouveau **Gran Caffè**

The beach in Viareggio.

Like everywhere in Tuscany, a meal in the Garfagnana begins with antipasti.

Margherita, is somewhat of a puffed-up architectural travesty—but it takes a great photo.

What you're really here for is the fine beach—a wide strip of manicured sand with a shallow shelf that's ideal for even little ones to paddle. Viareggio is also one of the few places in Tuscany you'll find things lively and youth-oriented well into the night, in season at least.

The town hosts Italy's second-most important February **Carnevale** (☎ 0584-1840750; www.viareggio. ilcarnevale.com), after Venice.

⑨ Torre del Lago. Music lovers should head 6km (3½ miles) south of Viareggio along lime-lined **Viale dei Tigli,** to pay homage to composer Giacomo Puccini (1858–1924). *Turandot,* his masterpiece and swansong, belongs among the great operas of all time. It is often featured at the annual summer, open-air **Festival Pucciniano** (☎ 0584-359322; www.puccinifestival.it). Tickets range from 33€ to 160€.

His home on Lago di Massaciuccoli, now the **Museo Villa Puccini** (☎ 0584-341445; www.giacomo puccini.it), holds mementos, autographed scores, and curios from the daily life of the maestro. The lakeside setting is delightful, with fruit

trees and bamboo thickets. *Admission 7€. Apr–Oct Tues–Sun 10am–12:40pm and 3–5:40pm; Nov–Jan Tues–Sun 10am–12:40pm and 2:30–5:10pm; Feb–Mar 10am–5:40pm and 2:30–5:50pm.*

Torre del Lago also has a reputation as one of the gay-friendliest beach resorts in Italy.

On day 7, make a final day trip—this time, into the highlands of the Garfagnana. The main town, Barga, is 37km (23 miles) north of Lucca via the S12 and S445.

⑩ ★★ kids The Garfagnana. Smothered in chestnut woods and littered with hiking trails, the Garfagnana valley offers a dose of wilderness within easy reach of Lucca. On the way up there, pause in Borgo a Mozzano to view the impossibly narrow, humpbacked 11th-century **Ponte del Diavolo (Devil's Bridge).**

On the return journey to Lucca, stop at the **Antica Locanda di Sesto** (p 139) to round out your trip to Tuscany's northwest with a special (and affordable) dinner of Lucchese and Garfagnana specialties.

For details on how to spend a day in the Garfagnana, see p 95, **③**.

Chianti & the Val d'Elsa

1. Greve in Chianti
2. Wineries of the Florentine Chianti
3. Panzano
4. Radda in Chianti
5. Castellina in Chianti
6. Monteriggioni
7. San Gimignano
8. Colle di Val d'Elsa

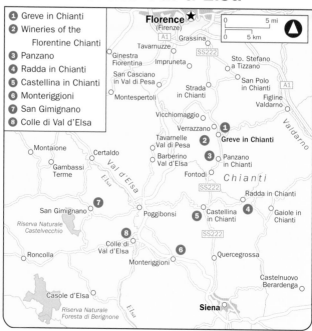

Wedged between Florence and Siena are the most famous—and perhaps the most photogenic—hills of Tuscany. The red sangiovese grape is king in the Chianti vineyards, known for wine since the Etruscans were calling the shots in central Italy. Switch to the Val d'Elsa for the atmospheric medieval settlements of Monteriggioni, Colle di Val d'Elsa, and especially San Gimignano. START: **Greve in Chianti, 27km (17 miles) south of Florence, where you'll spend your first 2 nights. Trip Length: 5 days.**

① ★ **Greve in Chianti.** Chianti's "capital" is arranged around triangular **Piazza Matteotti.** All over town you'll see the famous Black Rooster, symbol of the Classico winelands since 1716. The best-stocked wine shop is the **Enoteca del Chianti Classico,** Piazzetta Santa Croce 8 (☎ 055-853297). Butcher **Falorni,** Piazza Matteotti 71 (☎ 055-853029; www.falorni.it), is a wonderland for

meat lovers, with every species of salami and fresh cuts inside. ⏰ *1 hr.*

② ★★ **Wineries of the Florentine Chianti.** Greve makes the best base for exploring the Chianti cantinas—which you could spend anything between a half-day and a lifetime doing. Call in at Greve's **tourist office,** Piazza Matteotti 1 (☎ 055-8546299), for advice and a

Casks at Castello di Verrazzano.

map. My favorite local tasting spots include **Villa Vignamaggio** (☎ 055-854661; www.vignamaggio.com), 5km (3 miles) southeast of town off the road to Lamole. The estate where Da Vinci's subject for his *Mona Lisa* was raised was also the first whose wine was recorded as "chianti." Their Riserva is a dark, concentrated delight. Just north of Greve, **Castello di Verrazzano** (☎ 055-854243; www.verrazzano.com) produces a superlative 100% sangiovese called Sasello and a Super-Tuscan with 30% cabernet. Tasting at the roadside cantina is free. Both estates also offer cellar tours and more elaborate food-and-wine tastings, for which you should book a week ahead.

③ ★ Panzano. This little village is perched on a promontory above the Chianti's most famous stretch—the **Conca d'Oro (Golden Shell).** At **Antica Macelleria Cecchini,** Via XX Luglio 11 (☎ 055-852020), butcher Dario Cecchini entertains visitors with classical music and tastes of his excellent produce, while he recites Dante from memory. Uphill in the Old Town is the **Accademia del Buon Gusto,** Piazza Ricasoli 11 (☎ 055-8560159; www.accademiadelbuongusto.com),

where Stefano Salvadori's enoteca provides a unique wine education, and a particular insight into the smaller Chianti estates. Tasting is free and "without obligation." ⏱ *1½ hr.*

On day 3, divert southeast to Radda before returning to the Chiantigiana, the "Chianti Road," to overnight in Castellina (see p 115). Total distance is 46km (29 miles).

④ Radda in Chianti. This quaint little town was one of three players in the original Lega del Chianti (Chianti League). At its heart is the 15th-century **Palazzo del Podestà,** studded with the coats of arms of past rulers. A short drive (8km/5 miles) east of the walls is **Badia a Coltibuono** (☎ 0577-749479; www.coltibuono.com), a Vallombrosan abbey from the 1100s that's now an estate with a robust Chianti Classico Riserva. *Tasting free at roadside Osteria. Mar–Dec daily.*

⑤ ★ kids Castellina in Chianti. Castellina's central Piazza del Comune is dominated by the crenellated **Rocca,** which now houses the **Museo Archeologico** (☎ 0577-742090; www.museoarcheologicochianti.it; open Thurs–Tues, weekends only Nov–Mar)—after viewing Etruscan

Castellina in Chianti.

artifacts, climb the Torre for sweeping views of the Sienese Chianti. Stroll evocative "tunnel street" **Via delle Volte**, a soldiers' walk from the town's days as a Florentine bastion. **Andrea Rontini**, at no. 36 (☎ 0577-742016), sells stunning photographic prints of Tuscany from 15€. Castellina's gelateria, **Antica Delizia**, Via Fiorentina 4 (☎ 0577-741337; www.anticadelizia.it; closed Tues), sells the best gelato for miles in any direction.

On day 4, switch from the Chianti to the Val d'Elsa. First head south down the S222 as far as the SI-FI *raccordo*, then turn north. After a short stop in Monteriggioni, head to San Gimignano for 2 nights. Total driving distance is 53km (33 miles).

⑥ ★ kids Monteriggioni. In his *Commedia*, Dante compared the towers of Monteriggioni to giants. All 14 of the tiny town's turrets and its ring of walls are still here, more or less, and still look like that "circle of titans" guarding the lowest level of Dante's Hell. Scale the ramparts (1.50€; Apr–Sept only), admire the view, wander the two stone streets of this most perfectly preserved fortified village in Italy, grab a *caffè*, and continue on your way. 🕐 *1 hr.*

⑦ ★★★ kids San Gimignano. For a rundown of how to spend

your time here, and where to stay and dine, see p 160, in chapter 6.

Spend the morning of day 5 in San Gimignano, before driving 15km (10 miles) southeast to:

⑧ ★ Colle di Val d'Elsa. Colle's major marks on the history of Tuscany both happened in the 1200s: The pretty *città alta* ranged along a snaking ridge was the birthplace of master Gothic architect Arnolfo di Cambio (in 1240) and the site of a famous victory for Florence's Guelph army over Sienese Ghibellines, in 1269. Enter the oldest part of town across the viaduct and through Baccio d'Agnolo's **Palazzo Campana** gate (1539), then follow Via Campana to the **Duomo,** Piazza del Duomo. Inside there's a bronze *Crucifix* designed by Giambologna but cast by his student Pietro Tacca in 1608. The small **Museo Civico,** Via del Castello 33 (☎ 0577-923888), houses two ethereal Sienese *Madonnas* by near-contemporaries of Duccio. *Admission 3€. May–Sept Tues–Sun 11:30am–5pm; Oct–Apr Sat–Sun 10:30am–12:30pm and 3:30–8:30pm (Tues–Fri sometimes afternoons only).*

Return to San Gimignano to spend your final night there.

The intact walled village of Monteriggioni.

Where to **Stay & Dine**

For hotels and restaurants in San Gimignano, see p 165.

★★ **Albergaccio** CASTELLINA
MODERN TUSCAN   Reservations are essential at this outpost of creative, strictly seasonal Tuscan cuisine served in refined-rustic surrounds. *Via Fiorentina 63. ☎ 0577-741042. www.albergacciocast.com. Entrees 26€. MC, V. Lunch Mon–Tues, Fri–Sat; dinner Mon–Sat.*

★★ **Cetinelle** NEAR GREVE   A remote and secluded B&B, with unforgettable sunset views over the winelands toward Greve. Rooms are a good size, and simple yet comfortable with luxurious touches. *Via Canonica 13. ☎ 055-8544745. www. cetinelle.com. 8 units. Doubles 75€– 95€ w/breakfast. MC, V. Closed Jan to mid-Mar.*

Colombaio CASTELLINA   Great value roadside inn whose midsize rooms have sloping beam-and-tile ceilings and terra-cotta floors. Upstairs units are lighter and airier, and enjoy views over the vineyards. *Via Chiantigiana 29. ☎ 0577-740444. www.albergoilcolombaio.it. 13 units. Doubles 85€–100€ w/breakfast. AE, MC, V.*

★ **kids Dario DOC** PANZANO *FAST FOOD*   It's had a few changes of name—and is still best known as MacDario—but the winning formula has never altered: a fresh, bread-crumbed beefburger, oven-cooked "fries," sides, and relishes served fast and with a flourish at communal tables. Some evenings and during lunch on Sunday, the space morphs into Dario's **Officina della Bistecca** (set menu 50€). *Via XX Luglio 11. ☎ 055-852020. www.dariocecchini. com. Set menu 10€. MC, V. Lunch Mon–Sat.*

Vicchiomaggio.

★ **Nerbone di Greve** GREVE
TUSCAN   Traditional Tuscan dishes done right—and served in the atmospheric surrounds of a brick vault. Unusual cuts like *guancia* (cheek), roast meats, offal, and steak tartare are specialties. *Piazza Matteotti 22. ☎ 055-853308. www.nerbonedi greve.it. Entrees 12€–16€. MC, V. Lunch, dinner Wed–Mon.*

★★ **Officina della Cucina Popolare** COLLE VAL D'ELSA *TUSCAN* Dine in the modern, stylish interior or grab one of a few outside tables. A succinct menu is sustained by local producers, and includes simple, tasty fare like pork ribs or sausages on the grill. *Via Gracco del Secco 86. ☎ 0577-921796. www.cucina-popolare.com. Entrees 7€–13€. MC, V. Lunch Fri–Sun; dinner daily.*

★★ **Vicchiomaggio** NEAR GREVE Ten B&B units in the converted priest's house are the stars at this fine wine estate. Each consists of two rooms with cool tile floors, and decorated in antique creams for a clean, modern take on country styling. *Via Vicchiomaggio 4. ☎ 055-854079. www.vicchiomaggio.it. 16 units. Doubles 120€–158€ w/breakfast. AE, MC, V.*

The **Val d'Orcia & Valdichiana**

1 Buonconvento
2 Montalcino
3 Sant'Antimo
4 Bagno Vignoni
5 San Quirico d'Orcia
6 Pienza
7 Montepulciano
8 Sarteano
9 Chiusi
10 Lucignano
11 Monte San Savino
12 Castiglion Fiorentino
13 Arezzo
14 Cortona

T his road-trip itinerary covering southeastern Tuscany
takes in two of the region's great valleys. The silent, cypress-studded landscape of the Val d'Orcia—emerald green in spring, burnt copper in high summer—has become an iconic image that represents Tuscany itself. The sweeping trough cut by the Valdichiana is the only place a true *bistecca alla fiorentina* (T-bone-like beef-steak) can call home: White Chianina cattle are native here. Southeastern Tuscany is also home to fine medieval and Renaissance art, less-visited towns with quiet charm in abundance, and two great wines that surpass even chianti at its best. START: **Siena, 72km (45 miles) south of Florence. Trip length: 7 days.**

A Note on Hotels & Restaurants

For hotels, restaurants, and detailed information about attractions in Arezzo, see p 124; in Cortona, see p 128; in Montepulciano, see p 142; in Pienza, see p 146. For details of Tuscany's major local tourist offices, see p 182.

Head south down the S2 via Buonconvento, to Montalcino (44km/27 miles distant), where you'll spend your first night (below).

1 ★ **Buonconvento.** Park right at the roadside outside the well-tended medieval walls of this prim, tidy town—site of the death of Holy

Roman Emperor Henry VII in 1313 (his tomb is inside Pisa's Duomo). You'll find work by important Sienese artists such as Matteo di Giovanni, Pietro Lorenzetti, and Sano di Pietro hanging in the town's **Museo d'Arte Sacra della Val d'Arbia,** Via Soccini 18 (☎ 0577-807190; www.museo artesacra.it). The ticket desk doubles as the local tourist information office. *Admission 3.50€. Apr–Sept Wed 3–6pm, Thurs– Sun 10am–1pm and 3–6pm; Oct–Mar Thurs–Fri 2–5pm, Sat–Sun 10am– 1pm and 5pm.*

The nearby church of **SS Pietro e Paolo** was substantially remodeled in the 18th century, but still houses 15th-century panels by the prolific Matteo di Giovanni and Pietro di Francesco Orioli.

② ★★ **Montalcino.** As wine lovers well know, this rustic hilltown of cobbled stone streets and narrow stairways is the source of one of the world's greatest red vintages, **Brunello di Montalcino.** The walled town is visible for miles around, with the spires of its

The fortress in Montalcino.

A few of the wine bottles sold at the Enoteca La Fortezza.

medieval buildings studding the air like asparagus. The **Enoteca La Fortezza** (☎ 0577-849211; www. enotecalafortezza.com) is installed in the town's main attraction, a fortress where the Sienese Republic holed up for 4 years after final defeat by Florence in 1555. As well as wine, its former keep stocks local foodstuffs including pecorino cheese and Montalcino honey (famous among gourmets). Of course, most come here to taste and buy some of over 200 Brunellos. Mount the ramparts for a wide sweeping view from the Val d'Orcia to Monte Amiata. *Admission (ramparts) 4€. Apr–Oct daily 9am– 8pm; Nov–Mar daily 10am–6pm.*

The town's gathering place is **Fiaschetteria Italiana,** Piazza del Popolo 6 (☎ 0577-849043), an Art Nouveau cafe with comfortable banquettes and marble tables. It has served the celebrated local wine since 1888.

Don't leave town without a stop at one of Tuscany's best small museums, the **Musei di Montalcino,** Via Ricasoli (☎ 0577-864014), with its collection of mostly Sienese sacred art, including four carved Crucifixions from the 1300s. *Admission 4.50€. Tues–Sun 10am–1pm and 2–5:50pm.*

For details on wine tasting in and around Montalcino, see p 92, ❸.

On day 2, head south of town on the road to Castelnuovo dell'Abate; it's 9km (5½ miles) to:

❸ ★★★ **Sant'Antimo.** An idyllic glade below Castelnuovo dell'Abate is home to the photogenic Romanesque Abbazia di Sant'Antimo. In the 12th century, it became a Cistercian abbey, and remains Tuscany's most harmonious example of Romanesque architecture in the Lombard French style, with a semicircular apse, intricate carved capitals, and a 30m (100-ft.) bell tower. The French monks worship with chant seven times every day, and you're welcome to attend. Enquire at Montalcino's tourist office (see p 190) for precise timings. ⏱ *1 hr.* ☎ *0577-835659. www.antimo.it. Free admission. Mon–Sat 10:30am–12:30pm and 3–6:30pm; Sun 9:15–10:45am and 3–6pm.*

Return to the S2 via the S323 past Castiglione d'Orcia and the Rocca d'Orcia, a prominent medieval watchtower. It's 20km (12 miles) to:

❹ **Bagno Vignoni.** The steaming, sulfurous waters of this curious little village have been frequented since

Roman times, notably by Lorenzo de' Medici "the Magnificent" and St. Catherine of Siena. These days it's more likely to be amateur photographers coming to snap the *piazza d'acqua,* a 49m x 29m (161 ft. x 95 ft.) porticoed Renaissance pool built where the main village square used to be. ⏱ *45 min.*

Continue north on the S2, for 5km (3 miles) to:

❺ ★ **San Quirico d'Orcia.** This little walled farming town, with its magnificent travertine Gothic-Romanesque **Collegiata dei Santi Quirico e Giulitta,** was once an important stopover along the Via Francigena, the pilgrim route that linked Canterbury (in England) with Rome. Its quaint streets and formal 1540 gardens, the **Horta Leonini,** Piazza della Libertà, are a delightful spot to kill a couple of hours.

For a taste of 21st-century Tuscany, stop in at **Birrificio San Quirico,** Via Dante Alighieri 93a (☎ 0577-898193; www.birrificio sanquirico.it). Tuscany's artisan brewing industry is flourishing, and the blonde and amber ales brewed at this little place are among the best in the region. ⏱ *2 hr.*

Sant'Antimo.

San Quirico's Romanesque Collegiata.

Strike northeast on the S146 for Pienza, where you should spend your second night. Total distance from San Quirico is 10km (6 miles).

6 ★★ Pienza. The architectural jewel of southern Tuscany, Pienza is small enough to take in over an afternoon and evening. Don't leave without enjoying the breathtaking view over the entire Val d'Orcia from **Via del Casello.**

For details of hotels, restaurants, and what to see in Pienza, see p 146, in chapter 6.

On day 3, head east on the S146 for 13km (8 miles) to:

7 ★★★ Montepulciano. Take a full day to study the *palazzo* architecture, taste the wine, and sample the excellent restaurants in southern Tuscany's highest hilltown.

For hotels, restaurants, and details of how to spend 1 day in Montepulciano, see p 142, in chapter 6.

On your fourth morning, head south on the S146 past Chianciano, then follow signs for Sarteano, a total journey of 19km (12 miles).

8 ★ Sarteano. Distinctly off the regular tourist trail, this little walled town remains one of my favorite places to while away a morning (and have lunch; see p 122) in southern Tuscany. Come on a Saturday and you can join a tour run by the **Museo Civico,** Via Roma 24 (☎ 0578-269261), to see the **Tomba della Quadriga Infernale.** This unique Etruscan tomb frescoed with a demonic charioteer was only discovered in 2003; visits are strictly limited, and there's a replica of part of it downstairs in the museum if the tour is full, or you aren't here on a Saturday. Other tombs in the spectacularly-sited **Pianacce** necropolis are open daily (and free). *Tour plus museum: Admission 7€; Sat only; booking (by e-mailing museo@ comune.sarteano.siena.it) essential. Museum only: Admission 4€; Apr–Oct Tues–Sun 10:30am–12:30pm and 4–7pm; weekends only otherwise.*

Also worth tracking down is a 1546 *Annunciation* by the last great Sienese painter, Mannerist Domenico Beccafumi. It's in the boxy little church of **San Martino,** Piazza San Martino. If the church is locked, as it often is in low season, there's a key at the tiny tourist office (Corso Garibaldi 9; weekends only).

Follow signposts northeast for Chiusi, 12km (7 miles) away. Spend the afternoon and overnight here, your first stop in the Valdichiana.

9 ★ kids Chiusi. If you're on the trail of the Etruscans, head here to see what's left of one of the most powerful cities in their 12-city confederation (the *Dodecapoli*). Chiusi was then known as Clevsin; so

The rolling agricultural terrain of the Val d'Orcia.

powerful was the city, that its king, Lars Porsenna, attacked Rome in 508 B.C. What's left of Clevsin is buried under the little town today. Explore it for yourself with a subterranean tour of the **Labirinto di Porsenna,** Piazza Duomo (☎ 0578-226490). *Admission 3€. Guided visits June–Oct 15 daily 10:10am–12:10pm and 4:10–6:10pm; Oct 16–May Tues, Thurs, Sat–Sun 10:10am–12:10pm, Sun also 4:10–6:10pm.*

Chiusi's **Museo Archeologico Nazionale,** Via Porsenna (☎ 0578-20177), is one of Italy's outstanding Etruscan museums. Wander past alabaster funerary urns, black and orange Attic-style ceramics, Bucchero pottery, and a 6th-century B.C. sphinx. Most were recovered from necropoli around the town; those tombs are also open daily for visits (ask at the museum desk). *Admission 4€. Daily 9am–8pm.*

Day 5 makes a whistle-stop tour of the charming, less-visited small towns of the Valdichiana. Start early and take the A1 bound for Florence for 25km (15 miles) until the exit for Sinalunga/Lucignano. Follow signs for another 14km (9 miles) to:

⓾ ★ **Lucignano.** In an ideal world, you'd get your first sight of this little place from the air: Its elliptical street layout is unique in the annals of Tuscan town planning. Like a simplified maze, the village is laid out in four concentric ellipses with quaint little squares in the center. One is dominated by the **Collegiata,** with its 18th-century double half-oval staircase by Andrea Pozzo.

The highlight of the tiny **Museo di Lucignano,** Piazza del Tribunale (☎ 0575-838001; www.comune.lucignano.ar.it/turismo), is the *Albero della Vita* (*Tree of Life*), a complex 14th-century reliquary made by Sienese goldsmiths. The *Tree,* and the frescoed Sala di Buon Governo that houses it, is a popular spot for wedding vows. *Admission 5€. Mid-Mar to Oct Wed–Mon 10am–1pm and 2–6pm; off season Mon 10am–1pm, Wed–Sun 10am–1pm and 2–5pm.*

Drive a scenic road 8km (5 miles) north to:

⓫ ★ **Monte San Savino.** The birthplace of High Renaissance sculptor Andrea Sansovino (1460–1529) is another quiet little Valdichiana hilltown that's managed to avoid the perils (and riches) of commercial mass tourism. Dotted with medieval and Renaissance *palazzi*, it invites exploration and aimless wandering.

As you hoof it around the town, you can see some of Sansovino's works, notably his tabernacles at the little church of **Santa Chiara,** Piazza Gamurrini (☎ 0575-849418). There's also some trademark Luca della Robbia glazed terra-cotta work on display. If the church is locked, call at the tourist office (up the stairs immediately to the right) for the key. *Free admission. Wed–Fri (Apr–Oct also Tues) 9am–1pm; Sat–Sun 9am–1pm and 2:30–6pm.*

The 1520 **Loggia dei Mercanti,** Corso Sangallo, with its Corinthian columns, is also attributed to Sansovino. Across the street is Antonio da Sangallo the Elder's **Palazzo di Monte.** Farther up the hill, at the Piazza di Monte, is the church of **Sant'Agostino.** Sansovino renovated the building in 1532, adding the cloister and gallery, and there's a fine stained-glass window of *St. Augustine* by Guillaume de Marcillat. Schedule a late lunch on the panoramic terrace at **Belvedere** (p 122).

Drive 17km (10 miles) east to Castiglion Fiorentino, where you should spend the night (see p 122).

🕛 **★ Castiglion Fiorentino.** You can't miss it: As you approach, the **Torre del Cassero,** a pronglike tower built in the 1330s by the Perugians, looms over the town's skyline. (You can climb it on weekends May–Sept 10am–12:30pm and 4–6:30pm; admission 1.50€.) Wandering into the little hilltown takes you through a medieval girdle of fortified walls, leading to its hub, **Piazza del Municipio.** Dominating the square is the (now somewhat tattered) **Loggia di Vasari** reputedly designed by Renaissance man Giorgio Vasari in the 16th century.

The town's best museum is the **Pinacoteca Comunale,** inside

the deconsecrated church of Sant'Angelo al Cassero, directly uphill from Piazza del Municipio (☎ 0575-659457). It houses a 13th-century Umbrian Crucifix and a couple of panels by Bartolomeo della Gatta, including his bizarre *St. Francis Receiving the Stigmata.* There's also access to the church's atmospheric crypt. *Admission 3€. Tues–Sun 10am–12:30pm and 4–6:30pm (closes 6pm Nov–Mar).*

On day 6, drive north up the S71 for 18km (11 miles) to:

🕛 **★★ Arezzo.** Make your first stop at **San Francesco,** to reserve a slot to view Tuscany's greatest fresco cycle, before exploring the rest of eastern Tuscany's "capital" and overnighting in the center.

For a detailed rundown of hotels, restaurants, and sights in the city, see p 124, in chapter 6.

On your final morning, head south on the S71 for 29km (18 miles) to:

🕛 **★★ Cortona.** This steep, cobblestoned art city is your final stopover: There's no better spot to survey the entire Valdichiana, the so-called "breadbasket of Italy," than from the ramparts of its **Fortezza Medicea.**

For a complete rundown of Cortona's attractions, hotels, restaurants, shops, and nightlife, see the Cortona section in chapter 6.

A market in Arezzo.

Where to **Stay**

★ **Casa Toscana** CHIUSI   This B&B inside a handsome Liberty villa combines modern amenities with an eye for design: Rooms are color-washed in rich Tuscan tones, mattresses are firm, and furniture is modern but modeled on antique styles. *Via Baldetti 37.* ☎ *0578-222227. www. bandbcasatoscana.it. 8 units. Doubles 60€ w/breakfast. AE, DC, MC, V. Closed Mon–Wed in winter.*

★ **Porta Castellana** MONTALCINO   It's well worth booking ahead at this stylish three-room B&B built into brick-vaulted former storehouses on the edge of Montalcino. Breakfast in the garden as the mists rise from the Val d'Orcia below is unforgettable. *Via S. Lucia 20.* ☎ *0577-839001. www.portacastellana.it. 3 units. Doubles 85€. MC, V.*

★★ **Viziottavo** CASTIGLION FIORENTINO   With rooms themed around the seven deadly sins, this contemporary B&B opened in 2011 as "the eighth." Snug units come with modern amenities like air-conditioning and chromatherapy showers, but there's just enough terra cotta and exposed wood to retain some Tuscan ambience. *Via San Michele 69.* ☎ *0575-659534. www.viziottavo. com. 8 units. Doubles 70€–90€ w/breakfast. MC, V. Closed some weekdays Jan–Mar, Nov.*

Where to **Dine**

★ **Belvedere** MONTE SAN SAVINO *TUSCAN*   At this aptly-named, rural restaurant with splendid views over olive groves, service is formal—but that's not reflected in the value prices. The kitchen specializes in Valdichiana dishes like *polpette di Chianina* (veal meatballs). *Loc. Bano 226.* ☎ *0575-849588. www.ristorante belvedere.net. Entrees 7€–13€. DC, MC, V. Lunch, dinner Wed–Sun.*

★ **Da Gagliano** SARTEANO *TUSCAN*   At this small dining room, the menu follows the waxing and waning of the seasons—few ingredients are sourced from beyond the local hills. *Secondi* such as *coniglio al tegame con lardo e finocchio selvatico* (pan-fried rabbit with cured ham fat and wild fennel) are memorable. *Via Roma 5.* ☎ *0578-268022. Entrees 9€–13€. MC, V. Lunch, dinner Thurs–Mon (daily Aug; weekends only Nov–Mar).*

Re di Macchia MONTALCINO *SOUTHERN TUSCAN*   Local cooking around here means one thing: meat, especially game such as wild boar and hare, for *antipasto, primo,* and *secondo* if you dare. The powerful flavors and warren-like setting are just right to chase down a bottle of the iconic Brunello. *Via Saloni 21.* ☎ *0577-846116. Entrees 16€. MC, V. Lunch, dinner Fri–Wed.*

★★ **Zaira** CHIUSI *SOUTHERN TUS-CAN/ETRUSCAN*   The finest food in a town that punches above its weight when it comes to cooking: Try meat dishes like rabbit with lemon or duck cooked in Vino Nobile. Then ask to see the underground wine cellar, inside an Etruscan well that dates to 500 B.C. *Via Arunte 12.* ☎ *0578-20260. www.zaira.it. Entrees 8€–16€. AE, DC, MC, V. Lunch, dinner Tues–Sun (daily July–Sept and Dec).* ●

Arezzo

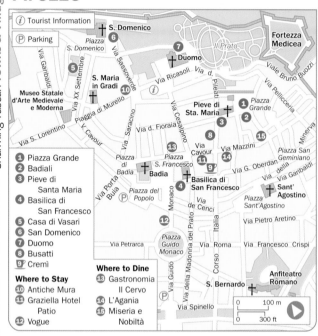

ⓘ Tourist Information

Ⓟ Parking

1 Piazza Grande
2 Badiali
3 Pieve di
   Santa Maria
4 Basilica di
   San Francesco
5 Casa di Vasari
6 San Domenico
7 Duomo
8 Busatti
9 Cremì

Where to Stay
10 Antiche Mura
11 Graziella Hotel
    Patio
12 Vogue

Where to Dine
13 Gastronomia
    Il Cervo
14 L'Agania
15 Miseria e
    Nobiltà

A retines are a proud and prosperous bunch, racing their Vespas through the Etruscan-era streets of their bustling town abutting fertile Valdarno and Valdichiana farmlands. Famous native sons include the poet Petrarch (1304–74); architect and author Giorgio Vasari (1512–74); and Roberto Benigni (b. 1952), who brought Arezzo to a world audience in *Life Is Beautiful*. Time here is best spent strolling the steep streets of the medieval core, and don't miss the frescoes by Piero della Francesca in the Basilica di San Francesco. START: **Arezzo is 81km (50 miles) southeast of Florence, well signpposted from the A1. Trip length: 1 day.**

1 ★★ kids **Piazza Grande.** This lopsided square began sinking at one end almost as soon as it was laid out around 1200, and it's been unstoppable since. The **Loggia di Vasari,** on the eastern (high) side was designed by the man himself, with obvious similarities to Florence's

Previous page: Siena's Piazza del Campo.

Uffizi. Note the semicircular apse at the rear of the Pieve di Santa Maria, typical of the Romanesque style.
🕐 *15 min.*

2 **Badiali.** A charming jumble of a shop where you can pick up a *faux*-antique print, small watercolor, or

souvenir calendar complete with all the saints' days. *Piazza Grande 2.* ☎ *0575-354720. MC, V.*

Shopping Tip

Diehard shoppers should time their visit to coincide with the **Arezzo Antique Market** (www.arezzofiera antiquaria.org), running for almost 50 years. It takes over Piazza Grande on the first Sunday of each month and the Saturday before. Bargains and rare finds usually disappear by 10am.

3 ★ Pieve di Santa Maria. This 12th-century church backing onto Piazza Grande is a stellar example of the Romanesque style, with each of 88 external columns on the facade uniquely sculpted. Its chief treasure inside is Pietro Lorenzetti's 1320 polyptych of the *Madonna and Child with Saints*, on the high altar above the crypt. Notice how St. Luke on the pinnacle panels looks up at the *Annunciation* and writes it down in

his Gospel, a unique narrative feature. ⏱ *20 min. Corso Italia 7.* ☎ *0575-22629. Free admission. Daily 8am–noon and 3–6pm.*

4 ★★★ Basilica di San Francesco. Between 1452 and 1466, Piero della Francesca painted his *Legend of the True Cross* inside San Francesco's Cappella Bacci—a cycle of frescoes based on Jacopo da Varazze's 1260 *Golden Legend*. They are rightly talked about in the same art-historical league as the Sistine Chapel. Each of the 10 panels is remarkable for its grace, ascetic severity, narrative detail, compositional precision, and dramatic light effects—"the most perfect morning light in all Renaissance painting," wrote art historian Kenneth Clark. They also feature some of the strangest hats ever frescoed. The church's rose window, from 1520, is by Guillaume de Marcillat. ⏱ *45 min. Piazza San Francesco.* ☎ *0575-352727. www.pierodella francesca.it. Admission 8€. Mon–Fri 9am–6:30pm; Sat 9am–5:30pm; Sun 1–5:30pm.*

Giorgio Vasari designed the loggia on Piazza Grande, under which atmospheric cafes now shelter.

5 ★ Casa di Vasari. The first art historian—who chronicled the lives of Michelangelo, da Vinci, Masaccio and others—Vasari (1511–74) bought this house in 1540. He decorated it with Mannerist artworks, often by his students, but executed the allegorical frescoes in the **Sala del Trionfo della Virtù** himself. Clearly he was a much better architect than he was a painter, but they do provide a fascinating window into High Renaissance mores and the influence of classical ideas on 16th-century Tuscan elites. *Via XX Settembre 55.* ☎ *0575-409040. Admission 2€. Wed–Mon 8:30am–7pm; Sun 8:30am–1pm.*

6 ★ San Domenico. The curious lopsided facade of this 13th-century basilica, which Vasari claimed was by Nicola Pisano, hides one of Arezzo's most ancient treasures: a Crucifix painted around 1260 by a young Cimabue, teacher of Giotto and "father" of Tuscan art. Fragmentary frescoes by Spinello Aretino (1350–1410) adorn both walls of the nave. *Piazza San Domenico 7.* ☎ *0575-23255. Free admission. Daily 9am–6:30pm.*

7 ★ Duomo. At the highest point in town, Arezzo's 13th-century cathedral is a rare Tuscan Gothic construction that symbolically towers over the civic Palazzo del Comune opposite. Don't miss Piero della Francesca's 1459 *Mary Magdalene* and the stained-glass windows (1521–26) recounting the *Life of Christ,* by Guillaume de Marcillat, in the right aisle. The adjacent park, **Il Prato,** is a good spot to take a breather, or let the kids run about. *Piazza del Duomo.* ☎ *0575-23991. Free admission. Daily 7am–12:30pm and 3–6:30pm.*

8 ★ Busatti. Since 1842, the Busatti-Sassolini family from Anghiari has been selling exquisite textiles and handmade fabrics—including sumptuous linens; and hemp, cotton, and wool items such as curtains, towels, cushions, tablecloths, and rugs in several colors. *Corso Italia 48.* ☎ *0575-355295. www.busatti.com. AE, MC, V.*

9 Cremi. Interrupt your shopping with a stop for the best artisan gelato in town. They also sell pancakes with a choice of sweet fillings. *Corso Italia 100. No phone. $.*

A market in Arezzo.

Where to Stay & Dine

★★ Antiche Mura CENTRO STORICO   Whitewashed stone-and-plaster walls, parquet floors, and baroque furnishings cut a contemporary *figura* at this stylish B&B just downhill from the Duomo. Rooms are midsize and modern—and ideal for a romantic getaway on a budget. *Piaggia di Murello 35.* ☎ *0575-20410. www.antichemura.info. 6 units. Doubles 75€ w/breakfast. No credit cards.*

★★ Gastronomia Il Cervo CENTRO STORICO *MODERN ITALIAN* There is a good à la carte menu here, but I prefer to pick from the downstairs deli bar, loaded with dishes prepared that morning. Filling, creative salads like pasta with zucchini, speck, and Parmesan, or squid with potato and celery always hit the mark. *Via Cavour 38–40 (at Via Guido Monaco).* ☎ *0575-20872. Entrees 8€–10€. MC, V. Lunch Tues–Sun; dinner Tues–Sat.*

★★ Graziella Hotel Patio CENTRO STORICO   For atmosphere, this ambitious hotel in the 18th-century Palazzo de' Giudici is our local favorite. Each of the large units is dedicated to one of Bruce Chatwin's travel tales, with furniture from the country it represents—like Emperor Wu-Ti accessories from China. *Via Cavour 23.* ☎ *0575-401962. www. hotelpatio.it. 10 units. Doubles 155€–175€ w/breakfast. Closed 2 weeks in Jan. AE, DC, MC, V.*

L'Agania CENTRO STORICO *TRADITIONAL ARETINE*   Locals and visitors have been packing this place since 1905 for rib-sticking *ribollita*, hand-rolled pasta, and robust, value fare such as *fegatelli* (pigs' liver). A bottle of local chianti will set you back just 5€. *Via*

One of the modern Italian dishes served at Gastronomia Il Cervo.

Mazzini 10. ☎ *0575-295381. www. agania.com. Entrees 6€–10€. AE, DC, MC, V. Lunch, dinner Tues–Sun.*

★ Miseria e Nobiltà CENTRO STORICO *MODERN ITALIAN*   A short menu, funky decor, and soft jazz soundtrack set this backstreet restaurant apart from the Aretine average. Modern offerings might include pasta with zucchini, saffron, and cherry tomatoes, or lard-wrapped roast pork with radicchio. After hours, it morphs into a wine bar. *Piaggia San Bartolomeo 2.* ☎ *0575-21245. Entrees 13€–18€. MC, V. Lunch Wed–Sun; dinner Tues–Sun.*

Vogue CENTRO STORICO   A stylish refit transformed this well-located boutique hotel into a safe bet for a sexy room in central Arezzo. Outside high season, haggle over the price. *Via Guido Monaco 54.* ☎ *0575-24361. www.voguehotel.it. 26 units. Doubles 180€–240€ w/breakfast. AE, MC, V.*

Cortona

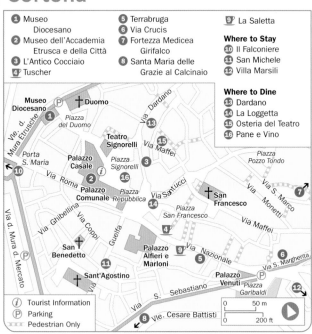

1 Museo Diocesano
2 Museo dell'Accademia Etrusca e della Città
3 L'Antico Cocciaio
4 Tuscher
5 Terrabruga
6 Via Crucis
7 Fortezza Medicea Girifalco
8 Santa Maria delle Grazie al Calcinaio
9 La Saletta

Where to Stay
10 Il Falconiere
11 San Michele
12 Villa Marsili

Where to Dine
13 Dardano
14 La Loggetta
15 Osteria del Teatro
16 Pane e Vino

Map labels: Museo Diocesano, Duomo, Piazza del Duomo, Via Dardano, Teatro Signorelli, Via Maffei, Piazza Pozzo Tondo, Porta S. Maria, Palazzo Casale, Piazza Signorelli, Via Roma, Palazzo Comunale, Piazza Repubblica, Via Satucci, Piazza San Francesco, San Francesco, Via S. Marco, Via Monetti, Via Maffei, Via Ghibellina, Via Coppi, Guelfa, Palazzo Alfieri e Marloni, Via Nazionale, Via S. Margherita, San Benedetto, Sant'Agostino, Palazzo Venuti, Piazza Garibaldi, Via S. Sebastiano, Vle. Cesare Battisti, Vle. d. Mura Etrusche, Via d. Mura di Mercato

(i) Tourist Information
(P) Parking
▪▪▪ Pedestrian Only

0   50 m
0   200 ft

Cortona, as much as anywhere in Tuscany, has a fair claim to the title "city of art." Luca Signorelli (1445–1523) and Sassetta (1392–1451) were both Cortonese; Fra' Angelico lived here for a decade. At its peak Cortona rivaled Arezzo and Perugia, and almost Florence, in power and prestige. Memories of its heyday linger in its art collections and medieval architecture, making it one of Tuscany's most romantic hilltowns. Despite this embarrassment of cultural riches, it was a much more recent phenomenon that placed Cortona on the tourist map: Frances Mayes' bestseller *Under the Tuscan Sun*.

START: **Cortona is 106km (63 miles) southeast of Florence on the S71. Trip length: 1 day.**

1 ★★ **Museo Diocesano.** Cortona's small yet outstanding collection of sacred art reflects the town's former glory, and its position at the crossroads of influences from Florence, Siena, and the neighboring region of Umbria. Native son Luca Signorelli is the predictable star, in particular his monumental 1502 *Lamentation,* complete with surreal background scenes including the Crucifixion and Resurrection. Elsewhere in this deconsecrated church turned museum, Fra' Angelico's gentle *Annunciation* (1436) over the former baptismal font reveals him in

top form, on his favorite subject. The narrative scenes from the *Life of the Virgin* on the predella are especially charming. Also represented are Sienese master Pietro Lorenzetti (1280–1348) and Florentine Bartolomeo della Gatta (1448–1502), and a fine Greco-Roman sarcophagus from the 2nd century even pops up. ⏱ *1 hr. Piazza del Duomo.* ☎ *0575-62830. Admission 5€ (13€ combined ticket with MAEC). Apr–Oct daily 10am–7pm; Nov–Mar closed Mon.*

② ★★ kids **Museo dell'Accademia Etrusca e della Città (MAEC).** Cortona's revamped civic museum, housed in the 13th-century Palazzo Casali, traces the history of the *città* from its prehistoric origins through its Etruscan pomp and Roman decline, using a sequence of multimedia displays from the area's many ancient digs. Upstairs, the eclectic collection of the Accademia Etrusca meanders through Egyptian mummies and a room dedicated to Futurist Gino Severini, to 17th-century celestial globes, Quattrocento ivories, and Etruscan bronze figurines. The prize find is an intact Etruscan bronze lamp from the 4th century B.C., in Room 5. ⏱ *1 hr. Piazza Signorelli 9.*

Shop wares in Cortona.

Cortona's Palazzo Comunale.

☎ *0575-637235. www.cortonamaec. org. Admission 10€ (13€ combined ticket with Museo Diocesano). Apr–Oct daily 10am–7pm; Nov–Mar closed Mon.*

③ ★ **L'Antico Cocciaio.** Cortona is known for its ceramics, and Cocciaio is the oldest of the town's outlets. The traditional patterns in green, cream, and dark yellow are prominent. Look for the symbolic stylized daisy, a design created by

The countryside by Cortona.

Gino Severini. This shop is unbelievably stuffed—don't bring your pet bull. *Via Benedetti 24.* ☎ *0575-605294. www.toscumbria.com/cocciaio. MC, V.*

4 **Tuscher.** Pause for sustenance at Cortona's most elegant bar-cafe, with an attractive mix of visitors and locals. Excellent pastries, snacks, and coffee are available. *Via Nazionale 43.* ☎ *0575-62053. $.*

5 ★ **Terrabruga.** The designs here are slightly more contemporary, but still offer a wide array of ceramics in traditional Cortonese colors and motifs. These authentic craftwares are designed and manufactured by hand in Giulio Lucarini's workshop. *Via Nazionale 56.* ☎ *0575-604405. www.terrabruga.com. AE, MC, V.*

6 ★ kids **Via Crucis.** The torturous, stepped ascent up Cortona's Via Santa Margherita is known as the "Path of the Cross": Fifteen

mosaics by Cortonese Futurist Gino Severini (1883–1966) depicting the *Stations of the Cross* line the route. The climb also passes the Porta Berarda, through which Margherita di Laviano entered Cortona in 1277, on her way to sainthood as St. Margaret of Cortona. Take water, and don't attempt the route if you have asthma or a heart condition: It's major-league steep. ⏱ *45 min.*

7 ★ kids **Fortezza Medicea Girifalco.** Built in 1556 by a relative of Pope Pius IV, Cortona's fortress has unmatched views over the Valdichiana, as far as Monte Amiata and Lago Trasimeno in Umbria. It's a magnificent sight—and makes the energy-sapping climb worthwhile. ⏱ *20 min. Viale Raimondo Bistacci.* ☎ *0575-637235. Admission 3€. Hours vary but usually Sat–Sun 10am–7pm.*

Drive 3km (2 miles) downhill from Cortona to:

8 **Santa Maria delle Grazie al Calcinaio.** This monument to High Renaissance architecture was built by Sienese polymath Francesco di Giorgio Martini between 1485 and 1513. Laid out on a Latin cross plan, the church enjoys a bucolic setting amid olive groves below the ancient walls. The 1516 rose window is by Guillaume de Marcillat. ⏱ *30 min. Via del Calcinaio. No phone. Free admission. Mon–Sat 4–7pm (3–5pm winter).*

9 ☕ **La Saletta,** Via Nazionale 26–28 (☎ 0575-603366), is my favorite wine bar in town, with live jazz on Saturday nights in winter. Patrons of all ages come for excellent Tuscan wines by the glass in elegant surroundings.

Where to Stay & Dine

★ **Dardano** CENTRO STORICO
TUSCAN The cooks at this family-owned, budget trattoria are known for their roasts—duck, chicken, and guinea hen (my favorite). *Via Dardano 24.* ☎ *0575-601944. www. trattoriadardano.com. Entrees 6€–12€. No credit cards. Lunch, dinner Thurs–Tues (daily in summer). Closed Jan–Feb.*

★★ **Il Falconiere** SAN MARTINO
Just 4.5km (3 miles) north of Cortona, a restored series of 17th-century buildings have the feeling of a sumptuous house in the Valdichiana countryside, with original furnishings, four-poster iron beds, and a large pool amid an olive grove. A luxe spa was added in 2009. *Loc. San Martino.* ☎ *0575-612679. www. ilfalconiere.com. 22 units. Doubles 290€–380€ w/breakfast. AE, MC, V. Closed 2 weeks in Jan.*

La Loggetta CENTRO STORICO
TUSCAN Innovative pasta dishes like *tagliolini* with cabbage and truffle or *pici* (thick, short spaghetti) with duck *ragù* complement the unique setting under a loggia above Piazza della Repubblica. *Piazza di Pescheria 4.* ☎ *0575-630575. www.locan danelloggiato.it. Entrees 7€–16€. AE, DC, MC, V. Lunch, dinner Thurs–Tues. Closed 2 weeks in Jan.*

★★ **Osteria del Teatro** CENTRO STORICO *TUSCAN* An atmospheric alley is the setting for a theatrical take on Cortonese cuisine. Come in season (summer through October-ish), and you can eat a full *porcini* mushroom menu. *Via Maffei 2.* ☎ *0575-630556. www.osteria-del-teatro.it. Entrees 11€–20€. AE, MC, V. Lunch, dinner Thurs–Tues.*

★★ **Pane e Vino** CENTRO STORICO *MODERN TUSCAN* This vaulted tavern has a vast wine list, creative vegetarian dishes, and a specialism in Chianina beef—on the grill, carpaccio, or tartare. *Piazza Signorelli 27.* ☎ *0575-631010. www. pane-vino.it. Entrees 6€–10€. MC, V. Lunch, dinner Tues–Sun.*

★ **San Michele** CENTRO STORICO
This central hotel in a barely-altered 11th-century palace has vaulted ceilings with *pietra serena* arches, midsize rooms under wood-beamed ceilings, and antique furnishings. The tower rooms are ideal for lovers. E-mail them for the best prices. *Via Guelfa 15.* ☎ *0575-604348. www.hotelsanmichele.net. 42 units. Doubles 79€–350€ w/breakfast. AE, DC, MC, V. Closed Nov to mid-Mar.*

★★ **Villa Marsili** OUTSIDE WALLS
With dignified lounges and finely furnished, frescoed bedrooms, this former gentleman's residence from 1786 is the coziest nest close to town, with outdoor gardens. Most rooms are elaborately furnished with views of the Valdichiana. *Via C. Battisti 13.* ☎ *0575-605252. www.villa marsili.com. 27 units. Doubles 110€–230€ w/breakfast. AE, DC, MC, V.*

Porcini mushrooms, which can be sampled at Osteria del Teatro.

Charming Tuscan Towns & Villages

Lucca

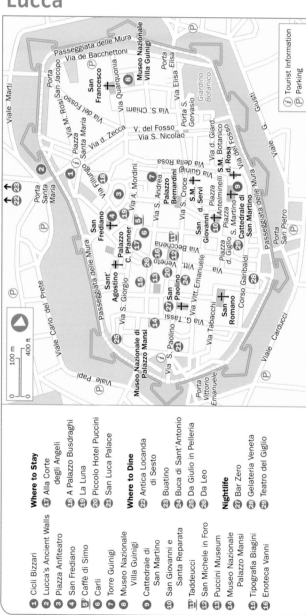

① Cicli Bizzari
② Lucca's Ancient Walls
③ Piazza Anfiteatro
④ San Frediano
⑤ Caffè di Simo
⑥ Carli
⑦ Torre Guinigi
⑧ Museo Nazionale Villa Guinigi
⑨ Cattedrale di San Martino
⑩ San Giovanni e Santa Reparata
⑪ Taddeucci
⑫ San Michele in Foro
⑬ Puccini Museum
⑭ Museo Nazionale Palazzo Mansi
⑮ Tipografia Biagini
⑯ Enoteca Vanni

Where to Stay
⑰ Alla Corte degli Angeli
⑱ A Palazzo Busdraghi
⑲ La Luna
⑳ Piccolo Hotel Puccini
㉑ San Luca Palace

Where to Dine
㉒ Antica Locanda di Sesto
㉓ Buatino
㉔ Buca di Sant'Antonio
㉕ Da Giulio in Pelleria
㉖ Da Leo

Nightlife
㉗ Bar Zero
㉘ Gelateria Veneta
㉙ Teatro del Giglio

ⓘ Tourist Information
Ⓟ Parking

Lucca is the most graceful provincial city in Tuscany, set within a ring of mighty medieval and Renaissance walls. At the heart of one of Italy's richest agricultural regions, locals eat and drink well, and have a deserved reputation for politeness. Hometown to Puccini, the entire city is dotted with grand *palazzi* and churches. Plus the popularity of the bike as the preferred form of local transport makes Lucca a pleasure to wander. START: **Lucca is 72km (45 miles) west of Florence on the A11, 21km (13 miles) north of Pisa on the S12r. Trip length: 2 days, with an overnight stay in the historic center, to see Lucca properly.**

1 kids **Cicli Bizzarri.** A bike rental shop (next door to the tourist office) might seem like a curious first stop, but you'll need wheels where we're heading. Rent yours here for 3€ to 4.50€ per hour; take your passport or a driver's license. *Piazza Santa Maria 32.* ☎ *0583-496682. www.ciclibizzarri.net. No credit cards.*

2 ★★★ kids **Lucca's Ancient Walls.** Planted with plane, chestnut, and ilex trees, Lucca's ramparts make for one of Tuscany's great bike rides. Now a city park stretching for 5km (2¾ miles), the **Passeggiata delle Mura** gives Lucca its special charm, and walking or cycling the circular route is the best way to get yourselves oriented. The only question is: clockwise or counterclockwise? I prefer the former, starting from Piazza Santa Maria, so my last view before descending is down into the manicured Baroque garden of the **Palazzo Pfanner.** ⏱ *1½ hr.*

3 ★ kids **Piazza Anfiteatro.** A 2nd-century Roman amphitheater stood here, off the northern end of the main shopping street, Via Fillungo ("long thread"), until its destruction in the 1100s: Locals used it as a quarry for the stone to construct Lucca's palaces and churches. The foundations of what were the grandstands today support an ellipse of medieval houses. ⏱ *10 min.*

4 ★ **San Frediano.** The original 6th-century basilica, built to honor an Irish hermit who became Bishop of Lucca, was reconstructed in the 12th century in the Lucchese-Romanesque style, using marble from the dismantled amphitheater. The dazzling 13th-century *Ascension* mosaic on the facade, probably by Bonaventura Berlinghieri, was restored in the 1800s. Just inside the entrance is the church's treasure, a 12th-century Romanesque baptismal font depicting the story of Moses. ⏱ *20 min. Piazza San Frediano.*

Via Fillungo, Lucca's main shopping street.

Lucca After Dark

Lucca is a typically drowsy Tuscan town after dark, with just a few nightspots. Strolling the center with a gelato is perhaps the best way to pass a warm evening. In business since 1927, **Gelateria Veneta,** Via Vittorio Veneto 74 (☎ 0583-467037; www.gelateria veneta.net), is the traditional choice. Summer drinkers at **Bar Zero,** Via S. Paolino 58 (no phone), usually spill out onto the steps of San Paolino church opposite. Beers, spirits, and wines by the glass are all popular, as is the nightly *aperitivo* buffet that arrives at 7pm. October to March is the season at the **Teatro del Giglio,** Piazza del Giglio (☎ 0583-467521; www.teatrodelgiglio.it), one of Tuscany's major houses. Rossini premiered *William Tell* here in 1831. The program has a mix of classical dance, theater, opera, and modern musical shows, Every evening throughout the year, the Chiesa di San Giovanni hosts an opera recital or orchestral concert dedicated to hometown composer Giacomo Puccini, in a series called **Puccini e la sua Lucca** (www.puccinielasualucca.com). Tickets are 17€ (13€ for ages 22 and under) and can be purchased all day inside San Giovanni.

☎ 0583-493627. Free admission. Mon–Sat 8:30am–noon and 3–5:30pm; Sun 9–11:30am and 3–5:30pm.

5 Caffè di Simo. On Lucca's main shopping drag, this is the most famous cafe in town. Puccini came here for a drink, perhaps humming his next aria. *Via Fillungo 58.* ☎ 0583-496234. $.

6 ★ Carli. One of the oldest jewelry stores in Tuscany, from 1655, Carli specializes in exquisite antique jewelry, silver, and watches. *Via Fillungo 95.* ☎ 0583-491119. AE, DC, MC, V.

7 ★ kids Torre Guinigi. This tower, rising 44m (146 ft.) with trademark ilex growing from the roof, was built by the city's ruling family in the

Mosaics on the facade of San Frediano.

One of Lucca's many handsome piazzas.

15th century. Climb its 230 steps to get a proper picture of Lucca enclosed by its ring of walls, with the Apennine mountain range beyond. ⏱ *30 min. Via Sant'Andrea (at Via Chiavi d'Oro).* ☎ *347-6270423. Admission 3.50€. Apr–May daily 9am–7:30pm; June–Sept daily 9am–6:30pm; Oct and Mar daily 9:30am–5:30pm; Nov–Feb daily 9:30am–4:30pm.*

⑧ ★ Museo Nazionale Villa Guinigi. Once owned by Paolo Guinigi, who ruled Lucca from 1400 to 1430, this museum displays the best from local archaeological digs as well as Romanesque, Gothic, and Renaissance sculpture (including a couple of terra cottas recently attributed to Donatello). Its painting collection is strong on works by regional artists; highlights include three fine panels by Florentine Fra' Bartolomeo. ⏱ *1 hr. Via della Quarquonia.* ☎ *0583-496033. www.luccamusei nazionali.it. Admission 4€; 6.50€ with Palazzo Mansi. Tues–Sat 8:30am–7pm; Sun 8:30am–1pm.*

⑨ ★★ Cattedrale di San Martino. Pope Alexander II consecrated Lucca's Duomo in 1070, but it took 4 centuries to finish. This ornate, asymmetrical structure was constructed around its *campanile* (bell tower) with an arched facade in the Pisan-Romanesque style. This facade was never completed; the topmost loggia and tympanum have yet to be built. Look for the reliefs under the portico, a stellar example of 13th-century stonework, including a fascinating 12-panel calendar of peasant life. The interior was given a Gothic dress in the 14th to 15th centuries, but remains dark and a touch grim. A highlight, in the sacristy, is Jacopo della Quercia's *Tomb of Ilaria del Carretto* (ca. 1406), his earliest surviving work and the first sculptural creation of the Renaissance to use Roman decorative motifs. Ruskin hailed it "the loveliest Christian tomb in Italy."

Adjacent to the cathedral is the **Museo della Cattedrale,** housing among its sacred art, the golden

San Michele in Foro.

accouterments worn by the *Volto Santo* on Lucca's Feast of the Lumi-nara, September 13th. ⏱ *1 hr. Piazza San Martino.* ☎ *0583-490530. www.museocattedrale lucca.it. Free admission to cathedral; 2€ sacristy; 6€ sacristy, Museo, and San Giovanni. Mon–Fri 9:30am–5:45pm (Nov–Mar closes 4:45pm); Sat 9:30am–6:45pm; Sun 9:30–10:45am and noon–6pm (Nov–Mar closes 5pm).*

🔟 ★ San Giovanni e Santa Reparata.

The main structure of the present church dates from the 1100s, although the facade is largely from the 1500s. Its roots, however, stretch much further back: Foundations under the nave, baptis-tery, and altar have been opened up to exploration and show an archeo-logical history that heads back past the 7th-century Lombard mauso-leum, past the Paleochristian 5th-century church to the 1st-century B.C. mosaic floor of Lucca's Roman

baths. ⏱ *30 min. Piazza San Giovanni.* ☎ *0583-490530. Admis-sion 2.50€; 6€ sacristy, Museo della Cattedrale, and San Giovanni. Apr–Nov daily 10am–6pm; Dec–Mar Mon–Fri 10am–2pm, Sat–Sun 10am–5pm.*

1️⃣1️⃣ ★ Taddeucci.

This pastry shop, founded in 1881, created a legendary confection called Buccel-lato Taddeucci, an anise-flavored cake studded with raisins that's still sold today. *Piazza San Michele 34.* ☎ *0583-494933. $.*

1️⃣2️⃣ ★★ San Michele in Foro.

The *foro* in the name of this 12th-century church comes from the fact that it was built atop the Roman forum. The facade, with its four gal-leries, blind arcades, and individu-ally unique, almost pagan columns, represents the zenith of the form that Romanesque architecture took around here (sometimes called "Luccan-Romanesque"). While the internal architecture is much altered, and disappointing after that blockbuster facade, worth a peek is Filippino Lippi's *Saints* in the right transept. ⏱ *20 min. Piazza San Michele.* ☎ *0583-48459. Free admis-sion. Daily 9am–noon and 3–6pm (Nov–Mar closes 5pm).*

1️⃣3️⃣ ★ Puccini Museum.

Reopened in 2011 after a long and controversial restoration process, the birthplace of Lucca's most famous son preserves objects and mementos relating to the great composer's life and works—includ-ing some of his paintings. ⏱ *40 min. Corte San Lorenzo 9.* ☎ *0583-584028. www.puccinimuseum.it. Admission 7€. Nov–Mar Wed–Mon 11am–5pm; Apr–Oct Wed–Mon 10am–6pm.*

14 Museo Nazionale Palazzo Mansi. It's almost a case of the frame outshining the painting at this lavishly decorated 16th-century palace, formerly owned by the powerful Mansi family. Fans of Baroque portraiture, though, should head upstairs to the gallery for works by Pontormo, Bronzino, Beccafumi, Correggio, Veronese, and others. ⏱ *45 min. Via Galli Tassi 43 (at Via del Toro).* ☎ *0583-55570. www.luccamuseinazionali.it. Admission 4€; 6.50€ with Villa Guinigi. Tues–Sat 8:30am–7pm; Sun 8:30am–1pm.*

15 ★ Tipografia Biagini. The highest quality paper is turned into bespoke stationery at this traditional typography workshop. Orders are designed and set by hand, and can be shipped home. *Via S. Giustina 20–24.* ☎ *0583-54292. www.tipografiabiagini.it. AE, DC, MC, V.*

16 ★★ Enoteca Vanni. Founded in 1965, this is Lucca's best wine cellar with great examples of the respectable local DOC,

A Puccini statue in Lucca.

Montecarlo. Lucca's hills are also acclaimed for olive oil, the best of which is stocked here. *Piazza S. Salvatore 7.* ☎ *0583-491902. www.enotecavanni.com. MC, V.*

Biking is one of the best ways to tour Lucca.

Where to Stay

One of the modern rooms at San Luca Palace.

★★ Alla Corte degli Angeli

CENTRO STORICO   A welcoming, warrenlike *palazzo* blessed with the most romantic rooms in town. Bedrooms are well proportioned, although not enormous, and kitted out with Italian antique furniture and embellished with a unique, hand-painted fresco. *Via degli Angeli 23.* ☎ *0583-496204. www.allacorte degliangeli.com. 10 units. Doubles 130€–210€ w/breakfast. AE, DC, MC, V.*

★ A Palazzo Busdraghi CENTRO

STORICO   This *residenza d'epoca* is located on an elegantly crumbling courtyard right in the heart of the city. Rooms vary in size and layout, but all retain their original *palazzo* furnishings and authentic 1600s feel. *Via Fillungo 170.* ☎ *0583-950856. www.apalazzobusdraghi.it. 7 units. Doubles 120€–160€ w/ breakfast. AE, DC, MC, V.*

La Luna CENTRO STORICO   You'll

find problems here if you look hard enough, but no one complains about the value. Rooms come in all sizes—from spacious to tiny, ditto for the bathrooms. Plus the hotel offers a consistently warm and welcoming atmosphere. *Corte Compagni 12 (off Via Fillungo).* ☎ *0583-493634. www. hotellaluna.com. 29 units. Doubles 105€–140€. AE, MC, V.*

★ Piccolo Hotel Puccini CEN-

TRO STORICO   The city's best value central hotel takes its name from the composer, who was born across the street. Small and friendly, the hotel offers clean, cozy bedrooms with modern furnishings. Only accept a room that opens out to the front. *Via di Poggio 9 (off Piazza San Michele).* ☎ *0583-55421. www. hotelpuccini.com. 14 units. Doubles 95€. AE, MC, V.*

★★ San Luca Palace CENTRO

STORICO   Opened in 2007, this crisp conversion of a 1540 *palazzo* has upped the ante for comfort within the walls. Modern, well-equipped rooms have retained some antique character. A good choice for business travelers. *Via San Paolino 103.* ☎ *0583-317446. www.sanlucapalace.com. 26 units. Doubles 170€–290€ w/breakfast. AE, DC, MC, V.*

Where to Dine

★★★ Antica Locanda di Sesto

SESTO DI MORIANO *LUCCHESE*
Local and seasonal specialties permeate the menu, which is delivered in a relaxed country dining room where friendly staff preserves a welcome nod to old-fashioned service. There's plenty of choice from the grill (*Cinta senese* pork, cuts of beef) and oven (piglet, rabbit, kid). *Via Ludovica 1660, Sesto di Moriano (signposted off S12, 11km/7 miles north of Lucca).* ☎ *0583-578181. www.anticalocanda disesto.it. Entrees 12€–18€. MC, V. Lunch, dinner Sun–Fri.*

★ Buatino NORTH LUCCA *ITALIAN/ LUCCHESE*

It's worth the walk 10 minutes north of Piazza Santa Maria to dine in the back room of this funky bar-cum-trattoria. *Antipasti* include Italian classics like bruschetta, and unfussy pasta dishes are all made fresh. For *secondi,* expect Lucchese ingredients like rabbit, *baccalà* (salt cod), and *farro* (spelt wheat). *Borgo Giannotti 508.* ☎ *0583-343207. Entrees 8€–14€. AE, MC, V. Lunch, dinner Mon–Sat.*

★ Buca di Sant'Antonio CENTRO STORICO *TUSCAN*

The most reliable fine dining in Lucca is served in a 1782 building where Puccini used to eat. The classic local dishes such as *capretto allo spiedo* (spit-roasted kid goat) are prepared with flavor, flair, and superb simplicity. *Via della Cervia 3.* ☎ *0583-55881. www.bucadisantantonio.it. Entrees 16€. AE, MC, V. Lunch Tues–Sun; dinner Tues–Sat.*

Da Giulio in Pelleria CENTRO STORICO *LUCCHESE*

There's no more authentic Lucchese dining within the city walls. Local specialties include horse tartar, veal snout, and Tuscan sausages with stewed white beans, plus, as ever, there are grilled meats and pasta. *Via delle Conce 45.* ☎ *0583-55948. Entrees 6€–13€. MC, V. Lunch Sat and 3rd Sun of month; dinner Mon–Sat.*

★★ Da Leo CENTRO STORICO *TUS-CAN/LUCCHESE*

The Buralli family makes everyone feel welcome at their unpretentious tavern in a 16th-century building. Guests come not for the charming 1930s decor, but for the affordable regional menu, including homemade pastas prepared daily and seasonal game roasts. *Via Tegrimi 1 (at Piazza San Salvatore).* ☎ *0583-492236. www. trattoriadaleo.it. Entrees 9€–16€. No credit cards. Lunch, dinner daily.*

The terrace at Buca di Sant'Antonio.

Massa Marittima

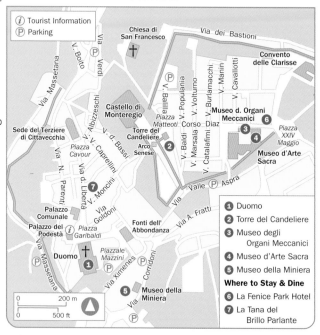

(i) Tourist Information
(P) Parking

1 Duomo
2 Torre del Candeliere
3 Museo degli Organi Meccanici
4 Museo d'Arte Sacra
5 Museo della Miniera

Where to Stay & Dine

6 La Fenice Park Hotel
7 La Tana del Brillo Parlante

Gripping the side of a hill 350m (1148 ft.) up in the Colline Metallifere (Metaliferous Hills) is the former mining community and capital of the Alta Maremma. Massa was overrun by Sienese soldiers then hit hard by plague in the 1300s, and is now a quiet hilltown with shuttered buildings, steep lanes, and a fine crop of small museums. Don't visit on a Monday, when most of the sights are closed. START: **Massa Marittima is 67km (41 miles) southwest of Siena, reached via the S73 and S441. Trip length: Half-a-day.**

---

1 ★ **Duomo.** Massa's Old (lower) Town clusters around triangular **Piazza Garibaldi,** with Massa's cathedral, a harmonious mixture in travertine of Pisan-Romanesque and Gothic styling. Above the main door lintel is a relief celebrating the life of Massa's patron saint and one-time bishop, 9th-century African immigrant Cerbonius, to whom the building is dedicated—spot the scene for which he's most famous, when he took a flock of geese to see the Pope. ⏱ *25 min. Piazza Garibaldi. No phone. Free admission. Daily 8am–noon and 3–6pm.*

Climb steep Via Moncini, heading through the Porta alla Silici and into the New (upper) Town.

2 kids **Torre del Candeliere.** A flying arch, made as a viaduct for

Sienese garrisons, connects the fortress ramparts to this 1228 tower. It has served as a clock tower since 1443 and is still impressive at two-thirds of its original 60m (197-ft.) height. ⏱ *20 min. Piazza Matteotti.* ☎ *0566-902289. www.massamaritti mamusei.it. Admission 2.50€. Apr–Oct Tues–Sun 10am–1pm and 3–6pm; Nov–Feb Tues–Sun 11am–1pm and 2:30–4:30pm.*

❸ ★ **Museo degli Organi Meccanici.** This is a unique collection of organs rescued from churches across Italy and restored to working order. Some of the instruments date back to 1600; there's also an early *ghironda* (hurdy-gurdy) and a line of fortepianos dating from 1700s Vienna to the early 20th century. ⏱ *20 min. Corso Diaz 28.* ☎ *0566-940282. www.museodegliorgani.it. Admission 4€. Mar–Sept 10am–1pm and 4–7pm (Mar–May closes 6pm); Oct to mid-Jan 10:30am–12:30pm and 3–6pm.*

❹ ★ **Museo d'Arte Sacra.** Massa's art highlight showcases Ambrogio Lorenzetti's glorious *Maestà*, painted in the 1330s. Considered "crude" by baroque tastes, it was lost and wasn't rediscovered until 1867, by which point it had been divided, nailed together, and was serving as a bin. Elsewhere in the small collection is a fine stained-glass *Crucifixion* by Ambrogio's brother, Pietro. ⏱ *40 min. Corso Diaz 36.* ☎ *0566-901954. www.massamaritti mamusei.it. Admission 5€. Apr–Oct Tues–Sun 10am–1pm and 3–6pm; Nov–Mar Tues–Sun 11am–1pm and 3–5pm.*

❺ 🧒 **Museo della Miniera.** To learn more about the town's mining heritage—the first mining code in European history was drawn up here in the 14th century—don your hard hat and head underground.

Massa Marittima.

The guided visit covers 700m (2,300 ft.) of reconstructed 1940s mineshaft. ⏱ *45 min. Via Corridoni.* ☎ *0566-902289. Admission 5€. Tours approximately hourly Tues–Sun 10am–noon and 3–5:45pm (Nov–Mar last tour 4:30pm).*

Eating & Staying in Massa

It may be small (just four tables), but country-styled **La Tana del Brillo Parlante,** Vicolo Ciambellano 4 (☎ 0566-901274; closed Wed), is one of my favorite places to dine in all Tuscany. The seasonal menu hosts familiar regional flavors, but they are combined with verve and originality. Entrees range from 14€ to 17€, reservations are essential, and they accept cash only. The standout lodgings in town are at **La Fenice Park Hotel,** Corso Diaz 63 (☎ 0566-903941; www.lafenice parkhotel.it), a handsome shuttered *palazzo* in the Città Nuova with 17 traditional Tuscan rooms. Doubles range from 90€ to 180€.

Montepulciano

- ⓘ Tourist Information
- ⓟ Parking

1. Palazzo Comunale
2. Cattedrale di Santa Maria
3. Palazzo Nobili-Tarugi
4. Museo Civico
5. Contucci
6. Gattavecchi
7. Santa Maria dei Servi
8. Frassineti
9. Mazzetti Albo Mosaics
10. Caffè Poliziano
11. Tempio di San Biagio

Where to Stay

12. Duomo
13. Il Riccio
14. La Dimora nel Corso

Where to Dine

15. Acquacheta
16. A Gambe di Gatto
17. La Grotta
18. Pulcino

T he garnet colored Vino Nobile, beloved by epicures, first put the handsome town of Montepulciano on the map in the Etruscan era. At an altitude of 605m (1,985 ft.), Montepulciano is also Tuscany's loftiest hilltown, with remarkable views over the vineyards from up on its volcanic crag. Before checking out individual sites, climb its steeply graded, serpentine main street—it has many names, but locals call it simply "Il Corso." Piazza Grande is at the summit of the Corso, where you can begin your tour of the individual attractions. START: **Montepulciano is on the S146, reached from Florence via the A1 (111km/69 miles) and Siena via the S2 (67km/40 miles). Trip length: 1 day.**

① ★ kids **Palazzo Comunale.** The highest point in town is **Piazza Grande,** enveloped by Renaissance *palazzi* and this Gothic town hall. The crenellated clock tower was added by Michelozzo (1396–1472), inspired by the Palazzo Vecchio (built in the 1200s), in Florence. A climb up the tower gives you a chance to get your Montepulciano geography straight—and take in expansive views over the Valdichiana below. ⏱ *30 min. Piazza Grande.* ☎ *0578-7121. Admission 2€. Mon–Sat 10am–6pm.*

② ★ Cattedrale di Santa Maria Assunta. To the world, this uncompleted Duomo presents a blank facade, but the sparse interior is not without its treasures. I visit just to gaze at Taddeo di Bartolo's 1401 triptych, *Assumption of the Virgin*, above the high altar. It glows, with the artist's use of subtle pinks, blood orange, eggplant purple, and plenty of gold leaf. ⏱ *20 min. Piazza Grande. No phone. Free admission. Daily 9am–12:30pm and 3:15–7pm.*

③ ★★ Palazzo Nobili-Tarugi. Facing the Duomo across Piazza Grande, this *palazzo*—with its half-moon arches, Ionic columns, and great portico—is attributed to Antonio da Sangallo the Elder. The much-photographed 1520 fountain out front incorporates two Etruscan columns, topped by two griffins and two lions bearing the Medici coat of arms. The interior is closed to the public. ⏱ *15 min. Piazza Grande.*

④ Museo Civico. The Sienese-Gothic Palazzo Neri-Orselli houses most of Montepulciano's art treasures. Its collection of some 200 Tuscan paintings features works from the 13th to 17th centuries. Other gems include 15th-century illuminated choir books, enameled terra cottas by Andrea Della Robbia

The "noble wine" of Montepulciano is the local specialty.

(1435–1525), and Etruscan funerary urns. ⏱ *30 min. Via Ricci 10. ☎ 0578-717300. Admission 5€. Tues–Sun 10am–6pm (Fri–Sun only in winter).*

Vino Nobile

Montepulciano's vintners have organized a consortium-cum-showroom, the **Consorzio del Vino Nobile di Montepulciano** (☎ 0578-757812; www.consorziovinonobile.it). The public can visit, at the Palazzo del Capitano del Popolo on Piazza Grande, and sample members' wines. Three tasting glasses 5€–10€. Easter–Oct Mon–Sat 1–5pm.

Piazza Grande, the highest point in Montepulciano.

Montepulciano is littered with *enoteches* and cantine (wine cellars) where you can sample (usually free) and purchase Vino Nobile and other local products.

⑤ ★ Contucci. In Montepulciano's main square, this renowned winery occupies the cellars of the 13th-century Palazzo Contucci, home to popes and Grand Dukes over the years. Contucci was one of the first makers of Vino Nobile, still a proud tradition today. *Palazzo Contucci, Piazza Grande.* ☎ *0578-757006. www.contucci.it. AE, DC, MC, V.*

⑥ ★★ Gattavecchi. Labels such as their outstanding Riserva dei Padri Serviti and 100% sangiovese Parceto have been well received worldwide. Ask to see the cellars: They have been in continuous use since before 1200, originally by the friars of the church next door. *Via di Collazzi 74.* ☎ *0578-757110. www. gattavecchi.it. AE, MC, V.*

⑦ Santa Maria dei Servi. The little parish church next to Gattavecchi is notable for a curious little

Tempio di San Biagio.

Madonna and Child inserted smack in the middle of another painting, to the left of the altar. The *Madonna* has been attributed to the 13th-century Sienese workshop of Duccio di Buoninsegna. ⏱ *10 min. Piazza di Santa Maria. No phone. Free admission. Irregular hours.*

⑧ ★ Frassineti. Intricate intarsia art handcrafted from wood sourced around the globe. Landscapes of the rural Val d'Orcia are a specialty, and cost around 200€ a piece. *Via dell'Opio nel Corso.* ☎ *0578-717295. No credit cards.*

⑨ ★ Mazzetti Albo Mosaics. Large framed mosaics, of scenes from Montepulciano and around, all handmade by Albo in his workshop. Prices from 350€. *Via dell'Opio nel Corso 14.* ☎ *0578-757272. No credit cards.*

⑩ ★★ Caffè Poliziano. This cafe-wine bar, which opened in 1868, has bounced back after decades of slumber, since the days when Pirandello and Fellini quaffed here. *Via Voltaia nel Corso 27.* ☎ *0578-758615. www. caffepoliziano.it. $–$$$.*

⑪ ★★ Tempio di San Biagio. This masterpiece of High Renaissance architecture was the greatest achievement of architect Antonio da Sangallo, who finished it in 1529. He was obviously inspired by Bramante's design for St. Peter's in Rome. Built on a Greek cross plan, it was designed to house a statue of the Madonna. Crowned by its dome, the church has two campaniles—one left unfinished. When shadows start to lengthen, the yellow travertine masonry glows like gold. ⏱ *20 min. Via di San Biagio (10-min. downhill walk from Porta di Grassi). No phone. Free admission. Daily 9am– 12:30pm and 3:30–7:30pm.*

Where to Stay & Dine

★★★ Acquacheta CENTRO STORICO *TUSCAN/GRILL* The menu's short at this informal little *osteria* inside a converted wine *cantina*: pasta five ways, flamegrilled meat, salads, plus a lengthy pecorino list. Their *fiorentina alla brace* is the best steak in town. *Via del Teatro 22.* ☎ *0578-717086. www.acquacheta.eu. Entrees 9€–18€. MC, V. Lunch, dinner Wed–Mon. Closed mid-Jan to mid-Mar.*

★★ A Gambe di Gatto CENTRO STORICO *MODERN TUSCAN* This tiny eatery offers elevated cooking in a relaxed setting. The best seasonal Tuscan ingredients go into such creative combinations as *Pratese mortadella* with white figs. *Via dell'Opio nel Corso 34.* ☎ *0578-757431. Entrees 12€–16€. DC, MC, V. Lunch, dinner Thurs–Tues. Closed Jan 10 to mid-Mar.*

Duomo CENTRO STORICO Small to midsize rooms at this family-run favorite, named for the cathedral opposite, are decorated in Tuscan *arte povera* style. *Via San Donato 14.* ☎ *0578-757473. www.albergo duomomontepulciano.it. 13 units. Doubles 75€–95€ w/breakfast. AE, MC, V.*

Il Riccio CENTRO STORICO Rooms are a bit featureless, but the friendly welcome, a unique setting above a 13th-century cloister in Montepulciano's oldest street, and the best roof terrace in town, ensure a memorable stay. *Via Talosa 21.* ☎ *0578-757713. www.ilriccio.net. 6 units. Doubles 100€. MC, V.*

★ kids La Dimora nel Corso CENTRO STORICO A surprisingly harmonious mix of wood-beam ceilings, terra-cotta tiles, and fresh, modern tones (and occasionally

Il Riccio's terrace.

furniture) grace this *palazzo* on the Corso. Rooms and mini-apartments were completely refitted in 2011. *Via di Gracciano nel Corso 33.* ☎ *0578-758757. www.trattoriadicagnano.it. 7 units. Doubles 85€–120€ w/breakfast. MC, V. Closed 2 weeks in Nov.*

★ La Grotta SAN BIAGIO *ITALIAN* This old-fashioned brick-vaulted restaurant serves upscale Italian classics, most of it harvested from the local countryside. *Via San Biagio 2.* ☎ *0578-757607. Entrees 21€. MC, V. Lunch, dinner Thurs–Tues. Closed Jan 10–Mar 10.*

★ kids Pulcino TOWARD CHIANCIANO *TUSCAN* Go for grilled meats straight from the farm, like the half-chicken or succulent veal, or *pici*, hand-rolled, short, thick spaghetti. One downer: Service can be slow. *S146 per Chianciano 37.* ☎ *0578-758711. www.pulcino.com. Entrees 10€–16€. AE, MC, V. Lunch, dinner daily. Irregular hours Nov–Easter.*

Pienza

To Siena
To Montepulciano, A1 Autostrada

Via della Madonnina

Piazza Dante Alighieri

Via Enzo Mangiavacchi

Via delle Mura

Corso Il Rossellino

Via Gozzante

Via Elisa

Piazza Spagna

Via Pia

Largo Roma

Via Dogale

Via Case Nuove

Chiesa di S. Francesco

Palazzo Piccolomini

Piazza Pio II

Palazzo Comunale

Corso Il Rossellino

Palazzo Borgia

Via Gozzante

Via di Circonvallazione

Duomo

Via del Casello

0   100 m
0   300 ft

P Parking

i Tourist Information

- ❶ Piazza Pio II
- ❷ Duomo
- ❸ Museo Diocesano
- ❹ Palazzo Piccolomini
- ❺ Ferro Biagiotti
- ❻ Nannetti e Bernardini
- ❼ Enoteca di Ghino
- ❽ Bar Il Casello

Where to Stay
- ❾ Chiostro di Pienza
- ❿ Città Ideale Suites
- ⓫ Giardino Segreto

Where to Dine
- ⓬ La Chiocciola
- ⓭ La Porta
- ⓮ Latte di Luna

This model Renaissance town was the creation of Pope Pius II, who wanted to transform the village of his birth, Corsignano, into a place that would glorify his name. He was born here as Silvio Piccolomini, in an impoverished branch of a noble Sienese family; he later added "Aeneas" as a first name out of love of the tales of Virgil, and after years as a humanist scholar, gout sufferer, and itinerant diplomat, served as pope from 1458 to 1464. His envisioned city never grew beyond a few blocks, but it remains a masterpiece. Zeffirelli recognized it for the stage setting it is, deserting Verona to film *Romeo and Juliet* here in 1968. START: **Pienza is 55km (33 miles) southwest of Siena, reached via the S2 and S146. Trip length: Half-a-day.**

❶ ★★ **Piazza Pio II.** Begin in the center of the tiny town: Virtually all the sights are on this set-piece piazza or nearby. The square is enclosed by the Duomo, Palazzo Piccolomini, and Palazzo Vescovile (Bishop's Palace).

The fourth side features the distinctly non-Renaissance **Palazzo Comunale,** home to the town hall and municipal offices. The bell tower, added later, was built lower than the Duomo's to emphasize the power of the Church over civil authority. ⏱ *15 min.*

2 ★★ Duomo. The classicized Renaissance facade complete with Roman arches and pediment conceals a Gothic interior influenced by the Austrian "hall churches" Pius admired on his travels. The Piccolomini family is honored with a coat of arms (cross and five upturned crescents) in the rose window and all over the church. Pius commissioned four leading Sienese artists to paint devotional altarpieces, and they're all still here: counterclockwise from the right aisle, works by Giovanni di Paolo, Matteo di Giovanni, Vecchietta, and Sano di Pietro. Alas, the whole thing is built on clay and sandstone, and may one day collapse: Check out the slope to the altar and ceiling cracks. ⏲ *30 min. Piazza Pio II.* ☎ *0578-748548. Free admission. Daily 7am–1pm and 2:30–7pm.*

Pienza's Duomo.

3 ★ Museo Diocesano. This neat little collection housed inside the Bishop's Palace looted local churches for its array of 14th- and 15th-century Sienese paintings, including a *Madonna and Child with Saints* by Vecchietta (1410–80). More surreal is a lifesize carved *San Regolo* holding his own severed head. ⏲ *30 min. Corso Rossellino*

30. ☎ *0578-749905. Admission 4.10€. Mid-Mar to Oct Wed–Mon 10am–1pm and 3–6pm; off season Sat–Sun 10am–1pm and 3–5pm.*

4 ★ Palazzo Piccolomini. The papal home of Pius II is architect Bernardo Rossellino's masterpiece, although it's obviously influenced by L. B. Alberti's Palazzo Rucellai in Florence (p 47, **8**). In Tuscan Renaissance architecture, it's usually the harmonious facade that's the star attraction. Not necessarily here: At the rear is a three-story loggia overlooking a hanging garden

Pienza gets very quiet after the day-trippers depart.

Pecorino for sale in Pienza.

with a drop-dead view over the Val d'Orcia. Descendants of Pius lived here until 1968. ⏱ *30 min. Piazza Pio II.* ☎ *0577-286300. www.palazzo piccolominipienza.it. Admission 7€. Guided tours only mid-Mar to mid-Oct Tues–Sun 10am–6pm; closes 4pm otherwise. Closed 2nd half of Nov and Jan 7–Feb 14.*

⑤ ★ Ferro Biagiotti. Browse for quality wrought-iron handcrafts, based on ancient designs. The products are made using the traditional technique, with fire, anvil, and hammer. *Corso Rossellino 67 (at Piazza Pio II).* ☎ *0578-748666. AE, MC, V.*

⑥ Nannetti e Bernardini. Italy's most famous pecorino, a sheep's-milk cheese, is sold in shops along Corso Rossellino, among which this rustic, artisan deli is my favorite. Fancier varieties are soaked in wine or dusted with truffles. For a lunchtime bite on the move, try their *porchetta* (salty herbed pork) *panino. Corso Rossellino 81.* ☎ *0578-748627. www. nannettiebernardinipienza.com. No credit cards.*

⑦ ★★ Enoteca di Ghino. Outstanding vintages of the very best wines from Tuscany and beyond. Bottles from 25€ to 10 times that. *Via del Leone 16.* ☎ *0578-748057. www.enotecadighino.it. AE, MC, V.*

⑧ Bar Il Casello. This sleek, air-conditioned bar and cafe is the social center of town, with snacks during the day, Tuscan reds and whites by the glass, and devastating views over the Val d'Orcia. In season, it's open Tuesday through Sunday until 1am, shockingly late by local standards. *Via del Casello 3.* ☎ *0578-749105. $.*

Where to Stay & Dine

★ Chiostro di Pienza CENTRO STORICO   Converted to a hotel in 2005, this 15th-century convent and cloister is the best full-service option within Pienza itself, and has a pool overlooking the wild expanses of the Val d'Orcia. Spacious rooms have frescoes; those in the wing are best. *Corso Rossellino 26.* ☎ *0578-748400.*

www.relaisilchiostrodipienza.com. 37 units. Doubles 70€–250€ w/breakfast. AE, DC, MC, V. Closed Mon–Thurs Jan to mid-Mar.

★ Città Ideale Suites CENTRO STORICO   Inside a quaint stone house on a quiet *piazzetta,* these elegant two-room suites offer refined B&B accommodations in the historic center. Go for "Bernardo" if you prefer contemporary to traditional design and furnishings. *Piazza San Carlo Borromeo 4.* ☎ *366-9311051. www.cittaidealesuites.com. 3 units. Doubles 120€–160€ w/breakfast. AE, DC, MC, V.*

kids Giardino Segreto CENTRO STORICO A haven of tranquility just a few paces off the Corso, these simple, central rooms are arranged around a peaceful herb garden, all with TVs and Wi-Fi (but no phones), Mini-apartments are a great choice for budget family travel. *Via Condotti 13.* ☎ *0578-748539. www.ilgiardinosegretopienza.com. 6 units. Doubles 50€–70€; apts (sleeping 4–5) 105€–125€ w/breakfast. AE, V. Closed Jan 15–Feb 15.*

La Chiocciola OUTSIDE WALLS *TUSCAN* Dishes at this rustic tavern with outdoor tables have stood the test of time. Pasta dishes are especially tasty (try the pappardelle with wild boar or hare sauce), or go for oven-baked pecorino cheese with a side. The cooking, with its abundant use of regional flavors, is never mannered. *Viale Mencattelli 2.* ☎ *0578-748683. www.trattoriala chiocciola.it. Entrees 8€–16€. AE, MC, V. Lunch, dinner Thurs–Tues. Closed 2 weeks in Jan.*

★ **La Porta** MONTICCHIELLO *TUSCAN* For a special treat, drive 6km (3¾ miles) southeast to the medieval village of Monticchiello to this renowned *osteria* right at the village gate. Regional fare includes favorites like *tagliata di manzo al Vino Nobile* (Valdichiana beef in red wine) and *faraona al vinsanto con patate arrosto* (guinea hen in sweet wine sauce with roast potato). There's terrace dining in fair weather; book ahead to ensure a berth. *Via del Piano 1, Monticchiello.* ☎ *0578-755163. www.osterialaporta.it. Entrees 12€–20€. MC, V. Lunch, dinner Fri–Wed. Closed last week in June and Jan 10–Feb 5.*

kids Latte di Luna CENTRO STORICO *TUSCAN* This laid-back trattoria near the eastern town gate draws a diverse regular crowd—from foreign exchange students to local *carabinieri*. Don't miss the homemade *semifreddi* (similar to ice cream) for dessert. *Via San Carlo 2–4.* ☎ *0578-748606. Entrees 7€–16€. MC, V. Lunch, dinner Wed–Mon. Closed Feb to mid-Mar.*

A spacious room at Città Ideale Suites.

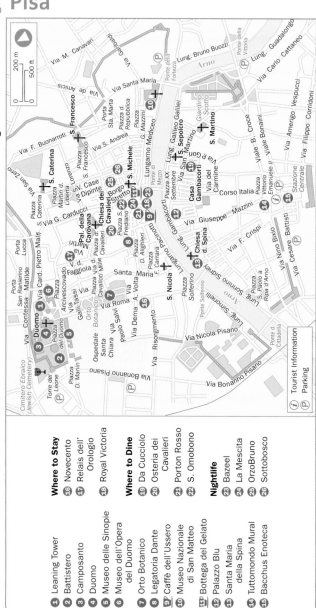

Pisa

Where to Stay

1 Leaning Tower
2 Battistero
3 Camposanto
4 Duomo
5 Museo delle Sinopie
6 Museo dell'Opera del Duomo
7 Orto Botanico
8 Legatoria Dante
9 Caffè dell'Ussero
10 Museo Nazionale di San Matteo
11 Bottega del Gelato
12 Palazzo Blu
13 Santa Maria della Spina
14 Tuttomondo Mural
15 Bacchus Enoteca

Where to Stay

16 Novecento
17 Relais dell' Orologio
18 Royal Victoria

Where to Dine

19 Da Cucciolo
20 Osteria dei Cavalieri
21 Porton Rosso
22 S. Omobono

Nightlife

23 Bazeel
24 La Mescita
25 OrzoBruno
26 Sottobosco

When Pisans discuss the good old days, they're talking about the 12th century. Buildings such as the Duomo and Leaning Tower were created in those heady days of Pisan power. Pisa enjoyed great maritime influence because of its harbor at the mouth of the Arno River, and the Pisan-Romanesque architecture that developed through the rich years of the 13th century is the reason so many outsiders pass through today. The city began to decline following its defeat at sea by the Genoese in 1285 and the silting up of its vital harbor, and eventually succumbed to Florence. I suggest you spend the night here, and get to know its lively center beyond the Campo dei Miracoli. START: **Pisa is 88km (55 miles) from Florence, taking the FI-PI-LI highway along the Valdarno. Trip length: 2 days to see the city properly.**

❶ ★★★ kids Leaning Tower (Torre Pendente). The freestanding *campanile,* or bell tower, of the cathedral, the most famous building in Italy, was begun in 1173. It was intended to be vertical but started to lurch almost immediately: You just can't stack that much marble on sinking subsoil. However, construction continued, with two long interruptions, until 1360, and in December 2001 it was righted to lean a mere 4m (14 ft.)—but you'll still notice the disorienting effects as you climb spiral steps to the top. It was supposedly from here that Galileo dropped balls of different masses, disproving Aristotle's theories about the acceleration of falling bodies. ⏱ *30 min. Piazza del Duomo.* ☎ *050-835011. www.opapisa.it. Admission 15€–17€ with reservation). Nov and Feb daily 10am–5pm; Dec and Jan daily 10am–4:30pm; Mar daily 9am–5:30pm; Oct daily 9am–7pm; Apr–Sept daily 8:30am–8pm. Minimum age 8.*

The Leaning Tower of Pisa, the Cattedrale, and the Baptistery on Pisa's Campo dei Miracoli.

2 ★★ **Battistero.** This stunning example of the Pisan-Romanesque style (with its own distinct lean) was begun in 1152 by Diotisalvi, and finally crowned with a Gothic dome in the 14th century. Don't miss the hexagonal pulpit (1260) by Nicola Pisano; it's supported by pillars resting on the backs of three marble lions, and carved with five scenes from the *Life of Christ*. ⏱ *30 min. Piazza del Duomo.* ☎ *050-835011. www.opapisa.it. Admission 5€; 10€ for entire Campo exc. Tower. Nov–Feb daily 10am–5pm; Mar daily 9am–6pm; Apr–Sept daily 8am–8pm; Oct daily 9am–7pm.*

3 ★★ **Camposanto.** In 1278, Giovanni di Simone designed this cemetery, allegedly over dirt from the Holy Land shipped to Pisa by the Crusaders. Some 600 members of medieval Pisan nobility are interred here. The entire building was once decorated with frescoes by Benozzo Gozzoli, Andrea di Bonaiuto, and others, many of which were destroyed when the Camposanto was hit by a U.S. incendiary bomb in 1944. The best of what remains is Buffalmacco's sobering *Triumph of Death*, painted in the late 1330s. ⏱ *45 min. Piazza del Duomo.*

☎ *050-835011. www.opapisa.it. Admission 5€; 10€ for entire Campo exc. Tower. Nov–Feb daily 10am–5pm; Mar daily 9am–6pm; Apr–Sept daily 8am–8pm; Oct daily 9am–7pm.*

4 ★★ **Duomo.** This cathedral, started by Buschetto in 1063 using a mix of classical and Arab styles, became the most influential Romanesque building in Tuscany. The facade was erected by Rainaldo in the 1200s, with arches that diminish in size as they ascend. The pulpit by Giovanni Pisano (1302–11) even outshines the one by his dad in the baptistery. ⏱ *40 min. Piazza del Duomo.* ☎ *050-835011. www. opapisa.it. Admission 2€ (free Nov–Feb); 10€ for entire Campo exc. Tower. Nov–Feb Mon–Sat 10am–12:45pm and 2–5pm, Sun 2–5pm; Mar and Oct Mon–Sat 10am–6pm, Sun 2–6pm; Apr–Sept Mon–Sat 10am–8pm, Sun 2–8pm.*

5 ★ **Museo delle Sinopie.** The sketches (or *sinopie*) displayed here survived beneath the Camposanto's ruined frescoes after the 1944 bombardment. (Fresco artists drew in red-brown pigment before applying their paint.) Compare the different drawing styles of such painters as

The interior of Pisa's baptistery.

Pisa After Dark

Away from the Campo, central Pisa has a lively nighttime scene, kept buzzing by the city's large student population. Stone-clad **Bazeel,** Lungarno Pacinotti 1 (☎ 340-2881113; www.bazeel.it), always seems to be the bar of the minute, attracting Pisa's fashionable set for *aperitivo,* live music, DJs, or big-screen sports. For beer lovers, **OrzoBruno,** Via Case Dipinte 6 (☎ 050-578802; www.orzobruno.it), has a selection of light and dark microbrews. Bookstore-cum-cafe **Sottobosco,** Piazza San Paolo all'Orto 3 (☎ 050-9912364), comes alive at night with live acoustic music, cocktails, and a beautiful clientele. Once dinner service is over, **La Mescita,** Via Cavalca 2 (☎ 050-957019; www.osterialamescitapisa.it), transforms itself into an atmospheric late-night enoteca with a respectable wine list.

Benozzo Gozzoli, Taddeo Gaddi, and Andrea di Bonaiuto. ⏱ *45 min. Piazza del Duomo.* ☎ *050-835011. www.opapisa.it. Admission 5€; 10€ for everything in Campo exc. Tower. Nov–Feb daily 10am–5pm; Mar daily 9am–6pm; Apr–Sept daily 8am–8pm; Oct daily 9am–7pm.*

6 ★ Museo dell'Opera del Duomo. Mostly Romanesque and Gothic art removed for safekeeping from the monuments of Piazza del Duomo is showcased here, including Bonnano Pisano's extraordinary 12th-century San Ranieri door (that originally hung on the Duomo right opposite the Tower) and plenty of *famiglia* Pisano sculpture. The courtyard has a unique view of the Campo dei Miracoli. ⏱ *45 min. Piazza Arcivescovado 6.* ☎ *050-835011. www.opapisa.it. Admission 5€; 10€ for entire Campo exc. Tower. Nov–Feb daily 10am–5pm; Mar daily 9am–6pm; Apr–Sept daily 8am–8pm; Oct daily 9am–7pm.*

7 kids Orto Botanico. Europe's oldest botanical garden, founded in 1543, is the perfect spot to breathe deep and wander unbothered after the chaos of the Campo. ⏱ *45 min. Via Ghini 5.* ☎ *050-2211313. Admission 2.50€. Mon–Fri 8:30am–5pm; Sat 8:30am–1pm. Closed 1 week around Aug 15.*

8 Legatoria Dante. This store by the university specializes in immaculately hand-bound leather writing journals. Prices start around 10€. *Via l'Arancio 4.* ☎ *050-9911619. www.legatoriadante.it. No credit cards.*

The grounds by the Duomo and Leaning Tower are a favorite photo stop.

Pisa's Palazzo Blu.

9 Caffè dell'Ussero. One of Italy's oldest literary cafe-bars, this was installed in 1775 on the ground floor of Palazzo Agostini. Young men of the Risorgimento drank and plotted here as students. The coffee and pastries are good choices. *Lungarno Pacinotti 27* ☎ *050-581100. Closed Sat and Aug. $.*

10 ★★ Museo Nazionale di San Matteo. An old convent that was once a prison today houses sacred art and sculpture gathered from Pisa's holy places. It's memorable largely for many less-known works by some major artists, like Masaccio's *St. Paul* (1426), the only piece of his much-studied *Pisa Altarpiece* still in Pisa. Look out too for Simone Martini's outstanding polyptych of the *Virgin and Child with Saints.* ⏱ *1¼ hr. Piazzetta San Matteo 1.* ☎ *050-541865. Admission 5€. Tues–Sat 8:30am–7pm; Sun 9am–1:30pm.*

11 ★ Bottega del Gelato. Pisa's best ice cream. Enough said. Slurp in the shade as you stroll under the arcades of adjacent Borgo Stretto, Pisa's main shopping street. *Piazza Garibaldi 11.* ☎ *050-575467. $.*

12 Palazzo Blu. It's easy to see why this handsome, Liberty-style riverside *palazzo* got its name. These days it's an intriguing space used to showcase the works of lesser known historical painters who worked in Pisa, as well as contemporary shows. ⏱ *45 min. Lungarno Gambacorti 9.* ☎ *050-916950. www.palazzoblu.org. Free admission. Tues–Sun 10am–1pm and 4–10pm.*

13 ★★ Santa Maria della Spina. All the truly ancient churches of Pisa face the sea, the original source of the maritime city's protection and wealth. This extravagant Gothic masterpiece, wrought by Pisa's leading Gothic sculptors, including Giovanni Pisano, is no exception. There's little point going inside. ⏱ *10 min. Lungarno Gambacorti (at Via Sant'Antonio).* ☎ *050-21441. Admission 2€. Hours vary but typically Tues–Sun 11am–12:45pm and 3–5:45pm.*

14 ★ Tuttomondo Mural. A few months before his death in 1990, New York street artist Keith Haring completed this giant mural on the theme of "peace and harmony." The dazzling and complex painting interweaves 30 of his trademark Pop Art figures. ⏱ *10 min. Via Zandonai.*

15 Bacchus Enoteca. This is the best wine shop in Pisa, especially strong on Tuscan vintages. Wines can be shipped worldwide. *Via Mascagni 1.* ☎ *050-500560. www.bacchusenoteca.com. AE, MC, V.*

Where to Stay

★ **Novecento** CENTRO STORICO This immaculately converted Liberty villa set around a courtyard garden is Pisa's best boutique offering. Rooms are small, but ooze style, and represent a good value so close to the Campo. *Via Roma 37.* ☎ *050-500323. www.hotelnovecentopisa.it. 14 units. Doubles 80€–120€ w/breakfast. AE, MC, V.*

★★ **Relais dell'Orologio** CEN-TRO STORICO A former private home of a noble family is the most intimate hotel in town, with a sophisticated yet welcoming ambience.

The same owners run a B&B, the nearby **Relais dei Fiori,** for tighter budgets. *Via della Faggiola 12.* ☎ *050-830361. www.hotelrelais orologio.com. 21 units. Doubles 135€–375€. AE, DC, MC, V.*

★ **Royal Victoria** CENTRO STORICO In business since 1839, this traditional hotel blends harmoniously with Pisa's colonial-style riverfront. Request a room overlooking the Arno. *Lungarno Pacinotti 12.* ☎ *050-940111. www.royalvictoria. it. 48 units. Doubles 65€–150€ w/breakfast. AE, DC, MC, V.*

Where to Dine

Dining Tip

Choose a restaurant that's well away from the Campo, to ensure you eat better food at better prices.

★★ **Da Cucciolo** SOUTH BANK *PISAN* Enchantingly old-fashioned backstreet trattoria frequented by locals who know good eating at a good price. It's the place to try simple Pisan classics like *seppie e bietole* (a stew of cuttlefish and chard). *Vicolo Rosselmini 9.* ☎ *050-26086. Entrees 8€–14€. AE, DC, MC, V. Lunch daily; dinner Mon–Sat.*

★ **Osteria dei Cavalieri** CENTRO STORICO *TUSCAN* The best food within a few minutes of the Campo. The menu is traditional, but skilled chefs lighten and modernize many of the region's robust classics. *Via San Frediano 16.* ☎ *050-580858.*

www.osteriacavalieri.pisa.it. Entrees 11€–16€. MC, V. Lunch Mon–Fri; dinner Mon–Sat. Closed Aug.

★ **Porton Rosso** CENTRO STORICO *TUSCAN/SEAFOOD* Tucked down a tiny alley, this seafood joint is highly rated by fish-loving locals. There's always a *"menu terra"* and pasta if you prefer the land-based route. *Vicolo del Tidi.* ☎ *050-580566. Entrees 10€–18€. AE, MC, V. Lunch, dinner Mon–Sat. Closed 3 weeks in Aug.*

S. Omobono CENTRO STORICO *PISAN* Dine among locals right on Pisa's market. The daily menu sticks to local classics such as *baccalà alla livornese* (salt cod stewed with tomatoes). *Piazza S. Omobono 6.* ☎ *050-540847. Entrees 8€–10€. MC, V. Dinner Mon–Sat. Closed 2 weeks in Aug.*

Pistoia

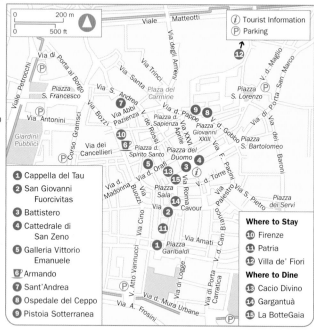

Tourist Information

Parking

1 Cappella del Tau
2 San Giovanni Fuorcivitas
3 Battistero
4 Cattedrale di San Zeno
5 Galleria Vittorio Emanuele
6 Armando
7 Sant'Andrea
8 Ospedale del Ceppo
9 Pistoia Sotterranea

Where to Stay

10 Firenze
11 Patria
12 Villa de' Fiori

Where to Dine

13 Cacio Divino
14 Gargantuà
15 La BotteGaia

Stuck midway between rivals Pisa and Florence, the ancient Roman city of Pistoia inherited Romanesque architecture and Gothic sculpture from the former and the best of the Renaissance through proximity to the latter. It can claim to be the birthplace of the pistol (or *pistolese*), but these days is better known for nurturing life—in both the plant nurseries that ring the city and the thriving produce market surrounded by excellent informal restaurants right at its heart. START: **Pistoia is 35km (22 miles) northwest of Florence, just off the A11. Trip length: 1 day.**

1 ★★ **Cappella del Tau.** This remarkable little chapel was completely frescoed in 1372 by Niccolò di Tommaso with scenes that covered every inch of the walls and ceiling. Now seriously damaged, what remains illustrates the *Life of St. Anthony Abbot* (lower register); *Stories from the New Testament* (middle register); and *Stories from the*

Old Testament (upper register and vaults). The wall facing the door is covered by a huge *Last Judgment*: The space is now shared, somewhat incongruously, with giant bronzes by Pistoiese sculptor Marino Marini (1901–80). ⏱ **20 min. Corso Fedi 28.** ☎ **0573-32204. Free admission. Mon–Sat 8:30am–1:30pm.**

2 ★ **San Giovanni Fuorcivitas.** The side facade of this small, supremely Romanesque church is an orderly festival of blind arcades, inlaid diamond lozenges, and stripes to put a zebra to shame. Inside the main attraction is the pulpit (1270) by Fra' Guglielmo da Pisa, a student of Nicola Pisano. ⏱ *15 min. Via Cavour.* ☎ *0573-24784. Free admission. Daily 8:30am–noon and 5–6:30pm.*

3 **Battistero.** Anchoring one corner of Pistoia's set-piece piazza, the city baptistery was built in characteristic bands of dark green and white by Cellino di Nese from 1337 to 1359, based on a design by Andrea Pisano. The Gothic pulpit was added in 1399, and the *Madonna* above the door is the work of Tommaso and Nino Pisano. ⏱ *10 min. Piazza del Duomo. No phone. Free admission. Tues–Wed and Fri–Sat 10am–1pm and 3–5pm; Sun 10am–1pm and 3–6pm.*

4 ★ **Cattedrale di San Zeno.** The current incarnation of Pistoia's Duomo dates from 1220, soon after which an old defensive tower close by, bristling with Ghibelline swallowtail crenellations, was given Romanesque striped arches and converted to serve as its bell tower.

The glazed terra-cotta decorations of the entrance barrel vault and the lunette above the main door are Andrea della Robbia creations. Inside the **Cappella di San Jacopo** is the Duomo's greatest treasure, the silver-gilded Altare di San Jacopo. In the crypt are the remains of the 5th-century church and marvelously medieval bits of a Guido da Como pulpit (1199), dismembered in the 17th century. Verocchio's 1485 *Madonna di Piazza* hangs on the right-hand wall of the chapel to the left of the high altar. ⏱ *20 min. Piazza del Duomo.* ☎ *0573-25095. Free admission. Daily 8:30am–12:30pm and 3:30–7pm.*

5 ★ **Galleria Vittorio Emanuele.** Skip forward 8 centuries from the Romanesque to Art Nouveau: This early 20th-century shopping mall (now rather tired) sports exuberant external decoration crafted by the town's Michelucci ironworks. ⏱ *10 min. Via degli Orafi (at Via della Nave).*

6 **Armando.** This lively place is both a favorite local coffee stop and a purveyor of sublime cream and fruit pastries. *Via Curtatone e Montanara 38.* ☎ *0573-23128. $.*

The Cattedrale di San Zeno.

Pistoia is known for its many plant nurseries.

7 ★★★ **Sant'Andrea.** Pistoia's undisputed artistic heavyweight is Giovanni Pisano's pulpit (1298–1301) inside this 12th-century church. The third of the four great Pisano pulpits (the others are in Pisa and Siena) and the first carved by Giovanni without the help of his dad, Nicola, this is the work with which the Pisan sculptor brought his art to absolute Gothic perfection, relying on his trademark narrative density and emotive power. Bring a .50€ coin for the light box. ⏲ *20 min. Piazzetta Sant'Andrea.* ☎ *0573-21912. Free admission. Daily 8am–12:30pm and 3–6pm.*

8 ★★ **Ospedale del Ceppo.** Pistoia's star outdoor attraction is the facade of this still-operational hospital: a Giovanni della Robbia frieze (1514–25) of glazed terra-cotta panels to surmount a Miche-lozzo-designed loggia. The six panels, plus a decaying one added later by Filippo Paladini, represent the seven acts of mercy, divided by the cardinal and theological virtues. ⏲ *10 min. Piazza Giovanni XXIII.*

9 ★ **kids Pistoia Sotterranea.** This fascinating guided under-ground visit follows the path of a diverted stream, under a couple of intact bridges now below the Ospedale del Ceppo, that over the centuries has served as a power source for an olive press, a public laundry, a refuse dump, and a source of drinking water—often simultaneously. The fascinating tour takes in the history of the hospital above (founded in 1277 and still going strong), and ends at the tiny, frescoed teaching and autopsy the-ater built in the 1700s. Tours in Eng-lish are available. ⏲ *1 hr. Piazza Giovanni XXIII 13.* ☎ *0573-368023. www.irsapt.it. Tour 9€. Daily at 10:30am, 11:30am, 12:30pm, 2pm, 3pm, 4pm, 5pm (Apr–Sept also 6pm).*

Giovanni della Robbia's frieze on the Ospedale del Ceppo.

Where to Stay

Firenze CENTRO STORICO The wisest budget choice in town has spacious, plain rooms that come with air-conditioning and are kept spotlessly clean. Extra beds for families cost 15€ to 25€. *Via Curtatone e Montanara 42.* ☎ *0573-23141. www.hotel-firenze.it. 20 units. Doubles 55€–88€ w/breakfast. No credit cards.*

★★ **Patria** CENTRO STORICO Completely refitted and reopened in 2011, the best hotel in central Pistoia has midsize, contemporary, yet warm rooms sporting parquet flooring and shiny chrome rainfall shower units. Ask about discounts if you're visiting on a weekend. *Via Crispi*

8–12.* ☎ *0573-358800. www.patria hotel.com. 27 units. Doubles 110€– 250€ w/breakfast. AE, DC, MC, V.*

★★ **Villa de' Fiori** PISTOIESE HILLS Inside a secluded Liberty villa, authentic antique-chic rooms come in all configurations, from suite-style family units divided by period screens, to romantic doubles with canopy beds, to mini-apartments suited to weeklong stays. Service is impeccable: You'll feel like a guest in an aristocratic home. *Via di Bigiano e Castel Bovani 39 (3km/2 miles north of center).* ☎ *0573-450351. www. villadefiori.it. 9 units. Doubles 94€– 182€ w/breakfast. AE, DC, MC, V. Closed Jan and weekdays Feb–Mar.*

Where to Dine

★★ **Cacio Divino** CENTRO STORICO *MODERN TUSCAN* Surprisingly daring Tuscan flavor combinations and contemporary presentation at fair prices. Dishes vary, but expect the likes of *pici alla lepre sul cacao amaro* (hand-rolled pasta with hare sauce on bitter chocolate) served with a smile. The two-course weekday lunch special is a steal at 13€. *Via del Lastrone 13.* ☎ *0573-1941058. www. cacio-divino.it. Entrees 9€–11€. MC, V. Lunch, dinner daily (mid-June to mid-Sept closed Sun lunch).*

★ **Gargantuà** CENTRO STORICO *MODERN ITALIAN* This lively enoteca-restaurant tucked into a tiny piazza sports bright, Catalan-style decor and a menu of pasta, *bruschetta*, and simple Tuscan mains.

There's a well-chosen wines-by-the-glass list, too, and you're welcome to just drink and snack if you're not too hungry. *Piazza dell'Ortaggio 12.* ☎ *0573-23330. www.taverna gargantua.com. Entrees 9€–15€. AE, MC, V. Lunch, dinner daily.*

★ **La BotteGaia** CENTRO STORICO *MODERN TUSCAN* This much recommended place serves classic Tuscan cuisine, elevated a notch above the norm, alongside more daring delicacies such as slow-cooked, milk-fed veal. Grab a table out back for views across to the Duomo and Baptistery. *Via del Lastrone 17 (also an entrance behind the Baptistery).* ☎ *0573-365602. www.labottegaia. it. Entrees 10€–14€. AE, DC, MC, V. Lunch Tues–Sat; dinner Tues–Sun. Closed 2 weeks in Aug.*

San Gimignano

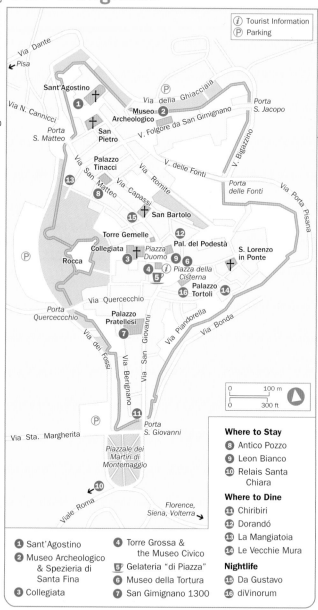

(i) Tourist Information
(P) Parking

Via Dante
← Pisa

Via N. Cannicci

Sant'Agostino ①

Via della Ghiacciaia

(P)

Porta
S. Jacopo

Museo ②
Archeologico

Porta
S. Matteo

San
Pietro

V. Folgore da San Gimignano

V. delle Fonti

Palazzo
Tinacci

Via Romite

Porta
delle Fonti

Via Porta Pisana

Via San Matteo

Via Capassi

⑬

⑧

⑮

San Bartolo

Torre Gemelle

⑫

Pal. del Podestà

S. Lorenzo
in Ponte

Collegiata ③

Piazza
Duomo

⑨ ⑥

Rocca

(P)

④
⑤ (i)

Piazza della
Cisterna

⑯

Palazzo
Tortoli

⑭

Porta
Quercecchio

Via Quercecchio

Via Piandorella

Via Bonda

Palazzo
Pratellesi
⑦

Via dei Fossi

Via San Giovanni

Via Berignano

(P)

⑪

Porta
S. Giovanni

Via Sta. Margherita

Piazzale dei
Martiri di
Montemaggio

0   100 m
0   300 ft

⑩

Viale Roma

Florence,
Siena, Volterra →

① Sant'Agostino
② Museo Archeologico
   & Spezieria di
   Santa Fina
③ Collegiata

④ Torre Grossa &
   the Museo Civico
⑤ Gelateria "di Piazza"
⑥ Museo della Tortura
⑦ San Gimignano 1300

Where to Stay
⑧ Antico Pozzo
⑨ Leon Bianco
⑩ Relais Santa
   Chiara

Where to Dine
⑪ Chiribiri
⑫ Dorandó
⑬ La Mangiatoia
⑭ Le Vecchie Mura

Nightlife
⑮ Da Gustavo
⑯ diVinorum

uscany's best-preserved medieval town once had more than 70 towers, symbols of local clan rivalry and one-upmanship, and a visible sign of the town's wealth in the years running up to the Black Death of 1348. The painter Benozzo Gozzoli was born here, and novelists and film directors have used it as a stage (E. M. Forster in *Where Angels Fear to Tread* and Franco Zeffirelli in *Tea with Mussolini*). Try to stay overnight: The place can feel like a theme park during the day, but San Gimignano at dusk is one of Tuscany's special places. START: **San Gimignano is off the Florence-Siena raccordo, 40km (24 miles) northwest of Siena and 52km (32 miles) southwest of Florence. Trip length: 1 day.**

1 ★★ Sant'Agostino. In 1464, a plague swept San Gimignano and the citizens prayed to St. Sebastian to end it. When the sickness passed, they dutifully hired native son Benozzo Gozzoli to paint a thankful scene on the nave's left wall showing this patron saint of plagues and his cloak of angels breaking the plague arrows being thrown down by a vengeful God. The town liked the results, so they commissioned Gozzoli to spend the next 2 years frescoing the apse of their Romanesque-Gothic church with *Scenes from the Life of St. Augustine.* Right

in front, Piero del Pollaiuolo's 1483 *Coronation of the Virgin* sits on Benedetto di Maiano's sculpted 1494 marble altar. ⏱ *20 min. Piazza Sant'Agostino.* ☎ *0577-907012. Free admission. Daily 7am–noon and 3–7pm (Nov–Apr closes 6pm); Jan–Apr closes Mon morning.*

2 Museo Archeologico & Spezieria di Santa Fina. San Gimignano's modest Etruscan collection proves the town's roots run much deeper than the Middle Ages. The museum is installed in the 1253 Spezieria, the pharmacy branch of

The backstreets of San Gimignano.

Two Beautiful Squares & Market Days

Two of Tuscany's loveliest squares, Piazza del Duomo and **Piazza della Cisterna,** stand side by side in the heart of town. On Thursday and Saturday mornings, vendors hawk their wares in Piazza del Duomo, in the long shadows of Gothic palaces and seven towers. Piazza della Cisterna, named for its 1237 well, is lined with 13th- and 14th-century buildings and hosts a fine hotel or two as well as the best gelato in town (**5** below).

the medieval Santa Fina hospital. Upstairs is the town's surprisingly large and sporadically interesting **Galleria di Arte Moderna e Contemporanea,** usually deserted. ⏱ *30 min. Via Folgore 3.* ☎ *0577-940348. Admission 3.50€. Daily 11am–6pm.*

3 ★★★ **Collegiata.** The city's principal church dates from the 11th century, but its present look is mostly from the 1400s. Inside, it's among Tuscany's most richly decorated, with scenes from the Old and New Testaments painted by Bartolo

San Gimignano is a picturesque place to shop.

di Fredi and (probably) Lippo Memmi facing each other across the nave. At the end of the nave on the right is one of my favorite spots in all Tuscany: Guiliano da Maiano's Renaissance Chapel of Santa Fina, frescoed in 1475 by Domenico Ghirlandaio with two scenes from the life of the local saint, a young girl named Fina. Look for the towers of 15th-century San Gimignano in the background of her funeral, on the left. ⏱ *45 min. Piazza del Duomo.* ☎ *0577-940316. Admission 3.50€. Feb–Mar, Nov, Dec–Jan Mon–Sat 10am–4:40pm, Sun 12:30–4:40pm; Apr–Oct Mon–Fri 10am–7:10pm, Sat 10am–5:10pm, Sun 12:30–7:10pm. Closed 1st Sun in Aug, Mar 12, Nov 16–30, and Jan 16–31.*

Travel Tip

For 7.50€ you can buy a discount ticket that covers the **Torre Grossa** and **Museo Civico** (**4**); the tiny **Museo Archeologico** (**2**); and the strange little **Museo Ornitologico** (☎ *0577-941-388*), a few glass cases containing stuffed birds in the confines of a dimly-lit, deconsecrated church.

4 ★★ **Museo Civico & Torre Grossa.** Climb 54m (175 ft.) up the highest tower in town for one of Tuscany's best panoramas, over the bucolic hills around San Gimignano and across the whole Val d'Elsa. (Though if you climb the hill to the right of the Collegiata, you'll get almost the same view for free from San Gimignano's ruined fortress.) The same ticket includes the art at the 13th-century **Palazzo del Popolo.** Lippo Memmi's impressive *Maestà* (from 1317) dominates the Council Chamber. Slightly racier are frescoes by his father, Memmi di Filippuccio, showing scenes from a medieval wedding night. The remainder of the collection is strong on pre-Renaissance painting. ⏱ *45 min. Piazza del Duomo 1.* ☎ *0577-990312. Admission 5€. Oct–Mar daily 10am–5:30pm; Apr–Sept daily 9:30am–7pm.*

Art work at the Museo Civico.

5 ★★ **Gelateria "di Piazza."** The queues out the door tell their own story: This place has been named Gelato World Champion more than once with good reason. My top choices are Vernaccia wine flavor and Crema di Santa Fina, made with saffron. (But not on the same cone.) *Piazza della Cisterna 4.* ☎ *0577-942244. www.gelateriadipiazza. com. $.*

6 kids **Museo della Tortura.** Though certainly not for young or easily frightened children, San Gimignano's original torture museum provides a fascinating, and reasonably scientific, presentation of some grim subject matter. The setting, in the Torre del Diavolo (Devil's Tower), and implements like the "Iron Maiden of Nuremberg" and

The medieval skyscrapers of San Gimignano.

Wine buffs will find San Gimignano well stocked with enotecas.

"Heretic's Fork," might just give you nightmares. Commentary in English completes a grisly experience. 🕐 *30 min. Via del Castello 1–3 (at Piazza della Cisterna).* ☎ *0577-942243. Admission 8€. Apr–Oct daily 10am–7pm (sometimes until midnight in midsummer); Nov–Feb Mon–Fri 10:30am–4:30pm, Sat–Sun 10am–6pm; Mar daily 10am–5pm.*

❼ ★ kids San Gimignano 1300. It took a team of five skilled craftsmen (two named Michelangelo and Raffaello, honestly) 3 years and a ton of clay to build the 800 structures that make up this enchanting 1:100 scale model of San Gimignano around 1300, with its 72 towers intact. Serious historical archive research by the universities at Florence and Pisa contributed to what is a unique reproduction of a medieval walled town, by digging up details of buildings long lost to history. 🕐 *20 min. Via Berignano 23.* ☎ *0577-941078. www.sangimignano 1300.com. Admission 5€. June–Aug daily 8am–11pm; Sept–May daily 8am–8pm.*

San Gimignano After Dark

Unsurprisingly, San Gim is a sleepy town after dark. However, it is blessed with a handful of excellent wine bars that serve the region's famed reds alongside Vernaccia di San Gimignano, the only DOCG white wine made in Tuscany. **Da Gustavo,** Via San Matteo 29 (☎ 0577-940057), draws a mixed crowd of visitors and locals. Vernaccias and chiantis (from 3€) are usually good, often sold by the glass, with snacks such as *crostini* or *bruschetta,* and Panforte for the sweet-toothed. My favorite spot to sip a glass or two is one of the handful of panoramic tables at **diVinorum,** Via degli Innocenti 5 (☎ 0577-907-192; www.divinorumwinebar.com). There are over 20 wines by the glass, and accompanying *bruschettoni* (large bruschettas) cost around 8€.

Where to Stay & Dine

★★ Antico Pozzo CENTRO STORICO   Dante slept in this 15th-century *palazzo*, now the ancient center's best hotel. Rooms vary in size, and superior units have frescoes. *Via San Matteo 87.* ☎ *0577-942014. www.anticopozzo.com. 18 units. Doubles 110€–180€ w/breakfast. DC, MC, V. Closed 3 weeks in Jan–Feb.*

★ 〔kids〕 **Chiribiri** CENTRO STORICO *ITALIAN*   The little basement eatery knocks out Italian and regional meat and pasta classics with gusto. A bonus: It's open 11am to 11pm nonstop, so if you or yours have odd meal times, they can feed you. *Piazzetta della Madonna 1.* ☎ *0577-941948. Entrees 7€–13€. No credit cards. Lunch, dinner daily.*

★★ Dorandó CENTRO STORICO *MODERN TUSCAN*   The city's most refined restaurant, with stone walls and a vaulted roof, serves creative, seasonal dishes based on medieval recipes. All with a slow food ethos. *Vicolo dell'Oro 2.* ☎ *0577-941862.*

One of the rooms at Antico Pozzo.

www.ristorantedorando.it. Entrees 20€–25€. AE, DC, MC, V. Lunch, dinner daily (Oct–Easter closed Mon). Closed Dec 10–Jan 31.

★ La Mangiatoia CENTRO STORICO *TUSCAN*   Many dishes at this intimate old-town restaurant—like *cinghiale di Remigio* (boar stewed in white wine)—derive from ancient Sangimignanese recipes. *Via Mainardi 5.* ☎ *0577-941528. Entrees 13€–16€. MC, V. Lunch, dinner Wed–Mon (June–Aug Mon–Sat). Closed Nov–Jan.*

★ Leon Bianco CENTRO STORICO   This 11th-century town house has many original features, views of the Val d'Elsa, and a location right on San Gim's principal piazza. Most of the medium to large rooms come with beamed ceilings. *Piazza della Cisterna 8.* ☎ *0577-941294. www. leonbianco.com. 26 units. Doubles 85€–138€ w/breakfast. AE, DC, MC, V.*

★★ Le Vecchie Mura CENTRO STORICO *TUSCAN*   Seasonal, quintessentially Tuscan dishes—*ribollita,* wild boar in Vernaccia wine—are served in a stylish vaulted interior or on the knockout panoramic terrace. *Via Piandornella 15.* ☎ *0577-940270. www.vecchiemura.it. Entrees 10€–18€. AE, MC, V. Dinner Wed–Mon. Closed Nov–Feb.*

Relais Santa Chiara OUTSIDE WALLS   For facilities (such as a swimming pool), this modern hotel away from the chaos of the center, but still walkable into town, is your best bet. Midsize rooms come with terra-cotta floors, marble mosaics, and terraces. *Via Matteotti 15.* ☎ *0577-940701. www.rsc.it. 41 units. Doubles 120€–220€ w/breakfast. AE, DC, MC, V.*

Siena

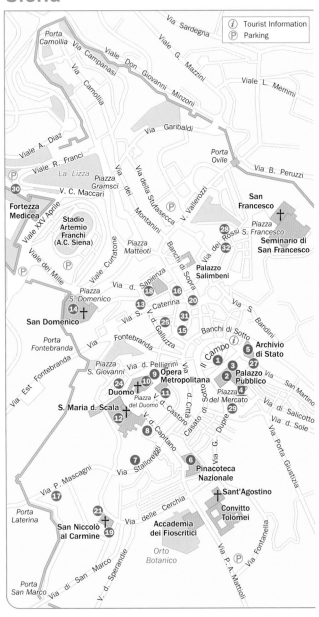

- (i) Tourist Information
- (P) Parking

Via Sardegna
Viale G. Mazzini
Viale L. Memmi
Porta Camollia
Via Campanasi
Viale Don Giovanni Minzoni
Via Camollia
Via Garibaldi
Porta Ovile
Via B. Peruzzi
Viale A. Diaz
Viale R. Franci
La Lizza
Piazza Gramsci
V. C. Maccari
Via dei
Via della Stufasecca
Via Vallerozzi
San Francesco
Piazza S. Francesco
Seminario di San Francesco
Fortezza Medicea
Viale XXV Aprile
Stadio Artemio Franchi (A.C. Siena)
Montanini
Banchi di Sopra
Via dei Rossi
Viale dei Mille
Piazza Matteoti
Via Curtatone
Via d. Sapienza
Via S. Caterina
Palazzo Salimbeni
Via S. Bandini
Piazza S. Domenico
San Domenico
Porta Fontebranda
Via Est Fontebranda
Via Fontebranda
Piazza S. Giovanni
Via d. Pellegrini
Via d. Galluzza
Banchi di Sotto
Il Campo
Archivio di Stato
Opera Metropolitana
Via di Città
Casato di Sotto
Palazzo Pubblico
Via San Martino
Duomo
Piazza V. d. Castoro
del Duomo
Piazza del Mercato
Via di Salicotto
S. Maria d. Scala
V. d. Capitano
Via d. Sole
Via G. Duprè
Via Porta Giustizia
Pinacoteca Nazionale
Via Stalloreggi
Sant'Agostino
Via P. Mascagni
Convitto Tolomei
Porta Laterina
Via delle Cerchia
San Niccolò al Carmine
Accademia dei Fioscritici
Orto Botanico
Via P. A. Mattioli
Via Fontanella
Porta San Marco
Via di San Marco
V. d. Sperandie

1 2 3 5 6 7 8 9 10 11 12 13 14 15 16 17 18 19 20 21 24 25 27 28 29 30 31 32

1. Piazza del Campo
2. Palazzo Pubblico
3. Torre del Mangia
4. Gino Cacino
5. Archivio di Stato
6. Pinacoteca Nazionale
7. Via Stalloreggi
8. Martini Marisa
9. Battistero
10. Duomo
11. Museo dell'Opera Metropolitana
12. Santa Maria della Scala
13. Casa di Santa Caterina
14. San Domenico
15. Vitra

Where to Stay
16. Antica Residenza Cicogna
17. Athena
18. Campo Regio Relais
19. Chiostro del Carmine
20. Grand Hotel Continental
21. Palazzo Ravizza
22. Santa Caterina

Where to Dine
23. Cane e Gatto
24. Da Divo
25. Grotta Santa Caterina da Bagoga
26. La Sosta di Violante
27. Le Logge
28. L'Osteria
29. Papei

Nightlife
30. Enoteca Italiana
31. Enoteca i Terzi
32. Kopa Kabana

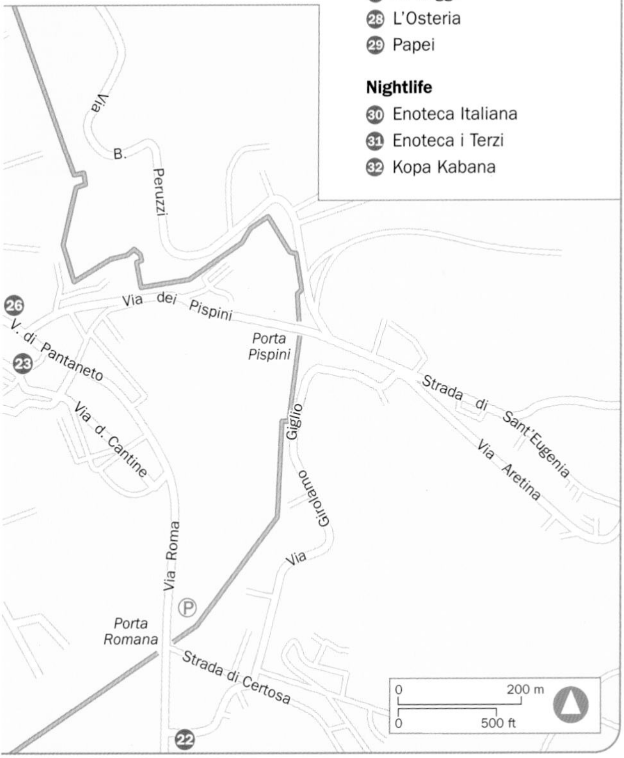

I f you have time for only one stop besides Florence, make it Siena. Dominating the medieval trade routes between France and Rome, the city in its day had Italy's richest banks and finest Gothic architecture, a quasi-democratic government under "the Nine," and its own constitution. Once Florence's rival in might and artistic patronage, Siena never fully recovered from the Black Death of 1348–49, which mowed down the population from 100,000 to 30,000. Now, the medieval character of its center appears frozen in time—the city is a living museum for art, architecture, and history buffs, with a vibrant civic culture. START: **Siena is 70km (43 miles) south of Florence along the Firenze–Siena raccordo. Trip length: 2 days to see the city properly.**

Siena's Piazza del Campo.

❶ ★★★ kids **Piazza del Campo.** The most dramatic piazza in Italy is Siena's "Campo." First laid out in the early 12th century on the site of the Roman forum, it is shaped like a sloping scallop shell or fan. By 1340, the city's leaders had paved the square in brick and divided it into nine sections in honor of the Council of Nine (the *Nove*), who ruled Siena during its golden age. Today it's the setting for the **Palio** (see below).

At the upper end of the square stands the **Fonte Gaia,** created from 1408 to 1419 by Jacopo della Quercia. What you see today is an inferior copy from 1868 (the badly damaged original is in Santa Maria della Scala, ⓬). ⏱ *15 min.*

❷ ★★★ **Palazzo Pubblico.** This Gothic *palazzo* was constructed in a crenellated style from 1297 to 1310 to house the city's government. Siena's remaining faithful added the loggia chapel by the entrance, the **Cappella della Piazza,** to thank God for delivering them from the Black Death.

Inside is one of Europe's outstanding civic museums, two rooms in particular marking the pinnacle of artistic achievement in Siena. In the **Sala del Mappamondo** is Simone Martini's 1315 *Maestà,* showing the city's protector under a huge canopy. It's not just a religious work: Christ's scroll reads: *Love Justice, ye who judge the Earth.*

Next door in the **Sala del Pace** (where "the Nine" sat), the walls are covered by Ambrogio Lorenzetti's *Allegories of Good and Bad Government* (1338). It's a work of medieval civic art without parallel, commissioned to remind rulers of the qualities of good government and a prosperous city: Justice, Wisdom, and Peace all appear. Alas, in the wake of the Black Death (that also killed Lorenzetti), *Bad Government* on the opposite wall came to pass: Fear, Treason, and War stalked Siena for decades. 🕐 *1½ hr. Piazza del Campo. ☎ 0577-292226. Admission 8€; 13€ with Torre del Mangia. Mid-Mar to Oct daily 10am–7pm; otherwise 10am–6pm.*

③ ★ kids Torre del Mangia. The 14th-century tower of the Palazzo Pubblico was named after a gluttonous bell-ringer, Giovanni di Duccio, nicknamed "Mangiaguadagni" or "eater of profits." At 102m (336 ft.), it is the tallest secular monument from the Middle Ages standing in Tuscany, so if you're expecting a great view you won't be disappointed. Don't attempt the climb if you're claustrophobic. 🕐 *30 min. Piazza del Campo. ☎ 0577-292262. Admission 8€; 13€ with Palazzo Pubblico. Mar to mid-Oct daily 10am–7pm; otherwise 10am–4pm.*

④ ★ kids Gino Cacino. This venerable deli, suppliers to some of Siena's notable restaurants, will load you a sandwich from whatever's behind the counter. *Piazza del Mercato 31. ☎ 0577-223076. $.*

⑤ ★ Archivio di Stato. Housed inside Bernardo Rossellino's Renaissance Palazzo Piccolomini, the State Archive preserves a remarkable set of wooden covers dating back to 1258 and made for the city's account books, called the *Tavolette di Biccherna*. They were painted from the 13th to 17th centuries with religious scenes, daily working life in the civic offices, and important events in Siena's history—Sano di

Pietro, Vecchietta, and Ambrogio Lorenzetti even did a few. 🕐 *45 min. Via Banchi di Sotto 52. ☎ 0577-241-745. Free admission. Mon–Sat hourly at 9:30, 10:30, and 11:30am.*

⑥ ★ Pinacoteca Nazionale. Although more famous works by Sienese masters are found elsewhere, this remains an impressive and representative showcase of the city's great artists. Look out for some Duccio, the charming narrative detail of Simone Martini's *Beato Agostino Novello* altarpiece, and Giovanni di Paolo's *Presentation at the Temple:* Despite two goes at a composition stolen straight from Ambrogio Lorenzetti (in the Uffizi), he still couldn't get the perspective right. Downstairs are the cartoons by Sienese Mannerist Domenico Beccafumi (1486–1551), from which some of the marble panels on the Duomo pavement were created. 🕐 *1 hr. Via San Pietro 29. ☎ 0577-286143. Admission 4€. Sun–Mon 9am–1pm; Tues–Sat 8:15am–7:15pm.*

⑦ ★ Via Stalloreggi. The little street where Duccio di Buoninsegna once had his studio still houses some of the last remaining artisan workshops within the walls. **Sator Print,** Via Stalloreggi 70 (☎ 0577-247478; www.satorprint.com), sells

Torre del Mangia.

Artwork at the Pinacoteca Nazionale.

hand-decorated prints and calligraphy based on historic Sienese designs. Nothing inside is cheap, but you'll find an affordable, authentic gift or souvenir with little trouble—or just stop by to see the maestro at work. At the **Bottega d'Arte,** Via Stalloreggi 47 (☎ 339-2700280; www.arteinsiena.it), buy original art in the style (and using the techniques) of the old Sienese masters. ⏱ *40 min.*

8 Martini Marisa. This fine purveyor of hand-painted Sienese *majolica* (ceramics) uses designs based on the traditional black, white, and burnt sienna motif, based on floor panels in the Duomo. *Via del Capitano 5–11.* ☎ *0577-288177. www.anticasiena.it. AE, MC, V.*

9 ★ Battistero. The 14th-century Baptistery stands on its own little square on top of a steep flight of steps, hiding behind a Gothic facade. Its prize possession is a baptismal font embellished with some of the finest sculpture of the Quattrocento (1400s). The hexagonal marble font (1411–30) is by Jacopo della Quercia in the Gothic–Renaissance style. Two of the bronze statues around the basin, *Faith* and *Hope*, are by

Donatello. Reliefs on the font include Ghiberti's *Baptism of Christ* and *John before Herod* (similar in style to his "Gates of Paradise" in Florence), and *Herod's Feast* by Donatello, all from 1427. Vecchietta frescoed the ceiling and lunettes around 1450. ⏱ *30 min. Piazza San Giovanni (behind Duomo).* ☎ *0577-283048. Admission 3€ or OPA Pass. Mid-June to mid-Sept daily 9:30am–8pm; mid-Sept to Oct and Mar to mid-June daily 9:30am–7pm; Nov–Feb daily 10am–5pm.*

10 ★★★ Duomo. The architectural highlight of Siena's golden age is the Cattedrale di Santa Maria Assunta (its formal name). Beginning in the 12th century, architects set out to create a dramatic facade with colored bands of marble mixing the Romanesque and Italian Gothic styles. Inside, between 1369 and 1547, over 40 Sienese artists, including Francesco di Giorgio and Domenico Beccafumi, created the 56 biblical and allegorical marble intarsia designs on the floor (only on view mid-Aug to Nov). The artistic highlight is the **Libreria Piccolominea,** added in 1485 by Cardinal Francesco Piccolomini (later Pope Pius III), to house the library of his more famous uncle, Pope Pius II. Frescoes by Umbrian painter Pinturicchio tell the story of Pius II's life, starting in the back right as you walk in. The nearby 13th-century pulpit is by Nicola Pisano (Giovanni's father). ⏱ *45 min. Piazza del Duomo.* ☎ *0577-283048. Admission 3€, 6€ when floor on display, or OPA Pass. Mar–May and Sept–Oct Mon–Sat 10:30am–7:30pm, Sun 1:30–5:30pm; Nov–Feb Mon–Sat 10:30am–6:30pm, Sun 1:30–5:30pm; June–Aug Mon–Sat 10:30am–8pm, Sun 1:30–6pm.*

11 ★★ Museo dell'Opera Metropolitana. Anyone with a serious interest in Sienese art should make

Bareback Anarchy: the Palio

Twice a year, on July 2 (the Provenzano) and August 16 (the Assunta), Europe's most daring horse race takes place on Siena's Campo. Jockeys representing 10 of the city's 17 districts *(contrade)* fly around the dirt-filled square three times with one aim: winning the banner, **il Palio.** Forget sportsmanship. The single rule is that no jockey can grab another horse's reins. But you can drug an opponent the morning of the race, kidnap him the night before, or "whip him with a leather belt made from the skin of the bull's penis," explains a marshal. The jockey, after all, is irrelevant: The horse wins whether there's a rider on it or not (both editions in 1989 were won by rider-less steeds).

All this has taken place in tribute to the Virgin Mary since at least 1310. In the weeks after a race, you'll often find the winning *contrada* out en masse, marching the streets banging drums and singing traditional songs. They may even be sucking child's pacifiers—in reference to the banner's nickname, *"il Bambino."*

for here: Duccio di Buoninsegna's 1311 *Maestà* is where it all began. Not only did Duccio invent a genre, he influenced the generation that included Simone Martini and the Lorenzettis. The Sienese were so pleased with his giant two-sided altarpiece it was paraded through the streets on its way to the Duomo. In the same room is Pietro Lorenzetti's 1342 *Birth of the Virgin*, which, fortunately for us, he managed to finish before the plague finished him. Downstairs are Giovanni Pisano's original sculptures for the Duomo.

The art is housed in a building originally intended to be the right aisle of a massive new cathedral, until the Black Death called a halt to Siena's golden age. A climb to its **Facciatone (Big Facade),** from inside the museum, rewards you with dizzying views down into the Campo. ⏱ *1 hr. Piazza del Duomo.* ☎ *0577-534571. Admission 6€ or OPA Pass. Mar 17–Oct 15 daily 10:30am–6:30pm; Oct 16–Mar 16 daily 10:30am–4:30pm.*

Siena's Duomo.

The pulpit inside Siena's Duomo.

Travel Tip

The best value way to see Siena's ecclesiastical sights is with the **OPA Si Pass.** Valid for 3 days, and costing 10€, it gets you into the Duomo, Battistero, Museo dell'Opera, and modest Oratorio di San Bernardino. It also allows access to the recently discovered Cripta, an overpriced though atmospheric trip through the frescoed (pre-Duccio) chambers of the ancient cathedral under the Duomo. See www.operaduomo. siena.it.

The view from atop the Museo dell'Opera Metropolitana.

⓬ ★★ **kids** **Santa Maria della Scala.** This 14th-century hospital, one of Europe's oldest, has gradually been turned into a museum and cultural complex displaying art and archaeological treasures. Most intriguing is the **Pellegrinaio,** the old Pilgrims' Ward, frescoed with scenes from everyday life in the hospital in the 1440s. Elsewhere seek out a disturbing *Massacre of the Innocents* by Matteo di Giovanni, in the **Cappella della Madonna;** the tiny oratory where St. Catherine used to pray all night; the restored **Sagrestia Vecchia** with a damaged and complex fresco cycle completed by Vecchietta in 1449; **Bambimus,** Siena's Museum of Children's Art, where paintings are hung at tot-friendly heights; and the labyrinthine basement—a great spot to get lost. ⏰ *1½ hr. Piazza del Duomo.* ☎ *0577-534571.*

*www.santamariadellascala.com.
Admission 6€. Mar 17–Oct 15 daily
10:30am–6:30pm; otherwise daily
10:30am–4:30pm.*

⑬ Casa di Santa Caterina.
Caterina Benincasa (1347–80), 24th
child of a Sienese dyer, grew up to
become the patron saint of Italy.
She took the veil at the age of 16,
and experienced what she called a
"mystical marriage" to Christ 3 years
later. The house where she lived as
a Dominican nun still stands today,
except it now has a Renaissance
loggia and two baroque oratories,
the **Oratorio della Cucina** being
the most lavishly appointed, with a
16th-century majolica floor. *🕐 20
min. Costa di San Antonio 6 (at Via
dei Pittori).* ☎ *0577-280801. Free
admission. Daily 9am–12:30pm and
3:30–6pm.*

⑭ ★ San Domenico. This severe-
looking church in the monastic
Gothic style was founded in 1125
and since the 1300s has been
closely linked with St. Catherine,
who is said to have had visions
here. Inside you can see a small
frescoed portrait by her contemporary, Andrea Vanni (1332–1414), the
only known picture by someone
who knew her. Slightly grislier, her
head is preserved and venerated
inside the **Cappella di Santa
Caterina.** It's surrounded by Sodoma's frescoed scenes from her life,
including her controversial appearance at the *Execution of Niccolò di
Toldo.* *🕐 20 min. Piazza San
Domenico. No phone. Free admission. Daily 7am–1pm and 3–6pm.*

⑮ ★ Vitra. Admire modern
designs in all shapes and sizes at
this funky artisan glassware store.
Everything is handmade in Siena.
Closed all Sunday and Monday
morning. *Via dei Termini 2 (at
Piazza Independencia).* ☎ *0577-
51208. MC, V.*

Siena After Dark

Besides enjoying the spectacle of an evening lounging in the
Campo, stop in at **Kopa Kabana,** Via de' Rossi 52 (☎ 0577-
223744), for the best homemade gelato in town—the *panpepato*
flavor is up there with the best I've ever tasted. **Enoteca Italiana,**
Fortezza Medicea (☎ 0577-228834; www.enoteca-italiana.it), is the
only state-sponsored wine bar in Italy, in vaults that were built for
Cosimo I de' Medici in 1560. Drink by the glass, or buy 1 of 1,600
bottles on sale. **Enoteca i Terzi,** Via dei Termini 7 (☎ 0577-44329;
www.enotecaiterzi.it), is under the vaulted ceiling of a 12th-century
tower, with wines by the glass and fine food if you're hungry. For
something younger, livelier, and more local, head down Via Pantaneto toward the university buildings. Names change, but the bars
always go on here til late. For the latest events happening around
town, look out for the free monthly listings publication ***Infor-
macittà*** (www.informacitta.net) at information offices, hotels, and
bars around the city.

Where to Stay

★★ Antica Residenza Cicogna

CENTRO STORICO   A friendly, family-run B&B whose rooms are compact, but dripping with character. All are thoughtfully furnished and come with carefully matched fabrics (the most spacious is "Liberty"). *Via dei Termini 67.* ☎ *0577-285613. www.anticaresidenzacicogna.com. 7 units. Doubles 80€–100€ w/breakfast. MC, V.*

Athena PORTA SAN MARCO

Although lacking the historic character of local rivals, this modern, board-rated four-star hotel offers tasteful (if unspectacular) rooms, an on-site car park, and great value within a 10-minute walk of the Duomo. *Via Mascagni 55.* ☎ *0577-286313. www.hotelathena.com. 100 units. Doubles 94€–270€ w/breakfast. AE, DC, MC, V. Closed Feb.*

★★★ Campo Regio Relais CEN-
TRO STORICO   This chic little town house hideaway whisks you from the bustle of the central streets. Rooms are decorated with traditional elegance, and there's a knockout

Palazzo Ravizza.

breakfast terrace facing the Duomo. *Via della Sapienza 25.* ☎ *0577-222073. www.camporegio.com. 6 units. Doubles 150€–450€ w/breakfast. AE, MC, V. Usually closed Jan to mid-Mar.*

★ Chiostro del Carmine PORTA
SAN MARCO   This atmospheric hotel set around a Carmelite cloister manages to combine proximity to the sights with a feeling of detached peace and tranquility. Well-equipped, modern rooms have retained some of the former convent's character. *Via della Diana 4.* ☎ *0577-223885. www.chiostrodelcarmine.com. 18 units. Doubles 99€–199€ w/breakfast. AE, DC, MC, V.*

★★ Grand Hotel Continental

CENTRO STORICO   This aristocratic hotel on Siena's most fashionable street has 15th-century architecture and stately frescoes, medium to large rooms with deluxe marble baths, and tasteful period decoration. *Banchi di Sopra 85.* ☎ *0577-56011. www.royaldemeure.com. 51 units. Doubles 430€–600€. AE, DC, MC, V.*

★ Palazzo Ravizza PORTA SAN
MARCO   Siena's coziest *pensione* since the 1920s, this Renaissance *palazzo* has antiques, frescoes, large, and high-ceilinged rooms, and a friendly welcome is guaranteed. *Pian dei Mantellini 34.* ☎ *0577-280462. www.palazzoravizza.it. 35 units. Doubles 90€–150€ w/breakfast. AE, DC, MC, V.*

★ Santa Caterina PORTA ROMANA
With Siena's most hospitable owners, this 18th-century villa with midsize rooms and chunky antique furniture is backed by a terraced garden overlooking the hills south. *Via E. S. Piccolomini 7.* ☎ *0577-221105. www.hscsiena.it. 22 units. Doubles 85€–195€ w/breakfast. AE, DC, MC, V.*

Where to Dine

★★ Cane e Gatto PORTA ROMANA *SIENESE* There's no menu at this intimate, romantic restaurant: You're served five gourmet courses of whatever was fresh at market, prepared with love in a traditional Sienese style. Wine matched to each course is extra. *Via Pagliaresi 6.* ☎ *0577-287545. Menu 80€ (less if you eat fewer courses). MC, V. Dinner Fri–Wed.*

★★ Da Divo CENTRO STORICO *MODERN TUSCAN* Innovative dishes rooted in Sienese tradition are served in an Etruscan cave with a classy atmosphere of soft jazz. Main dishes include a side (unusual in Tuscany). *Via Franciosa 25–29.* ☎ *0577-284381. www.osteriada divo.it. Entrees 20€–24€. MC, V. Lunch, dinner Wed–Mon. Closed 2 weeks in Jan–Feb.*

★ Grotta Santa Caterina da Bagoga CENTRO STORICO *SIENESE* This tiny, brick-vaulted dining room is run by former Palio-winning jockey "Bagoga." The kitchen is especially strong on stews, such as *coniglio alla Senese* (rabbit on the bone with capers, tomatoes, and herbs). *Via della Galluzza 26.* ☎ *0577-282208. Entrees 7€–15€. AE, MC, V. Lunch, dinner Tues–Sun.*

★★ La Sosta di Violante PORTA ROMANA *MODERN ITALIAN* Sticking less rigidly to Tuscan flavors— and occasionally abandoning them altogether— this place offers fresh, modern cooking comfortably away from the Campo scrum. *Pollo al mattone* (brick-baked chicken) is succulent beyond belief. *Via Pantaneto 115.* ☎ *0577-43774. www. lasostadiviolante.it. Entrees 10€– 16€. AE, MC, V. Lunch, dinner Mon– Sat. Closed 1 week in Jan.*

The atmospheric interior of Da Divo.

★ Le Logge CENTRO STORICO *TUSCAN* The best seasonal cuisine close to the Campo, in a refined and old-fashioned atmosphere. The veal is the tastiest in town, and the delicate black truffle is used liberally in season. Reservations recommended. *Via del Porrione 33.* ☎ *0577-48013. Entrees 16€–26€. AE, DC, MC, V. Lunch, dinner Mon–Sat.*

★★ L'Osteria CENTRO STORICO *TUSCAN* This neighborhood *osteria* halfway downhill to San Francesco is as local as it comes in the old center. The grill is the star: beef all ways, veal, and *cinta senese*, the finest breed of pig, native to the Chianti. *Via de' Rossi 79–81.* ☎ *0577-287592. Entrees 8.50€–15€. AE, MC, V. Lunch, dinner Mon–Sat.*

★ Papei CENTRO STORICO *SIENESE* Trust this family-run trattoria for simple yet well-prepared classic Sienese fare such as rabbit in white wine with rosemary and sage or pappardelle in wild boar *ragù*. *Piazza del Mercato 6.* ☎ *0577-280894. Entrees 8€–15€. AE, MC, V. Lunch, dinner Tues–Sun.*

Volterra

1. Porta all'Arco
2. L'Incontro
3. Palazzo dei Priori
4. Duomo
5. San Francesco
6. Pinacoteca e Museo Civico
7. Camillo Rossi
8. Teatro Romano
9. Fabula Etrusca
10. Museo Etrusco Guarnacci
11. alab'Arte

Where to Stay
12. Foresteria Volterra
13. La Locanda
14. Podere Marcampo
15. San Lino

Where to Dine
16. Enoteca del Duca
17. Lo Sgherro
18. Vecchia Osteria dei Poeti

Nightlife
19. La Vena di Vino
20. Web & Wine

Volterra rises like a fortress, 540m (1,800 ft.) above the rolling agricultural plains of the Valdicecina. The Etruscans who settled here in the 9th century B.C. made their living trading and working what's under your feet: alabaster (for sculpting) and alum (for dyes). The town still has a medieval appearance, with foreboding *palazzi,* cobblestone streets and alleyways, and shops hawking craftswares. Come for the artisan shopping, the *Twilight: New Moon* connections, a Mannerist masterpiece on canvas, and a major Etruscan museum. START: **Volterra is 72km (45 miles) from Florence, on the S68 30km (19 miles) west of where it branches off the Florence–Siena raccordo. Trip length: 1 day.**

1 ★ Porta all'Arco. Volterra's remaining ancient gate, all that's left of what were once 7.5km (4½ miles) of Etruscan city walls, marks the start of a steep ascent into the *centro storico.* So important is the gate to the town that Partisans defending Volterra in 1944 risked their lives bricking it up in case it became the target of a Nazi assault. ⏲ **10 min.**

2 L'Incontro. My favorite cafe in the historic center sells artisan chocolates, homemade pastries, and crazy gelato flavors like biscuit or mojito. Later on, you can also enjoy Tuscan vintages by the glass. *Via Matteotti 18.* ☎ *0588-80500. $.*

Crumbling Etruria

Northwest of the city center (3.5km/2 miles), Le Balze is one of Tuscany's more quietly frightening scenes—a bowl-shaped ravine where fast-paced erosion is devouring the edges of Volterra. Aided by periodic earthquakes, it has already exposed and then destroyed much of the Etruscan necropolis at this end of town. Now it threatens the medieval Badia church, abandoned after an 1846 quake brought the precipice to its doorstep. The best spot to appreciate the scale of the erosion is from the minor road out of town towards Montecatini Valdicecina.

❸ ★ **Palazzo dei Priori.** Built between 1208 and 1257, this is the oldest Gothic town hall in Tuscany; Florence's Palazzo Vecchio was modeled after it. The council hall and antechamber are open to the public. On view is a damaged *Annunciation with Four Saints* by Jacopo di Cione (or perhaps Orcagna) from 1383. Opposite, across Piazza dei Priori, is the Palazzo Pretorio, with its **Torre del Porcellino,** a tower named for the stone piglet that protrudes near the top. ⏰ *20 min. Piazza dei Priori.* ☎ *0588-86050. Admission 1.50€. Mid-Mar to Oct daily 10:30am–5:30pm; Nov to mid-Mar Sat–Sun 10am–5pm.*

❹ ★ **Duomo.** A simple 12th-century facade hides a lush interior with a coffered Renaissance ceiling. Immediately left of the entrance is the **Cappella dell'Addolorata,** with a charming terra-cotta *Nativity* embellished with frescoes by Benozzo Gozzoli. More moving still is the wooden *Deposition* in the right transept, carved by an anonymous Pisan in 1228.

The octagonal **Baptistery** across the little piazza, from 1283, has an inlaid marble font (1502) by Andrea Sansovino. ⏰ *30 min. Piazza San Giovanni. No phone. Free admission. Mon–Thurs, Sat–Sun 8am–noon and*

Palazzo dei Priori.

Alabaster, or *Pietra Candida*

Volterra is often nicknamed "the town of alabaster." Since the era of the Etruscans, locals have shaped objects both practical and artistic from these calcium sulphate deposits. Revived in the late 19th century, the local artisan industry has been going strong since, turning out ghostly-white lampshades, sculptures, jewel boxes, and even elegant sinks. To learn more, visit the town's alabaster museum, the **Ecomuseo dell'Alabastro,** Piazzetta Minucci (☎ 0588-87580). Admission costs 3.50€ and daily hours are 11am to 5pm in summer; in winter it's open weekends only 9am to 1:30pm.

3–6pm; Fri 8am–noon and 4–6pm *(closes 5pm daily in winter).*

⑤ ★ San Francesco. Dating to just a few years after St. Francis's death, this former convent at the western edge of the medieval town rewards a 5-minute downhill trek. The highlight is the **Cappella Croce del Giorno,** frescoed in 1410 by Cenni di Francesco. His subject matter, like Piero della Francesca 40 years later in Arezzo (p 79, **⑧**), is the *Legend of the True Cross.* ⏱ *15 min. Piazza San Francesco 3. No phone. Free admission. Daily 9am–6pm. Hours erratic, especially off season.*

⑥ ★★ Pinacoteca e Museo Civico. This combined picture gallery

A detail of Volterra's Duomo.

and museum of artifacts is acclaimed for its religious paintings—mostly the work of Tuscan artists from the 14th to the 17th centuries. Taddeo di Bartolo's *Enthroned Madonna* altarpiece from 1411 is a glory in gold. Room 12 houses the real treasures, including an astoundingly modern, angst-ridden *Deposition* painted by a young Rosso Fiorentino in 1521, and two large 1491 Luca Signorelli panels, notably an intricate, fantastical *Annunciation.* ⏱ *45 min. Via dei Sarti 1.* ☎ *0588-87580. Admission 10€ (includes Museo Etrusco and Museo d'Arte Sacra). Mid-Mar to Oct daily 9am–7pm; otherwise daily 8:30am–1:45pm.*

⑦ ★ Camillo Rossi. This workshop, founded in 1912, is one of Volterra's best outlets for alabaster *objets. Piazza Pescheria 1.* ☎ *0588-86133. www.rossialabastri.com. AE, DC, MC, V.*

Crafts Shopping Tip

Prints and lithographs created from hand-engraved zinc plates are another local artisan specialty. My two favorite workshops, where everything is created on-site, are **L'Istrice,** Via Porta all'Arco 23 (☎ 0588-85422; www.labositrice.it), and **Bubo Bubo,** Via Roma 24 (☎ 0588-80307).

Teatro Romano.

8 kids **Teatro Romano.** From Volterra's medieval ramparts, you can look down on the remains of a 1st-century Roman theater, and later spa baths, among the best preserved in central Italy. ⏱ *10 min. Viale Francesco Ferrucci (at Porta Fiorentina).* ☎ *0588-86050. Admission 3.50€. Mid-Mar to Oct daily 10:30am–5:30pm; otherwise Sat–Sun 10am–4pm.*

9 ★ **Fabula Etrusca.** Intricate handmade jewelry cast using ancient goldsmith techniques and modeled after original Etruscan designs. Prepare your credit card before entering. *Via Lungo le Mura del Mandorlo 10.* ☎ *0588–87401. www.fabulaetrusca.it. AE, DC, MC, V.*

10 ★★ **Museo Etrusco Guarnacci.** This place has one of the best (yet most poorly displayed) Etruscan collections in Italy. The 600 cinerary urns, dating from the 6th to the 1st century B.C., are made variously of alabaster, tufa, and terra cotta. The most celebrated piece is in Room XV: an elongated bronze known as the *Ombra della Sera,* an early-3rd-century B.C. votive figure of a young boy—look at it side-on to spot some anatomical "innovations" added by the unknown creator.

Other highlights include the *Urna degli Sposi,* depicting a grumpy looking pair of newlyweds, and a series of reliefs of Homer's *Odyssey.* ⏱ *45 min. Via Minzoni 15.* ☎ *0588-86347. Admission 10€ (includes Pinacoteca and Museo d'Arte Sacra). Mid-Mar to Oct daily 9am–7pm; otherwise daily 8:30am–1:45pm.*

11 **alab'Arte.** To see alabaster in various stages of completion, have a poke around Volterra's last open sculptural workshop. You're free to buy anything that takes your fancy. *Via Orti S. Agostino 28.* ☎ *0588-87968. www.alabarte.com. MC, V.*

Volterra After Dark

Nightlife here is on the quiet side. Grottolike **La Vena di Vino,** Via Don Minzoni 30 (☎ 0588-81491; www. lavenadivino.com), is a reliable and friendly wine bar with an especially good range of reds, plus cheese platters to accompany them. Glasses range from 2€ to 6€. At **Web & Wine,** Via Porta all'Arco 13 (☎ 0588-81531; www.webandwine. com), you can order a plate of salami, sample fine Tuscan vintages (including biodynamic and organic wines), and check your e-mail.

Where to Stay

★ **Foresteria Volterra** OUTSIDE WALLS   Excellent choice for budget travelers: Rooms are slightly institutional, but spotless, cheery, and well-equipped—and come in all configurations from single up to quad. *Borgo San Lazzero.* ☎ *0588-80050. www.foresteriavolterra.it. 35 units. Doubles 62€–82€ w/breakfast. AE, DC, MC, V.*

La Locanda CENTRO STORICO Rooms in this converted convent are color-schemed by floor. In the heart of the old town, all are a good size, clean, and comfortable. A couple of doubles have hydromassage baths. *Via Guarnacci 24–28.* ☎ *0588-81547. www.hotel-lalocanda.com. 18 units. Doubles 93€–189€ w/breakfast. AE, MC, V.*

★★ kids **Podere Marcampo** OUTSIDE WALLS   In addition to 360-degree views of Volterra and Le Balze, plus a swimming pool, this place has retained its traditional farmhouse feel, with terra-cotta flooring, exposed beams, and dark-wood fittings that keep the large, fully-equipped apartments and hotel-style doubles rooted in their Tuscan heritage. *Signposted by road, 1.5km (1 mile) northwest of Volterra.* ☎ *0588-85393. www.agriturismo-marcampo.com. 6 units. Doubles 80€–118€ w/breakfast; apts sleeping 4–5 105€–160€. AE, MC, V.*

★ **San Lino** CENTRO STORICO The best lodging inside the medieval walls, this place was originally built as a convent in 1480. Superior rooms on the second floor cost little extra but have more space, more character, and the choice of a view over the rear garden and small pool. *Via S. Lino 26.* ☎ *0588-85250. www.hotel sanlino.com. 44 units. Doubles 90€–105€ w/breakfast. AE, DC, MC, V.*

Where to Dine

★ **Enoteca del Duca** CENTRO STORICO *MODERN TUSCAN*   The town's most refined dining is installed in a 16th-century building with high ceilings and terra-cotta floors. Try the *lavagnette* (homemade egg pasta) with celery and pecorino pesto, or the pigeon breast. *Via di Castello 2.* ☎ *0588-81510. Entrees 12€–28€. www.enotecadel duca-ristorante.it. AE, DC, MC, V. Lunch, dinner Wed–Mon (also Tues dinner in summer).*

★ **Lo Sgherro** OUTSIDE WALLS *TUSCAN*   There's no ceremony at this neighborhood trattoria, just solid, regional cooking at prices that have gone out of fashion elsewhere in Tuscany. Your order is hollered through a hole in the wall at *mamma* in the kitchen. *Borgo San Giusto 74 (10-min. downhill walk from Porta San Francesco).* ☎ *0588-86-473. Entrees 7.50€–17€. MC, V. Lunch; dinner Tues–Sun.*

Vecchia Osteria dei Poeti CENTRO STORICO *TUSCAN*   For Tuscan staples like pappardelle with hare or Volterran cooking, try this traditional dining room right on the main drag. The lengthy Tuscan wine list has options from 10€ to over 100€ a bottle. *Via Matteotti 54.* ☎ *0588-86029. Entrees 9€–22€. AE, MC, V. Lunch, dinner Fri–Wed.* ●

The **Savvy**
Traveler

Before You Go

Government Tourist Offices

In the U.S.: 630 Fifth Ave., Ste 1565, New York, NY 10111 ☎ 212/245-5618; 500 N. Michigan Ave., Chicago, IL 60611 ☎ 312/644-0996; and 12400 Wilshire Blvd., Ste 550, Los Angeles, CA 90025 ☎ 310/820-1898.

In Canada: 110 Yonge St., Ste 503, Toronto, ONT, M4W 3R8 ☎ 416/925-4882; www.italiantourism.com.

In the U.K. & Ireland: 1 Princes St., London, W1B 2AY ☎ 020/7408-1254; www.italiantouristboard.co.uk.

In Australia and New Zealand: Level 4, 46 Market St., Sydney, NSW 2000 ☎ 02/9262-1666; www.italiantourism.com.au.

Entry Requirements

U.S., Canadian, U.K., Irish, Australian, and New Zealand citizens with a valid passport don't need a visa to enter Italy if they don't expect to stay more than 90 days and don't expect to work there. If after entering Italy you find you want to stay more than 90 days, you can apply for a permit for an extra 90 days, which as a rule is granted immediately. Go to the nearest *questura* (police headquarters) or your home country's consulate.

For passport information and applications in the **U.S.,** call ☎ **877/487-2778** or check http://travel.state.gov; in **Canada,** call ☎ **800/567-6868** or check www.passportcanada.gc.ca; in the **U.K.,** call ☎ **0300/222-0000** or visit www.ips.gov.uk; in **Ireland,** call ☎ **01/671-1633** or check http://foreignaffairs.gov.ie; in **Australia,** call

☎ **131-232** or visit www.passports.gov.au; and in **New Zealand,** call ☎ **0800/225050** or check www.passports.govt.nz. Allow plenty of time before your trip to apply for a passport; processing usually takes a few weeks but can take longer during busy periods (especially spring). When traveling, safeguard your passport and keep a copy of the critical pages with your passport number in a separate place. If you lose your passport, visit the nearest consulate of your native country as soon as possible for a replacement.

The Best Times to Go

April to June and late September to October are the best months to visit Tuscany. However, they are also the most expensive: Hotels are generally on high-season rates, for May, June, and September at least.

From late June through mid-September, when the summer rush is full blown, Siena and the Tuscan hilltowns can teem with visitors. August is the worst month weatherwise, when it's usually uncomfortably hot and muggy; but it's also a good month to bag a deal on a room in Florence. (When you get there, expect theaters, many upscale restaurants, and some nightclubs to be closed, however.) And from August 15 to the end of the month, the entire region goes on vacation, and many family-run restaurants and shops are closed (except at the spas, beaches, and islands—where the Italians head en masse).

From late October to Easter, many attractions go on shorter winter hours, or occasionally close for renovation. Some hotels and restaurants take a month or two off between November and February, spa and beach destinations such as Viareggio become padlocked ghost towns, and it can get much colder than you'd expect; it might even snow in the hills.

Festivals & Special Events

SPRING. Easter is always a big event in Tuscany, especially in Florence at the **Scoppio del Carro** (Explosion of the Cart), with its Renaissance pyrotechnics on Easter Sunday. An 18th-century cart, pulled by two snowy white oxen loaded with fireworks, arrives at the Piazza del Duomo, where it's ignited.

More cultural, Florence's **Maggio Musicale Fiorentino** (Musical May; www.maggiofiorentino.com) features a month's worth of opera, concerts, and dance recitals in *palazzi* and churches around the city; these days it continues through June.

The **Festa del Grillo** (Cricket Festival) takes place in mid- to late May, the first Sunday after Ascension Day. In Florence's Cascine Park, vendors sell crickets in decorated cages. After a parade along the Arno, participants release the crickets into the grass.

The last weekend in May, Cortona hosts the **Giostra dell'Archidado** (☎ 0575-630352), a crossbow competition with participants clad in 14th-century costume.

One Sunday early in June, the **Regatta of the Ancient Maritime Republics** takes place—a rowing competition among the four medieval maritime republics of Venice, Amalfi, Genoa, and Pisa. Its location rotates annually between the four.

Also in Pisa, the **Luminara di San Ranieri** celebrates the city's patron saint by lining the Arno with flickering torches, from dusk on June 16.

SUMMER. Pisa's liveliest month ends on the final Sunday, with the **Gioco del Ponte** (Game of the Bridge)— teams in Renaissance costumes on opposite banks of the river have a push-of-war over the Ponte di Mezzo with a 7-ton cart.

St. John the Baptist's Day, June 24, sees the first in the week-long series of **Calcio Storico Fiorentino**. Florence's Piazza Santa Croce is transformed into a pitch for these ancient, and rough, "football" matches.

From mid-June to late August, Fiesole hosts the **Estate Fiesolana** (www.estatefiesolana.it), a summertime festival of music, ballet, film, and theater. Most performances take place in the ruined Roman amphitheater, which seats 3,000 spectators.

The biggest event of the Tuscan calendar is the **Palio delle Contrade,** the twice-annual bareback horse race between the 17 districts of Siena. The race occurs around the dirt-packed main square, with parades and partying before and afterwards. The first (the Palio di Provenzano) is on July 2; the second (the Palio dell'Assunta) on August 16. See p 171.

The **Giostra dell'Orso** (Joust of the Bear; www.giostradellorso.it) takes place in Pistoia on July 25. The match pits mounted knights in medieval garb against targets shaped like bears.

In San Gimignano, **Dentro e Fuori le Mura** is a festival of concerts, opera, and film staged in late July (some outdoors). For 2 weeks in either July or August, Siena's Accademia Musicale Chigiana presents the **Settimana Musicale Senese** (www.chigiana.it), one of Italy's best concert and opera programs.

Montepulciano's major festival happens on the last Sunday in August. The town's districts race wine barrels up the length of the steep Corso to the Duomo, in the **Bravio delle Botti.**

Tuscany Bookmarks

www.yourwaytoflorence.com: Accommodations, shopping, tourism, art, history, wines, even weather forecasts—a city catchall.

www.ioamofirenze.com: Florence food, wine, nightlife, and events blog, written (in Italian) by a savvy local.

www.ilpalio.org: The all-things Palio site has history, race trivia, video of recent Palios, and a list of winners since 1644.

www.pisa-airport.com: Information about Pisa's Galileo Galilei International Airport, Tuscany's international gateway.

www.theflorentine.net: The website of Florence's major English-language magazine.

www.turismo.intoscana.it: This official resource is useful for an overview of Tuscany as a whole.

www.trenitalia.com: The state railway website is an essential planning tool for train travel across Tuscany.

www.arttrav.com: News, views, and reviews from Florence and Tuscany, written by an expat art historian.

www.wga.hu: Online art museum with a comprehensive Renaissance collection.

www.summerinitaly.com/planning/strike.asp: Information on pending strikes throughout Italy.

The first Sunday of September in Arezzo, the **Giostra del Saracino** (Saracen's Joust; www.giostradel saracino.arezzo.it) takes place—a tournament between mounted knights in 13th-century armor and the effigy of a Saracen warrior.

AUTUMN. All Lucca is festooned with candles on the evening of September 13, for the **Luminara di Santa Croce.** A holy procession also starts from the cathedral.

The second week of September also sees the **Rassegna del Chianti Classico,** a 4-day wine festival centered around Greve.

In Montalcino, on the last weekend of October, residents celebrate the **Sagra del Tordo** or "Feast of the Thrush." Locals in medieval costume stage an archery tournament, parades, and plenty of gastronomy, including barbeque thrush.

WINTER. On December 25, the year's final **Display of the Virgin's Girdle** (the Sacro Cingolo) takes place in Prato. The belt that the Virgin handed to "Doubting" Thomas on her Assumption is revealed from the Duomo balcony, with Renaissance-styled drummers in attendance. The solemn ceremony is repeated on Easter Day, May 1, August 15 (the Feast of the Assumption), and most importantly September 8, the Virgin's Birthday.

Italy's second-largest **Carnevale** (☎ 0584-58071; www.viareggio. ilcarnevale.com) is hosted by Viareggio. Events and parades take place throughout February.

Cellphones (Mobiles)
Italy (like most of the world) is on the GSM (Global System for Mobiles) wireless system. GSM phones

function with a removable SIM card, encoded with your phone number and account information. World phones are the only U.S. phones that are compatible.

If necessary, U.S. visitors can rent a GSM phone before leaving home from **InTouch USA** (☎ 800/872-7626; www.intouch usa.us) or **Cellhire** (☎ 877/244-7242; www.cellhire.com). Alternatively, you can buy a local handset for well under 50€. A basic smartphone costs around 100€.

U.K. and Irish mobiles all work in Italy; call your service provider before departing to ensure that the international call bar is off, and to check call and (especially) data

charges, which can be high. Remember that you are also charged for calls you *receive* on a U.K. mobile used abroad. All travelers should remember that some smartphone apps work in the background and will consume data if you don't switch data functions off.

The cheapest option, for everyone with an unlocked handset, is to buy a SIM card when you get to Tuscany. The major Italian networks are **Vodafone, Wind, TIM,** and **3.** A local rechargeable SIM costs about 5€ and gives you far cheaper local calls (around .12€/min.) and data (2€/ week for 250MB is standard). You must show photo I.D. when buying.

Money

Italy falls somewhere in the middle of pricing in Europe—not as expensive as, say, Paris or Scandinavia, but not as cheap as Spain or Greece. Tuscany comes just behind Venice in terms of the costliest bit of Italy to travel, but the advice in this book should guide you to the best options to fit any budget.

It's a good idea to exchange at least some money—just enough to cover airport incidentals and transportation to your hotel—before you leave home, so you can avoid lines at airport ATMs.

Currency
In January 2002, Italy retired the lira and joined most of Western Europe in switching to the **euro.** Coins are issued in denominations of .01€, .02€, .05€, .10€, .20€, and .50€, as well as 1€ and 2€; bills come in denominations of 5€, 10€, 20€, 50€, 100€, 200€, and 500€.

Exchange rates are listed in most international newspapers and

constantly updated at **XE.com.** To get a transaction as close to this rate as possible, pay with your credit card (although check foreign transaction fees with your card provider before leaving home).

Traveler's checks, while still the safest way to carry paper money, are going the way of the dinosaur. The evolution of international computerized banking and consolidated ATM networks has led to the triumph of plastic throughout the Italian peninsula—even if cold cash is still the most trusted currency in family joints, where credit cards may not be accepted.

You'll get the best rate locally if you **exchange money** at a bank or use one of its ATMs. The rates at "Cambio/change/wechsel" exchange booths are invariably less favorable but still a good deal better than what you'd get exchanging money at a hotel or shop (a last-resort tactic only).

ATMs

The ability to access your personal bank account through the **Cirrus** (www.mastercard.com) or **PLUS** (www.visa.com) network of ATMs (or "cashpoints")—or get a cash advance on an enabled Visa or MasterCard—is now standard throughout Italy. All you need to do is search out a machine that has your network's symbol displayed, pop in your card, and punch in your PIN (make sure it's four digits; six-digit PINs won't work). It'll spit out local currency drawn directly from your home account (and at a more favorable rate than converting cash). Keep in mind that many banks impose a fee every time a card is used at a foreign bank's ATM (up to $5 or more). Banks in Italy do not usually charge you a second fee to use their ATMs.

An ATM in Italian is a *Bancomat* (although Bancomat is a private company, its name has become the generic word for ATMs). Increased internationalism has been slowly doing away with the old worry that your card's PIN, be it on a bank card or credit card, need be specially enabled to work abroad, but it always pays to check with your issuing bank to be sure. Many banks also request pre-notification of foreign travel as an anti-fraud measure—and this is a wise precaution if you want to be sure your card won't be stopped. If at the ATM you get a message saying your card isn't valid for international transactions, it's possible the bank just can't make the phone connection to check it (occasionally this can be a citywide epidemic); try another ATM or another town.

If your card is equipped with the "Chip and PIN" security technology, be prepared to enter your PIN when you use the card to make purchases. This is increasingly common across Tuscany, although for now, traditional "swipe" cards are still accepted in central Italy (even while they are being phased out elsewhere in Europe).

Credit Cards

Visa and MasterCard are almost universally accepted at hotels, restaurants, and shops; some also accept American Express. Diners Club is gaining a little ground, especially in Florence and in more expensive establishments throughout the region. If you arrange with your card issuer to enable the card's cash advance option (and get a PIN as well), you can also use them at ATMs. To use "Chip and PIN" credit cards, you'll need to know your PIN number to make a purchase.

Wire Services

If you find yourself out of money, a wire service can help you tap willing friends and family for funds. Through **MoneyGram** (☎ 800/328-5678 in U.S.; ☎ 0800-8971-8971 in U.K.; www.moneygram.com), you can get money sent around the world in less than 10 minutes. MoneyGram's fees can vary, but a good estimate from the U.S. is $10 for sums up to $500 and $16 for up to $1,000, with a sliding scale for larger amounts. From the U.K, sending £500 costs £36, with a sliding scale for larger sums. A similar service is offered by **Western Union** (☎ 800/325-6000 in U.S.; ☎ 0800-833833 in U.K.; www.westernunion. com).

For all wire transfer companies, a currency exchange rate also applies. Additionally, the sender's credit card company may charge a fee for the cash advance as well as a higher interest rate.

Getting **There** & Getting **Around**

By Plane

The logical air entry point to Tuscany is Pisa's **Galileo Galilei Airport** (☎ 050-849300; www.pisa-airport.com), 3km (2 miles) south of Pisa and 84km (52 miles) west of Florence. Major budget and regular airlines such as **Ryanair** (www.ryanair.com), **easyJet** (www.easyjet.com), and **British Airways** (www.ba.com) connect Pisa to several European cities, and there are between three and six flights a week with **Delta** (www.delta.com) direct to **New York's J.F.K.** Two trains an hour whizz you from the airport to Pisa Centrale station in 5 minutes (1.20€); occasionally you can connect directly to Florence (60–90 min., 5.80€) without changing at Pisa Centrale. A faster alternative for anyone heading straight to Florence is the airport shuttle bus operated by **Terravision** (☎ 050-26080; www.terravision.eu). The 70-minute journey runs 10 times a day and costs 10€. A taxi from Pisa airport to Pisa Centrale station costs 10€.

Tuscany's other major airport is **Amerigo Vespucci** (☎ 055-3061300; www.aeroporto.firenze.it), in the suburb of Peretola, 5km (3 miles) west of central Florence. It's partly a domestic airport—**Alitalia** (www.alitalia.it) connects daily with Rome and Sicily. **CityJet** (www.cityjet.com) flies 6 days a week to London City Airport. **Meridiana–Eurofly** (www.meridiana.it) also flies there direct from London's Gatwick Airport, Madrid, and Barcelona; **Lufthansa** (www.lufthansa.com) connects daily to Munich and Frankfurt. To reach the center, take the half-hourly "Vola in bus" service (5€) operated by **ATAF** (☎ 800-424500; www.ataf.net). It terminates next to Santa Maria Novella. A **taxi** (☎ 055-4242; www.socota.

it) from the air terminal to anywhere in the center (or vice versa) costs 20€ during the day, 22€ on Sundays and holidays, and 23€ at night.

Italy's major intercontinental gateways are Milan's **Malpensa Airport** (☎ 02-232323; www.seamilano.eu), and Rome's **Fiumicino Airport** (www.adr.it). Both are connected by major airlines to hubs across North America. **Alitalia** (www.alitalia.it) can connect you on to Florence from Rome, but if you're spending time touring locally before heading to Tuscany, the train is the best bet. By rail, Florence is within 2 hours of Milan, Venice, or Rome (☎ 892021; www.trenitalia.it). See "By Train," below.

By Train

Every day, around 15 **Eurostar** trains (☎ 08432-186186 in U.K.; ☎ +44 1233/617-575 elsewhere; www.eurostar.com) zip from London St. Pancras to Paris's Gare du Nord via the Channel Tunnel, in 2¼ hours. In Paris, you can transfer to Gare de Lyon station for one of two daily direct TGV trains to Milan (7½ hr.), from where you can connect to Pisa (3¼–4 hr.) or Florence (1¾ hr.). There is also a daily night train direct from Paris to Florence with multiperson sleeping cars that can be reserved. The night train leaves Gare de Lyon in the evening and gets into Florence's Santa Maria Novella for breakfast. One-way tickets cost from 35€ to 100€ per person for a (cramped) six-berth couchette, to between 145€ and 180€ per person for a two-berth cabin. Paris-Italy trains are operated by Thello (www.thello.com). All international trains need seat reservations in advance. The main Tuscan rail stations, receiving trains from most parts of Italy, are Florence and Pisa. Siena is an important provincial hub, although only served by slow *Regionale* services. Most arrivals in Florence are at the Modernist **Stazione Santa Maria Novella,** Piazza della Stazione (☎ 892021 or www.trenitalia.com for nationwide rail information). Occasional trains halt at the less convenient **Stazione Rifredi** (connect for the short hop to Santa Maria Novella) or **Stazione Campo di Marte,** on the eastern fringe of the center; a 24-hour bus service (#12) links these two terminals. Fast (Frecciarossa) trains arrive from Milan in under 2 hours, and from Rome, in around 1½ hours. Standard one-way fares on these high-speed services are 53€ and 45€, respectively, but advance and special fares are available if you hunt. Slower trains are cheaper.

In Pisa, trains arrive at **Stazione Pisa Centrale,** Piazza della Stazione, at the southern end of town. Of the major terminals in Tuscany, the best links are between Florence and Pisa, with trains departing every half-hour, at least. The trip between the two cities takes about an hour, costing 5.90€ for a one-way, second-class ticket.

Hourly trains also run directly between Rome and Pisa, taking 2½ to 4 hours and costing 18€ to 47€ for a one-way ticket, depending on the train.

Trains link Lucca and Pisa half-hourly, taking only 30 minutes and costing 2.50€ for a one-way ticket.

In Siena, trains arrive at **Stazione Siena,** Piazza Rosselli. The station is 15 minutes by frequent bus from the heart of Siena. The most useful link is the hourly service between Florence and Siena, taking 1½ hours and costing 6.40€ for a one-way ticket. (However, a bus between the two cities is more convenient—see "By Bus," below.) Frequency and journey time between Siena and Chiusi, which lies on the

main Rome–Florence–Milan line, is about the same; a one-way ticket costs 5.90€. Journeys between Pisa and Siena (1¾ hr.) require a change in Empoli.

See p 98 for my recommended Tuscan rail & bus itinerary.

By Bus

A number of regional bus companies provide the best links between rail hubs like Florence, Siena, or Pisa, and the smaller towns of Tuscany. Among the most useful are: **CPT** (Pisa–Volterra link; ☎ 050-505511; www.cpt.pisa.it); **LFI** (Arezzo; ☎ 0575-39881; www.lfi.it); **SITA** (Florence–Siena and Chianti link; ☎ 055-214721; www.sitabus.it); **TRA.IN** (Siena and around; ☎ 0577-204111; www.trainspa.it); and **VaiBus** (Lucca and around; www.vaibus.it). Most have downloadable timetables online. Tickets are usually sold at newsstands, small general stores, and the bus travel office.

See p 98 for my recommended Tuscan rail and bus itinerary.

By Car

For motorists, the main link is the most traveled road in Italy—the **A1** autostrada (Italy's spinal expressway). This route comes in from the north and Milan, moving southeast toward Bologna before cutting abruptly south across the Apennines to Florence. If you're already in the south, you can travel the same road north between Rome and Florence.

Skirting the western coast of Italy, including the Versilia Riviera, the **A12** heads down from Genoa. North of Pisa the A12 meets up with **A11**, which cuts east toward Florence. Florence and Siena are also linked by an expressway (the *raccordo*) with no route number; from Florence just follow the green signs for Siena.

For visitors heading to Arezzo and eastern Tuscany, follow the autostrada (A1) as though you're going to Rome, until you reach the exits for Arezzo to the immediate east of the road.

Autostrade are superhighways, denoted by green signs and a number prefaced with an A, like the A1 from Rome to Florence. A few aren't numbered and are simply called a *raccordo,* a connecting road between two cities (such as Florence–Siena and Florence–Pisa–Livorno, the "FI–PI–LI"). Autostrade are usually toll roads, although not too expensive. There's a toll calculator at www.autostrade.it: Florence to Lucca, for example, costs 4.30€; Florence to Rome is 16€.

Strade Statali are state roads, usually two lanes wide, indicated by blue signs. Their route numbers are prefaced with an SS or an S, as in the S222 from Florence to Siena. On signs, however, these official route numbers are used infrequently. Usually, you'll just see blue signs listing destinations by name with arrows pointing off in the appropriate directions. Even if it's just a few miles down the road, often the town you're looking for won't be mentioned on the sign at the appropriate turnoff. It's impossible to predict which of all the towns that lie along a road will be the ones chosen to list on a particular sign. Sometimes, the sign gives only the first minuscule village that lies past the turnoff; at other times it lists the first major town down that road, and some signs mention only the major city the road eventually leads to, even if it's hundreds of miles away. It pays to study the map and fix in your mind the names of all the possibilities before coming to an intersection.

The **speed limit** on roads in built-up areas around towns and cities is 50kmph (31 mph). On the

autostrada it's 130kmph (81 mph), except during wet conditions when it's 110kmph (68 mph). Italians have an astounding disregard for these limits—perhaps one reason why Italy, statistically-speaking, has Western Europe's most dangerous roads. Nevertheless, police can ticket you and collect the fine on the spot. At 0.5 mg/l, Italy's official blood alcohol limit is stricter than in the U.S or U.K. The traffic police will throw you in jail if they pull you over and find you inebriated.

If you're from outside the E.U. but driving a private car in Tuscany, before leaving home apply for an **International Driver's Permit,** in the U.S, from your local American Automobile Association (AAA; www.aaa.com). In Canada, the permit is available from the Canadian Automobile Association (CAA; www.caa.ca). Technically, you need this permit, your actual driver's license, and an Italian translation of the latter (also available from the AAA and CAA) to drive in Italy, although in practice the license itself generally suffices. If you're driving a rented car, a valid driver's license from your home country is usually fine—but check with the rental company ahead of time.

If someone races up behind you and flashes their lights, that's the signal for you to slow down so they can pass you quickly and safely. Stay in the right lane on highways; the left is only for passing and for cars with large engines and the pedal to the metal. On a two-lane road, the idiot passing someone in the opposing traffic who has swerved into your lane expects you to veer obligingly over into the shoulder so three lanes of traffic can fit—he would do the same for you. Probably.

Benzina (gas or petrol) is even more expensive in Italy than elsewhere in Europe. Even a small rental

Tuscan Tourist Offices

Arezzo: Palazzo Comunale, Piazza della Libertà (☎ 0575-401945)

Chiusi: Via Porsenna 79 (☎ 0578-227667; www.prolocochiusi.it)

Colle Val d'Elsa: Via Campana 43 (☎ 0577-922791)

Cortona: Palazzo Casali, Piazza Signorelli 9 (☎ 0575-637223)

Elba: Viale Elba 4, Portoferraio (☎ 0565-914671; www.aptelba.it)

Florence: Piazza della Stazione 4 (☎ 055-212245; www.firenze turismo.it); Via Cavour 1R (☎ 055-290832); Loggia di Bigallo, Piazza del Duomo (at Via dei Calzaiuoli)

Livorno: Piazza del Municipio (☎ 0586-820454; www.comune. livorno.it/portaleturismo)

Lucca: Piazza Santa Maria 35 (☎ 0583-919931; www.luccaturismo.it)

Massa Marittima: Via Todini 3–5 (☎ 0566-902756; www.altama remmaturismo.it)

Montalcino: Costa del Municipio 1 (☎ 0577-849331; www.proloco montalcino.it)

Montecatini: Viale Verdi 66 (☎ 0572-772244; www.montecatini turismo.it)

Montepulciano: Piazza Don Minzoni 1 (☎ 0578-757341; www. prolocomontepulciano.it)

Pienza: Palazzo Vescovile, Corso Rossellino 30 (☎ 0578-749905; www.comunedipienza.it)

Pisa: Piazza Vittorio Emanuele II 16 (☎ 050-42291; www.pisa unicaterra.it)

Pistoia: Via Roma 1 (at Piazza del Duomo; ☎ 0573-61622; www. turismo.pistoia.it)

Prato: Piazza del Duomo 4 (☎ 0574-24112; www.pratoturismo.it)

San Gimignano: Piazza del Duomo 1 (☎ 0577-940008; www.san gimignano.com)

Sansepolcro: Via Matteotti (☎ 0575-740536; www.lavalledipiero.it)

Siena: Piazza del Campo 56 (☎ 0577-280551; www.terresiena.it)

Viareggio: Viale Carducci 10 (☎ 0584-962233; www.aptversilia.it); Piazza Dante (☎ 0584-46382)

Volterra: Piazza dei Priori 19–20 (☎ 0588-87257; www.volterratur.it)

---

car guzzles between 60€ and 80€ for a full tank.

There are many pull-in filling stations along major roads and on the outskirts of towns, as well as 24-hour rest stops along the autostrada. Almost all stations are closed for *riposo* and on Sundays, but many have a pump fitted with a machine that accepts bills so you can self-service your tank at 3am. Unleaded gas is *senza piombo*. Diesel (which is cheaper) is *gasolio*.

Car Rentals

In Tuscany, all roads lead to Florence, but you won't need a car once you get there: The Centro Storico is best explored on foot, and parking is expensive. Your best tactic is to tour Tuscany by car at the start or end of your trip, picking it up or returning it as you leave or arrive in Florence. You're usually allowed to park in front of your hotel long enough to unload your luggage. You'll then want to proceed to a garage. (Ask at your hotel; most have a deal with their nearest.)

You'll save money by booking a car before leaving home. The major global rental companies operating in Italy are **Avis** (www.avis.com), **Budget** (www.budget.com), and **Hertz** (www.hertz.com). U.S.-based agents offering European car rental include **Auto Europe** (☎ 888/223-5555; www.autoeurope.com), **Europe by Car** (☎ 800/223-1516; www.ebctravel.com), and **Kemwel Holiday Auto** (☎ 877/820-0668; www.kemwel.com). In some cases, members of the **American Automobile Association (AAA)** or AARP qualify for discounts.

From the U.K., we recommend **Holiday Autos** (☎ 0871/472-5229; www.holidayautos.co.uk). Its pre-paid vouchers include insurance, which is sky-high in Italy. A reliable

local alternative is **Europcar** (☎ 199-307030; www.europcar.it). Meta-search sites like **Kayak.com** are also worth checking to compare rates across various agents.

Both stick shift (manual) and automatic are commonly available at car-rental companies. The former is preferable for negotiating Tuscany's hilly terrain.

We'd also recommend you opt for the **Collision Damage Waiver (CDW),** even though it can be expensive and likely comes with a minimum contribution you are required to pay toward any claim. A bump in Italy isn't that uncommon. To protect against nasty excess charges, consider a Europe policy from **Insurance4CarHire.com**: A 31-day policy costs $83.

Car-rental agencies also require you to purchase theft protection (it will probably be included in the price, however). Before buying added insurance, check your own personal auto insurance policy and credit card terms and conditions to see if they already provide coverage.

Fast **Facts**

AREA CODES Italy no longer uses separate city codes. Dial all numbers as written in this book, including the initial "0" when dialing from overseas.

BUSINESS HOURS General hours of operation for **stores, offices,** and **churches** are from 9:30am to noon or 1pm and again from 3 or 3:30pm to 7pm. That early afternoon shutdown is the *riposo,* the Italian *siesta.* Most stores close on Sunday or on Monday (morning only or all day). Some government services and business offices are open to the public only in the mornings. Traditionally, state museums are closed

Mondays, but check entries in the relevant chapters for exact hours. The biggest "sights" generally stay open all day, but many smaller ones close for *riposo* or open only in the morning (9am–2pm is common). Some churches open earlier than 9am, and the largest often stay open all day. **Bank hours** tend to be Monday through Friday from 8:30am to 1:30pm and 2:30 to 3:30pm or 3 to 4pm.

Use the *riposo* as the Italians do—take a long lunch, stroll through a park, travel to the next town, or return to your hotel to recoup your energy. The *riposo* is especially welcome in August.

CRIME   See "Safety," below. Also note that it is illegal for you to knowingly buy **counterfeit goods** (and, yes, paying 10€ for a "Rolex" counts as *knowingly*). Tourists have left Florence with large fines among their holiday souvenirs.

DRUGSTORES   You'll find **green neon crosses** above the entrances to most *farmacie* (pharmacies). You'll also find many *erboriste* (herbalist shops), which usually offer more traditional herbal remedies along with pharmaceuticals. Most keep everything behind the counter, so be prepared to point or mime. *Language tip:* Most minor ailments start with the phrase *mal di,* so you can just say "Mahl dee" and point to your head, stomach, throat, or whatever. Pharmacies rotate which will stay open all night and on Sundays, and each store has a poster outside showing the month's rotation.

ELECTRICITY   Italy operates on a 220 volts AC (50 cycles) system. You'll need a simple adapter plug and, for non-Europeans, a current converter for some appliances. Get whatever you need before leaving home, as they can be devilish to find in Italy.

EMBASSIES/CONSULATES   The **U.S. Embassy** is in Rome at Via Vittorio Veneto 119A (☎ 06-46741; www. usembassy.it). The **U.S. consulate** in Florence—for passport and consular services but not visas—is at Lungarno Vespucci 38 (☎ 055-266951; http://florence.usconsulate. gov), open to emergency drop-ins Monday through Friday from 9am to 12:30pm. Afternoons and for non-emergencies, the consulate is open by appointment only; call ahead or book online.

The **U.K. Embassy** is in Rome at Via XX Settembre 80 (☎ 06-4220-0001; http://ukinitaly.fco.gov.uk), open Monday and Friday from 9am

to 2pm, Tuesday and Thursday from 9am to 3:30pm. The **U.K. consulate** in Florence is at Lungarno Corsini 2 (☎ 055-284133). It's open Monday to Thursday 9:30am to noon.

Of English-speaking countries, only the U.S. and U.K. have consulates in Florence. Citizens of other countries must go to Rome for help: The **Canadian Embassy** in Rome is at Via Zara 30 (☎ 06-85444-2911; www.canada.it), open Monday through Thursday from 9am to noon. **Australia's** Rome embassy is at Via Bosio 5 (☎ 06-852721; www. italy.embassy.gov.au). The consular section is open Monday through Friday from 9am to 5pm. **New Zealand's** Rome representation is at Via Clitunno 44 (☎ 06-853-7501; www.nzembassy.com/italy), open Monday through Friday from 8:30am to 12:30pm and 1:30 to 5pm. The embassy for **Ireland** is at Piazza di Campitelli 3, Rome (☎ 06-6979-121; www.ambasciata-irlanda.it), open weekdays 10am to 12:30pm and 3 to 4:30pm.

EMERGENCIES   Dial ☎ 113 for any emergency. You can also call ☎ 112 for the *carabinieri* (gendarmerie-style police), ☎ 118 for an ambulance, or ☎ 115 for the fire department. If your car breaks down, dial ☎ 116 for roadside aid from the Automotive Club of Italy.

HOLIDAYS   Businesses, banks, and shops are closed on the following national holidays: January 1; January 6 (Epiphany); Easter Sunday *(Pasqua);* Easter Monday *(Pasquetta);* April 25 (Liberation Day); May 1 (Labor Day); August 15 *(Ferragosto);* November 1 (All Saints' Day); December 8 (Immaculate Conception); December 25 (Christmas Day); December 26 *(Santo Stefano).* Towns and cities also largely shut on their patron saint's day (for example, June 24, St. John the Baptist, for Florence).

HOSPITALS The emergency ambulance number is ☎ 118. Hospitals in Italy are partially socialized, and the care is efficient, personalized, and of a high quality. The most central hospital in Florence is **Santa Maria Nuova,** a block northeast of the Duomo on Piazza Santa Maria Nuova (☎ 055-27581), open 24 hours. Pharmacy staff tend also to be competent health-care providers, so for less serious problems their advice will do fine. For significant but non-life-threatening ailments, you can walk into most hospitals and get speedy care—with no questions about insurance policies, no forms to fill out, and no fees to pay. Obviously it's still crucial to carry an appropriate travel health insurance policy. E.U. citizens should take an **EHIC** card to be certain of free reciprocal health care; forms are available in the U.K. from post offices or at **www.ehic.org.uk**. Most hospitals will be able to find someone who speaks English, but there's also a Florence-based **free medical translator** available at ☎ 055-2344567; hours are Monday, Wednesday, and Friday 4 to 6pm, Tuesday and Thursday 10am to noon.

INTERNET ACCESS Cybercafes and Wi-Fi points are increasingly common in cities. In smaller towns you may have a bit of trouble, but most hotels now offer Wi-Fi throughout (or at least in the lobby, and often free). In a pinch, hostels, local libraries, and, sometimes, bars will have a terminal for access or Wi-Fi. **Internet Train** (www.internettrain.it) is a franchise-based chain of Internet points across Italy. Charge your prepayment card at one branch and you can use it again at any of 14 across Tuscany. Antiterror laws in Italy mean that all Internet point users must present their passports.

LANGUAGE Although Italian is the local language around these parts, English is common, especially among under 40s. Anyone in the tourism industry will know the English they need to facilitate transactions. Most Italians are delighted to help you learn a bit of their lingo as you go, and they will certainly appreciate your attempts to converse with them in their native tongue. To help, we've compiled a lists of key phrases and menu terms later in this chapter; see p 204.

LIQUOR LAWS Driving drunk is illegal, and unwise on Italy's twisty, narrow roads (or anywhere, for that matter). The legal drinking age in Italy is 16. Public drunkenness (aside from people getting noisily tipsy at big dinners) is unusual.

LOST & FOUND Be sure to tell all of your credit card companies the minute you discover your wallet has been lost or stolen and file a report at the nearest police precinct *(questura)*. Your credit card issuer and insurer may require a police report number or record of the loss. Most credit card companies have an emergency toll-free number to call if your card is lost or stolen; they may be able to wire you a cash advance or deliver an emergency credit card in a day or two.

To report a lost or stolen card, call the following Italian toll-free numbers: **Visa** at ☎ 800-819-014, **MasterCard** at ☎ 800-870-866, or **American Express** at ☎ 800-874-333, or for U.S. cardholders collect at ☎ 336-393-1111 from anywhere in the world. As a backup, write down the emergency number that appears on the back of each of your cards (*not* the toll-free or freephone number—you can't dial those from abroad; if one doesn't appear, call the card issuer and ask).

Identity theft and fraud are potential complications of losing your wallet, especially if you've lost your driver's license along with cash and credit cards. Placing a fraud alert on your credit records may protect you, and you can do so online with the three major U.S. credit-reporting agencies, **Equifax** (www.equifax.com), **Experian** (www.experian.com), and **TransUnion** (☎ 800-719-1636; www.transunion.com). Finally, if you've lost all forms of photo I.D., call your airline and explain the situation; they might allow you to board the plane if you have a copy of your passport or birth certificate and a copy of the police report you've filed.

MAIL   The Italian mail system is notoriously slow, and friends back home may not receive your postcards before they see you again in person. Postcards, aerograms, and letters, weighing up to 20g (.7 oz.), cost .75€ to send. Buy stamps from postal offices or wherever you see the black-and-white "T" *(tabacchi)* sign. Ask for *"un francobollo per gli Stati Uniti / per Gran Bretagna,"* and so on.

NEWSPAPERS & MAGAZINES   Visitors will see plenty of familiar mastheads. The *International Herald Tribune, Wall Street Journal Europe,* and *USA Today* are available at many newsstands, even in small (tourist) towns. U.K. daily and Sunday newspapers are available (a day or 2 behind) at all good-size newsstands. Florence's biweekly the *Florentine* is the major English-language publication; Lucca's monthly *Grapevine* serves English speakers living in or visiting that town. For comprehensive Florence listings, pick up *Firenze Spettacolo.* Italian-speakers should go for *La Nazione,* a national daily published in Florence, or *Il Tirreno,* more widespread closer to the coast.

POLICE   For emergencies, call ☎ 113. Italy has several different police forces, but you'll most likely only ever deal with two. The first is the urban *polizia,* whose city headquarters is called the *questura* and who can help with lost and stolen

property. More useful for serious crimes is the *carabinieri* (☎ 112).

RESTROOMS   Public toilets are going out of fashion, but most bars will let you use their bathrooms without a scowl or forcing you to buy anything. It's polite to buy a *caffè* anyhow. Ask *"Posso usare il bagno?"* (poh-soh oo-zar-eh eel ban-yo). Donne/signore are women and *uomini/signori* men. Train stations usually have a bathroom, for a fee. In many of the public toilets that remain, the little old lady with a basket has been replaced by a coin-op turnstile.

SAFETY   Other than the inevitable pickpockets, especially in Florence, random violent crime is practically unheard of in Tuscany. However, the area around Florence's Santa Maria Novella, and the Cascine Park, are best avoided at night, ditto the alleys around Santo Spirito and Santa Croce in the small hours.

In general, just be smart, especially in crowded spots. Keep your passport, credit and ATM cards, and photocopies of important documents under your clothes in a money belt or neck pouch. Use the hotel safe, if there is one. **For women:** Beware of drive-by purse snatchings, by young thieves on mopeds, particularly in Florence. Keep your purse on the wall side of the sidewalk and sling the strap across your chest. If your purse has a flap, keep the clasp facing your body. **For men:** Keep your wallet in a front pocket and perhaps loop a rubber band around it. (The rubber catches on the fabric of your pocket and makes it harder for a thief to slip the wallet out.)

SMOKING   Italy banned smoking inside all bars, restaurants, and offices in 2005. Note, however, that smoking on outdoor terraces (including in restaurants) is allowed.

TAXES   There's no sales tax added to the price tag of your purchases, but there is a **value-added tax** (in Italy, IVA) automatically included in just about everything. For major purchases, you can get this refunded (see p 63). Florence also introduced an additional **accommodation tax** in 2011. You will be charged 1€ per person per night per government-star rating of the hotel, up to a maximum of 10 nights. Children 9 and under are exempt. This tax is not usually included in any published room rate.

TELEPHONES & FAX There are several types of public pay phones: those that take coins only, those that take both coins and phone cards, and those that take only **phone cards** (*carta* or *scheda telefonica*). You can buy prepaid phone cards at any *tabacchi* (tobacconists), most newsstands, and some bars in several denominations. Break off the corner before inserting it; a display tracks how much money is left as you talk. Don't forget to take the card with you when you leave! Some public phones also take credit cards.

For **operator-assisted international calls** (in English), dial toll-free ☎ 170. Note, however, that you'll get better rates by calling a home operator for collect calls, as detailed here: To make calling card calls, insert a phone card or coin—it'll be refunded at the end of your call—and dial the local number for your service. For **Americans:** AT&T is at ☎ 800-172-444, MCI at ☎ 800-90-5825, and Sprint at ☎ 800-172-405. These numbers will raise an American operator for you. **Canadians** can reach Canada Direct at ☎ 800-172-213. **Brits** can call BT at ☎ 800-172-441. **Australians** can use Optus by calling ☎ 800-172-611 or Telstra at ☎ 800-172-610.

To **dial direct internationally** from Italy, dial ☎ 00, then the country code, the area code, and the number. Country codes are as follows: the United States and

Canada 1; United Kingdom 44; Ireland 353; Australia 61; New Zealand 64. Make calls from a public phone if possible because hotels charge inflated rates, but take along plenty of *schede* to feed the phone. Many Internet points are equipped with headsets for **VoIP** (Voice over Internet Protocol) calling using services like Skype. Cellphones (see "Before You Go," above) often offer affordable international calling tariffs. Ask at a phone shop.

To access free **national telephone information** (in Italian), check **Paginegialle.it** (for business numbers) and **Paginebianche.it** (for personal numbers).

Your hotel will most likely be able to send or receive **faxes** for you, sometimes at inflated prices, sometimes at cost. Otherwise, most *cartolerie* (stationery stores), *copista* or *fotocopie* (photocopy shops), Internet cafes, and some *tabacchi* (tobacconists) offer fax services.

TIME ZONE Italy is 6 hours ahead of Eastern Standard Time in the United States, 1 hour ahead of GMT or BST in the U.K. and Ireland.

TIPPING In **hotels,** a service charge is usually included in your bill. In family-run operations, additional tips are unnecessary and sometimes considered rude. In fancier places with a hired staff, however, you may want to leave a .50€ daily tip for the maid, pay the bellhop or porter 1€ per bag, and a helpful concierge 2€ for his or her troubles. In **restaurants,** 10% to 15% is usually included in the bill, alongside a fixed charge for *"pane e coperto"* (bread and cover)—to be sure, ask *"è incluso il servizio?"* You may want to leave up to an additional 10% for good service, but don't feel obliged. At **bars and cafes,** leave your change up to the next euro on the counter for the barman; if you sit at a table, you're being charged extra anyway, so there's no need to feel a duty to leave more for a barman. **Taxi** drivers appreciate a euro or two.

WATER   Although most Italians take mineral water with their meals, tap water is safe everywhere, as are any public drinking fountains you run

across. Unsafe sources will be marked *"acqua non potabile."* If tap water comes out cloudy, it's only calcium or other minerals inherent in a water supply that often comes untreated from fresh springs.

A Brief **History**

1100–700 B.C.   Villanovan culture thrives in what we now call Tuscany.

800–300 B.C.   The Etruscans are the major power in central Italy.

600–510 B.C.   The Etruscan Tarquin dynasty rules as kings of Rome.

508 B.C.   Lars Porsena, Etruscan king of Clusium (now Chiusi), attacks the young Roman Republic and wins.

295–265 B.C.   Rome conquers Etruria and allies with Umbria. The Roman Empire spreads throughout central Italy and Latinizes local culture.

59 B.C.   Julius Caesar founds Florentia, and Florence is born.

56 B.C.   The First Triumvirate (Caesar, Pompey, and Crassus) meets in Lucca.

A.D. 250   Florence's first Christian martyr, St. Minias, is beheaded in the city.

313   Roman Emperor Constantine the Great, a convert himself, declares religious freedom for Christians.

476   After a long decline, the Roman Empire falls.

570–774   The Lombard duchies rule over much of Tuscany and neighboring Umbria.

774–800s   Charlemagne and the Carolingian dynasty picks up where the Lombards left off.

1115   Florence is granted independent status within the Holy Roman Empire (a territory that covered modern-day central Europe).

1125   Florence razes neighbor Fiesole to the ground. Florentine expansion begins.

1155   Frederick I Barbarossa is crowned Holy Roman Emperor and attempts to take control of part of Italy.

1173   Pisa begins its bell tower. Eleven years later, someone notices the tilt.

1215   Florentine families form factions reflecting the conflict between emperor and pope. Those favoring the pope are known as Guelphs, pro-Imperial supporters as Ghibellines.

1250–1600   Intellectual pursuit of knowledge and study of the classical and Arab worlds begins to take precedence over Christian doctrine and superstition: the Humanist era.

1260   Ghibelline Siena defeats Guelph Florence at the Battle of Montaperti. Siena dedicates itself to the Virgin Mary in thanks.

1284   Genoa trounces Pisa's fleet in the naval Battle of Meloria. A long Pisan decline begins.

1300   The Guelph triumph in Florence is secure, but they

immediately split into the White and the Black factions.

1302 Dante is exiled from Florence on trumped-up charges. He never returns, and is buried in Ravenna in 1321.

1303–77 The pope moves from Rome to Avignon. St. Catherine of Siena is instrumental in returning the papacy to Italy.

1304–10 Florentine Giotto frescoes the Scrovegni Chapel, in Padua. Western painting would never be the same.

1308–21 Dante writes the *Divine Comedy*, which sets the Tuscan dialect as the precursor of modern Italian.

1310 Siena runs its first Palio on record.

1348 The Black Death rips through Italy, killing more than half the population. Siena loses more than two-thirds of its citizens.

1355 Siena's government of the Nine (the *"Nove"*) falls, ending almost a century of stability.

1361 Florence conquers Volterra.

1378–1417 The Western Schism: Avignon, Rome, and Pisa each appoint a pope, and the competing pontiffs get busy excommunicating one another.

1384 Florence conquers Arezzo.

1401 Lorenzo Ghiberti wins the competition to cast the Baptistery doors in Florence. May the Renaissance begin!

1406 Florence conquers Pisa.

1434–64 Cosimo "il Vecchio" consolidates Medici power over Florence.

1435 Leon Battista Alberti publishes *De Pictura,* the seminal work of Renaissance art theory, largely on optics and perspective.

1439 The Council of Florence: Eastern and Western churches briefly reconcile their ancient differences.

1458 The coronation, in Rome, of Sienese Pope Pius II is re-created outside the Palazzo Pubblico for the benefit of citizens of Siena.

1469–92 The rule of Lorenzo de' Medici "the Magnificent" in Florence, under whose patronage the arts flourish.

1475 Michelangelo Buonarotti is born in Caprese, near Arezzo.

1494 Puritanical Dominican Fra' Girolamo Savonarola helps drive the Medici from Florence and takes control of the city.

1495 The "Bonfire of the Vanities": At Savonarola's urging, Florentines carry material goods seen as decadent—including paintings by Botticelli, Lorenzo di Credi, and others—to Piazza della Signoria and burn them.

1498 At the pope's urging, Florentines carry Savonarola to Piazza della Signoria and set him on fire.

1498–1512 The Florentine Republic is free from the Medici.

1501–04 Michelangelo carves *David, "Il Gigante."*

1505 For a few months, Leonardo da Vinci, Michelangelo, and Raphael all live and work in Florence at the same time.

1527 Emperor Charles V sacks Rome. Medici Pope Clement VII escapes to Orvieto, where by papal bull he refuses to annul Henry VIII's marriage to Catherine of Aragon and helps give rise to the Anglican Church.

1530 The Medici firmly take back power in Florence.

1550   Vasari publishes his *Lives of the Artists,* effectively the first art history book.

1555–57   Florence conquers Siena. The Sienese Republic makes a last stand at Montalcino.

1569   Cosimo I de' Medici is the first Grand Duke of Tuscany.

1581   The Uffizi opens as a painting gallery.

1633   Despite being championed by the Medici, Galileo is forced by the Church to recant his idea that Earth revolves around the Sun.

1737   Gian Gastone, last of the Medici Grand Dukes, dies.

1796–1806   Napoléon sweeps through Tuscany, eventually declaring himself king of Italy.

1805   Napoléon gives Lucca to his sister Elisa Baciocchi as a duchy.

1814–15   Napoléon is exiled on Elba, which he rules as governor.

1824   Lorraine Grand Duke Leopold II starts draining the marshes of the Maremma. The reclamation is complete in 1950 with the defeat of malaria.

1848–60   The *Risorgimento* movement struggles for a unified Italy.

1860   Tuscany joins the new Kingdom of Italy.

1865–70   Florence serves as Italy's capital.

1921   The Italian Communist Party is founded, in Livorno, and goes on to play a major part in postwar democratic politics.

1922   Mussolini becomes the Fascist dictator of Italy.

1940–45   World War II. Fascist Italy initially participates as an Axis power, before descending into civil war between Fascists and Partisans.

1944   Nazi troops withdraw from Florence, blowing up the Arno bridges. Supposedly on Hitler's direct order, the Ponte Vecchio is spared.

1946   Italy votes to become a republic.

1948   Italy's regions are created: Tuscany and Umbria finally get an official dividing line between them.

1966   The Arno flood in Florence. Up to 6m (20 ft.) of water and mud destroys or damages countless works of art. Over 100 people die.

1985   Italy's worst winter on record; the frost hits grapevines heavily and comes close to destroying all the olive trees in Tuscany.

1988   Pedestrian zones go into effect in major cities, making historic centers traffic-free (almost).

1993   On May 27, a car bomb rips through the west wing of the Uffizi, killing five people and damaging many paintings.

1997   In Assisi, in neighboring Umbria, a series of earthquakes hit, and part of the basilica's ceiling collapses, destroying frescoes and damaging Giotto's *Life of St. Francis.*

1999   Tuscany rejoices when local filmmaker Roberto Benigni, after victory at Cannes, gathers three Oscars for his Holocaust fable *La Vita è Bella (Life is Beautiful).*

2001   The first cases of BSE (mad cow disease) in Italy are confirmed. Beef consumption plummets 70%, and the government considers banning such culinary institutions as the *bistecca alla fiorentina.* The year ends on a high note when the Leaning Tower of Pisa reopens to the public, after more than a decade of desperate measures to keep it from collapsing. (Don't worry—it still leans.)

2002   Florence's football team, Fiorentina, known as *I Viola,* goes out of business. But her return to the highest echelons of European competition will take just 6 years.

2008   The city of Florence makes the first moves toward issuing a formal pardon for Dante, exiled 700 years previously. For the third time since the Millennium, Bruco wins Siena's Palio.

2009   Young center-left candidate Matteo Renzi is elected Mayor of Florence, and immediately sets about making the city more friendly to pedestrians (and less friendly toward car traffic).

2011   Despite last-minute legal wrangles, Florence introduces a controversial accommodations tax.

Art & Architecture

Architecture

Ambulatory   Continuation of the side aisles to make a walkway around the chancel space behind the main altar of a church.

Apse   The semicircular or polygonal space behind the main altar of a church.

Arcade   A series of arches supported by columns, piers, or pilasters.

Architrave   The long vertical element lying directly across the tops of a series of columns (the lowest part of an entablature); or, the molding around a door or window.

Badia   Abbey.

Baldacchino   A stone canopy over a church altar.

Basilica   A form of architecture first used for public halls and law courts in ancient Roman cities. Early Christians adopted the form—a long rectangular room, divided into a central nave with side aisles but no transept—to build their first large churches. A "basilica" is now sometimes used to denote an important church without a bishop's seat.

Bay   The space between two columns or piers.

Bifore   Divided vertically into two sections.

Blind Arcade   An arcade of pilasters (the arches are all filled in), a defining architectural feature of the Romanesque style.

Caldarium   The hot tub or steam room of a Roman bath.

Campanile   A bell tower, usually of a church but also of public buildings; it's often detached or flush against the church rather than sprouting directly from it.

Cantoria   Small church singing gallery, usually set into the wall above the congregation's heads.

Capital   The top of a column. The classical "orders" (types) are Doric (plain), Ionic (with scrolls, called

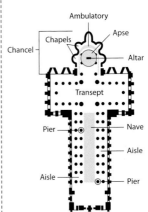

Church Floor Plan.

volutes, at the corners), and Corinthian (leafy). There's also Tuscan (even simpler than Doric; the column is never fluted or grooved, and usually has no base) and Composite (Corinthian superimposed with Ionic). In many Paleochristian and Romanesque churches, the capital is carved with primitive animal and human heads or simple biblical scenes.

Cappella Italian for chapel.

Caryatid A column carved to resemble a woman (see also *telamon*).

Cattedrale Cathedral (also Duomo).

Cavea The semicircle of seats in a classical theater.

Cella The innermost, most sacred room of a Roman pagan temple.

Chancel Space around the high altar of a church, generally reserved for the clergy and the choir.

Chiesa Italian for church.

Chiostro Italian for cloister.

Ciborium (1) Another word for *baldacchino* (above); (2) Box or tabernacle containing the Host (the symbolic body and blood of Christ taken during communion).

Cloister A roofed walkway open on one side and supported by columns; usually used in the plural because often four of them faced one another to make interior open-air courtyards, centered around small gardens, found in monasteries and convents.

Collegiata A collegiate church, having a chapter of canons and a dean or provost to rule over it but lacking the bishop's seat that would make it a cathedral.

Colonnaded Lined with columns.

Cornice Protruding section, usually along the very top of a wall, a facade, or an entablature; a pediment is usually framed by a lower cornice and two sloping ones.

Cortile Italian for courtyard.

Crenellated Topped by a regular series of teethlike protrusions and crevices; these battlements often ring medieval buildings or fortresses to aid in defense.

Crypt An underground burial vault; in churches, usually found below the altar end, and in Italy often the remnant of an older version of the church.

Cupola Dome.

Cyclopian Adjective describing an unmortared wall built of enormous stones by an unknown, central Italian, pre-Etruscan people. The sheer size led the ancients to think they were built by the Cyclopses.

Duomo Cathedral (from *domus*, "house of God"), often used to refer to the main church in town even if it doesn't have a *cathedra,* or bishop's seat—the prerequisite for a cathedral.

Entablature Section riding above a colonnade, made up of the

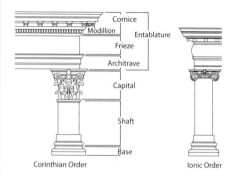

Corinthian Order

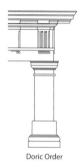

Ionic Order   Doric Order

Classical Orders.

architrave (bottom), frieze (middle), and cornice (top).

Forum The main square in a Roman town; a public space used for assemblies, courts, and speeches, and on which important temples and civic buildings were located.

Frieze A decorative horizontal band or series of panels, usually carved in relief and at the center of an entablature.

Frigidarium Room for cold baths in a Roman bath.

Greek Cross Building ground plan in the shape of a cross whose arms are of equal length.

Latin Cross Building ground plan in the shape of a Crucifix-style cross, where one arm is longer than the other three (this is the nave).

Liberty Italian version of Art Nouveau or Art Deco, popular in the late 19th and early 20th centuries.

Loggia Roofed porch, balcony, or gallery.

Lozenge A decorative, regularly sided diamond (square on its corners), made of either marble inlay or a sunken depression, often centered in the arcs of a blind arcade on Romanesque architecture.

Lunette Semicircular wall space created by various ceiling vaultings or above a door or window; often it's decorated with a painting, mosaic, or relief.

Matroneum In some Paleochristian and early Romanesque churches, the gallery (often on the second floor) reserved for women, who were kept separate from the men during Mass.

Narthex Interior vestibule of a church.

Nave The longest section of a church, usually leading from the front door to the altar, where the worshipers sit; often divided into aisles.

Palazzo Traditionally a palace or other important building; in contemporary Italian it refers to any large structure, including office buildings (and has become the common way to refer to a city block, no matter how many separate structures form it).

Paleochristian Early Christian, used generally to describe the era from the 5th to the early 11th century.

Pediment A wide gable at the top of a facade or above a doorway.

Piano nobile The primary floor of a palace where the family would live, usually the second (American) but sometimes the third floor. It tends to have higher ceilings and larger rooms and be more lavishly decorated than the rest of the *palazzo*. The ground floor was usually for storage or shops and the attic for servants.

Pier A rectangular vertical support (like a column).

Pietra forte A dark gray, ocher-tinged limestone mined near Florence. Harder than its cousin *pietra serena* (below), it was used more sparingly in Florentine architecture.

Pietra serena A soft, light-gray limestone mined in the Florentine hills around Fiesole and one of the major building blocks of Florence's architecture—for both the ease with which it could be worked and its color, used to accent door jambs and window frames in houses and columns and chapels in churches.

Pieve A parish church; in the countryside, often primarily a baptismal site.

Pilaster Often called pilaster strip, it's a column, either rounded or squared off, set into a wall rather than separate from it.

Porta Italian for door or city gate.

Portico A porch.

Refectory The dining room of a convent or monastery—which, from the Renaissance on, was often painted with a *Last Supper* to aid religious contemplation at the dinner table.

Sacristy The room in a church that houses (or housed) the sacred vestments and vessels.

Sanctuary   Technically the holiest part of a church, the term is used to refer to the area just around or behind the high altar.

Spandrel   Triangular wall space created when two arches in an arcade curve away from each other (or from the end wall).

Spoglio   Architectural recycling; the practice of using pieces of an older building to help raise a new one. (Roman temples were popular mines for both marble and columns to build early churches.)

Sporti   Overhanging second story of a medieval or Renaissance building supported by wooden or stone brackets.

Stele   A headstone.

Stemma   Coat of arms.

Stucco   Plaster composed of sand, powdered marble, water, and lime; often molded into decorative relief, formed into statuary, or applied in a thin layer to the exterior of a building.

Telamon   A column sculpted to look like a man (also see *caryatid*).

Tepidarium   The room for a warm bath in Roman baths.

Terme   Roman baths, usually divided into the calidarium, tepidarium, and frigidarium.

Torre   Italian for tower.

Transept   The lateral cross-arm of a cruciform church, perpendicular to the nave.

Travertine   A whitish or honey-colored form of porous volcanic tufa mined near Tivoli. The stone from which much of ancient Rome (and Montepulciano) was built.

Tribune   The raised platform from which an orator speaks; used to describe the raised section of some churches around and behind the altar from which Mass is performed.

Two-light   Of a window, divided vertically into two sections (see also *bifore*). A three-light window is divided vertically into three sections.

Tympanum   The triangular or semi-circular space between the cornices of a pediment or between the lintel above a door and the arch above it.

Painting, Sculpture & Ceramics

Aerial perspective   The tendency of objects to blur toward the background color as they approach the horizon, a phenomenon mastered by Tuscan painters by the mid-1400s.

Altarpiece   A painting placed on or hung above the altar, often made from poplar wood and consisting of two or more panels. After 1310, all churches were required to have one.

Ambone   Italian for pulpit.

Amphora   A two-handled jar with a tapered neck used by the ancients to keep wine, oil, and other liquids.

Arriccio   The first, rough layer of plaster laid down when applying fresco to a wall. On this layer, the artist makes the *sinopia* sketches.

Bottega   The workshop of an artist. (On museum signs, the word means the work was created or carried out by apprentices or assistants in the stated master's workshop.)

Bozzetto   A small model for a larger sculpture (or sketch for a painting); in the later Renaissance and Baroque eras, it also came to mean the tiny statuettes turned out for their own sake to satisfy the growing demand among the rich for table art.

Bucchero   Etruscan black earthenware pottery.

Canopic vase   Etruscan funerary vase housing the entrails of the deceased.

Cartoon   In Italian *cartone*, literally "big paper," the full-size preparatory sketch made for a fresco or mosaic.

Chiaroscuro   Using patches of light and dark colors in painting to model figures and create the illusion of three dimensions. (Caravaggio was a master at also using the technique to create mood and tension.)

Cinerary urn Vase or other vessel containing the ashes of the deceased; Etruscan ones were often carved with a relief on the front and, on the lid, a half-reclining figure representing the deceased at a banquet.

Contrapposto A twisted pose in a figure, first used by the ancients and revived by Michelangelo; a hallmark of the Mannerist school.

Diptych A painting with two sections or panels.

Ex voto A small plaque, statue, painting, or other memento left by a supplicant, signifying either his or her gratitude to a saint or the Madonna, or imploring the saint's help in some matter.

Fresco The multistep art of creating a painting on fresh plaster (*fresco* means "fresh").

Gesso Calcium sulphate, or gypsum, applied in up to seven layers to treat a wooden panel before painting.

Graffiti Incised decorative designs, made by painting the surface in two thin layers (one light, the other dark), then scratching away the top layer to leave the designs in contrast. Called *"sgraffito"* in Italian.

Grotesques Carved or painted faces, animals, and designs, often deliberately exaggerated or ugly; used to decorate surfaces and composite sculptures (such as fountains) and to illuminate manuscripts.

Illuminated Describing a manuscript or book, usually a choir book or Bible, that has been decorated with colorful designs, miniatures, figures, scenes, and fancy letters, often produced by anonymous monks.

Intarsia Inlaid wood, marble, precious stones, or metal.

International Gothic Highly decorative style of painting with its roots in the art of Simone Martini. Leading Florentine exponents were Fra' Angelico and Gentile da Fabriano.

Majolica Tin-glazed earthenware pottery usually elaborately painted; a process pioneered and mastered in Italy in the 14th to 17th century.

Pala Altarpiece.

Pietra dura The art of inlaying semiprecious stones to form patterns and pictures; often called "Florentine mosaic" and increasingly popular from the late 15th century.

Pinacoteca Painting gallery.

Polyptych A panel painting having more than one section that's hinged so it can be folded up. Two-paneled ones are called diptychs (see above), three-paneled ones triptychs (see below). Any more panels use the general term.

Porphyry Any igneous rock with visible shards of crystals suspended in a matrix of fine particles.

Predella Small panel or series of panels below the main part of an altarpiece, often used to tell a story of Christ's Passion or a saint's life comic-strip style.

Putti Cherubs (sing. *putto*); chubby naked toddler boys sculpted or painted, often with wings.

Sacra conversazione Type of painting in which saints are arranged with the Madonna in a unified space, rather than relegated to wings, as in a polyptych (see above).

Sarcophagus A stone coffin or casket.

Schiacciato Literally, "flattened." A sculpture form pioneered by Donatello; figures are carved in extremely low relief so that from straight on they give the illusion of three-dimensionality and great depth, but from the side are oddly squashed.

Sfumato A painting technique, popularized by Leonardo da Vinci, as important as perspective in achieving the illusion of great depth. The artist cloaks objects (landscape features like hills, or facial features) in a filmy haziness; the farther away the object, the blurrier it appears, and the more realistic the distance seems.

Sinpoia Underpainting or sketch made in red-brown pigment, the first drawing made on a wall to be frescoed.

Stoup A holy-water basin.

Tempera Type of paint in which pigments are bound with egg yolk; used for almost all paintings before oil took over around 1500.

Tondo A round painting or sculpture.

Trecento The 14th century (in Italian, literally "300s"), often used to describe that era of art dominated by the styles of Giotto and the International Gothic.

Triptych A painting with three sections or panels.

Useful **Terms** & **Phrases**

Tuscan, being the local lingo of Dante, is considered the purest form of Italian. (In Siena they will tell you that, actually, it's Sienese dialect that's perfect.) That means travel in Tuscany will help you learn the most word-perfect Italian there is. Here are some key phrases to get you started.

Molto Italiano: A Basic Italian Vocabulary

English	Italian	Pronunciation
Thank you	Grazie	graht-tzee-yey
Please	Per favore	pehr fah-vohr-eh
Yes	Sì	see
No	No	noh
Good morning or Good day	Buongiorno	bwohn-djor-noh
Good evening	Buona sera	Bwohn-ah say-rah
Good night	Buona notte	Bwohn-ah noht-tay
How are you?	Come sta?	koh-may stah?
Very well	Molto bene	mohl-toh behn-ney
Goodbye	Arrivederci	ahr-ree-vah-dehr-chee
Excuse me (to get attention)	Scusi	skoo-zee
Excuse me (to get past someone on the bus)	Permesso	pehr-mehs-soh
Where is . . . ?	Dovè . . . ?	doh-veH?
the station	la stazione	lah stat-tzee-oh-neh
a hotel	un albergo	oon ahl-behr-goh
a restaurant	un ristorante	oon reest-ohr-ahnt-eh
the bathroom	il bagno	eel bahn-nyoh
To the right	A destra	ah dehy-stra

English	Italian	Pronunciation
Straight ahead	Avanti (or sempre diritto)	ahv-vahn-tee (*sehm*-pray dee-*reet*-toh)
I would like	Vorrei	voh-*ray*
This/that	Questo/quello	*qway*-sto/*qwell*-oh
A glass of	Un bicchiere di	oon bee-key-*air*-ay-dee
(mineral) water	acqua (minerale)	*ah*-kwah (min-air-*ahl*-lay)
carbonated	gassata (or con gas)	gahs-*sah*-tah (kohn gahs)
uncarbonated	senza gas	*sen*-zah gahs
red wine	vino rosso	*vee*-no *roh*-soh
white wine	vino bianco	*vee*-no bee-*ahn*-koh
How much is it?	Quanto costa?	*kwan*-toh *coh*-sta?
It's too much.	È troppo.	ay *tro*-poh
The check, please.	Il conto, per favore.	eel kon-toh *pehr* fah-*vohr*-eh
Can I see . . . ?	Posso vedere . . . ?	*poh*-soh veh-*dare*-eh?
the church	la chiesa	la key-*ay*-zah
the fresco	l'affresco	lahf-*fres*-coh
When?	Quando?	*kwan*-doh
Is it open?	È aperto?	ay ah-*pair*-toe
Is it closed?	È chiuso?	ay key-*you*-zoh
Yesterday	Ieri	ee-*yehr*-ree
Today	Oggi	*oh*-jee
Tomorrow	Domani	doh-*mah*-nee
Breakfast	Prima colazione	*pree*-mah coh-laht-tzee-*ohn*-ay
Lunch	Pranzo	*prahn*-zoh
Dinner	Cena	*chay*-nah
What time is it?	Che ore sono?	kay *or*-ay *soh*-noh
Monday	Lunedì	loo-nay-*dee*
Tuesday	Martedì	mart-ay-*dee*
Wednesday	Mercoledì	mehr-cohl-ay-*dee*
Thursday	Giovedì	joh-vay-*dee*
Friday	Venerdì	ven-nehr-*dee*
Saturday	Sabato	*sah*-bah-toh
Sunday	Domenica	doh-*mehn*-nee-kah

Numbers

1	uno	(*oo*-noh)
2	due	(*doo*-ay)
3	tre	(tray)
4	quattro	(*kwah*-troh)
5	cinque	(*cheen*-kway)
6	sei	(say)
7	sette	(*set*-tay)
8	otto	(*oh*-toh)
9	nove	(*noh*-vey)

English	Italian	Pronunciation
10	dieci	(dee-*ay*-chee)
100	cento	(*chen*-toh)
1,000	mille	(*mee*-lay)

Italian **Menu & Food Terms**

Acciughe or Alici   Anchovies.

Acquacotta   "Cooked water," a watery vegetable soup thickened with egg and poured over stale bread.

Affettato misto   Mix of various salami, prosciutto, and other cured meats; served as an appetizer.

Agnello   Lamb.

Agnolotti   Semicircular ravioli (often stuffed with meat and/or cheese).

Anatra   Duck.

Anguilla   Eel.

Antipasti   Appetizers.

Aragosta   Lobster.

Arista di maiale   Roast pork loin, usually served in slices, flavored with rosemary, garlic, and cloves.

Baccalà (alla livornese)   Dried salted codfish (cooked in olive oil, white wine, garlic, and tomatoes).

Bistecca alla fiorentina   Florentine-style steak, made with Chianina beef, grilled over wood coals, and then brushed with olive oil and sprinkled with pepper and salt.

Bocconcini   Small veal chunks sautéed in white wine, butter, and herbs. (Also the word for ball-shaped portions of any food, especially mozzarella.)

Braciola   Loin pork chop.

Branzino   Sea bass.

Bresaola   Air-dried, thinly sliced beef filet, dressed with olive oil, lemon, and pepper—usually an appetizer.

Bruschetta   A slab of bread grilled and then rubbed with garlic, drizzled with olive oil, and sprinkled with salt; often served *al pomodoro* (with tomatoes).

Bucatini   Fat, hollow spaghetti. Classically served *all'amatriciana* (with a spicy, hot tomato sauce studded with pancetta [bacon]).

Cacciucco   Seafood soup-stew of Livrono in a spicy tomato base poured over stale bread.

Cacio or Caciotto   Southern Tuscan name for pecorino (sheep's-milk) cheese.

Cannellini   White beans, the Tuscan's primary vegetable.

Cannelloni   Pasta tubes filled with meat and baked in a sauce (cream or tomato). The cheese version is usually called *manicotti* (although either name may be used for either stuffing).

Cantuccini   Twice-baked hard almond cookies, vaguely crescent-shaped and best made in Prato (where they're known as *biscotti di Prato*).

Capocollo   Aged sausage made mainly from pork necks.

Caprese   A salad of sliced mozzarella and tomatoes lightly dressed with olive oil, salt, and pepper.

Capretto   Kid goat.

Caprino   Soft goat's-milk cheese.

Carciofi   Artichokes.

Carpaccio   Thin slices of raw cured beef, pounded flat and often served topped with arugula (rocket) and Parmesan cheese shavings.

Casalinga   Home cooking.

Cavolo   Cabbage.

Ceci   Chickpeas (garbanzo beans).

Cervelli   Brains, often served *fritti* (fried).

Cervo   Venison.

Cibrèo   Stew of chicken livers, cockscombs, and eggs.

Cinghiale   Wild boar.

Cipolla   Onion.

Coniglio   Rabbit.

Cozze   Mussels.

Crespelle alla fiorentina   Thin pancakes wrapped around ricotta and spinach, covered with tomatoes and cheese, and baked in a casserole.

Crostini   Small rounds of bread toasted and covered with various pâtés, most commonly a tasty liver paste.

Dentice   Dentex; a fish similar to perch.

Fagioli   Beans, almost always white cannellini beans.

Faraona   Guinea hen.

Farro   Emmer or spelt, a barley-like grain (often in soups).

Fave   Broad (fava) beans.

Fegato   Liver.

Focaccia   Like pizza dough with nothing on it, this bready snack is laden with olive oil, baked in sheets, sprinkled with coarse salt, and eaten in slices plain or split to stuff as a sandwich. In Florence, it's also popularly called *schiacciato*.

Formaggio   Cheese.

Frittata   Thick omelet stuffed with meats, cheese, and vegetables; sometimes eaten between slices of bread as a sandwich.

Fritto misto   A deep-fried mix of meats, often paired with fried artichokes. By the coast, usually a mixed fry of seafood.

Frutte di mare   A selection of shellfish, often boosted with a couple of shrimp and some squid.

Funghi   Mushrooms.

Fusilli   Spiral-shaped pasta; usually long like a telephone cord, not the short macaroni style.

Gamberi (gamberetti)   Prawns (shrimp).

Gelato   Dense version of ice cream (*produzione propria* means homemade).

Gnocchi   Pasta dumplings usually made from potato.

Granchio   Crab.

Granita   Flavored ice; *limone* (lemon) is the classic.

Involtini   Thinly sliced beef or veal rolled with veggies (often celery or artichokes) and simmered in its own juices.

Lampreda   Lamprey (an eel-like fish).

Lenticchie   Lentil beans; Italy's best come from Castellúccio, in Umbria.

Lepre   Wild hare.

Lombatina di vitello   Loin of veal.

Maiale   Pork.

Manzo   Beef.

Mascarpone   Technically a cheese but more like heavy cream, already slightly sweet and sweetened more to use in desserts like tiramisù.

Melanzana   Eggplant (aubergine).

Merluzzo   Cod.

Minestrone   A little-bit-of-everything vegetable soup, usually flavored with chunks of cured ham.

Mortadella   A very thick, mild pork sausage; the original bologna (because the best comes from Bologna).

Mozzarella   A nonfermented cheese, made from the fresh milk of a buffalo (but increasingly these days from a cow), boiled and then kneaded into a rounded ball; served as fresh as possible.

Oca   Goose.

Orata   Sea bream.

Orecchiette   Small, thick pasta disks (literally, "little ears").

Osso buco   Beef or veal knuckle braised in wine, butter, garlic, lemon, and rosemary; the marrow is a delicacy.

Ostriche   Oysters.

Paglio e fieno   Literally, "hay and straw," yellow (egg) and green (spinach) tagliatelle mixed and served with sauce.

Pancetta   Salt-cured pork belly, rolled into a cylinder and sliced—the Italian bacon.

Panforte   Any of a number of huge barlike candies vaguely akin to fruitcake; a dense, flat honey-sweetened mass of nuts, candied fruits, and spices.

Panino   A sandwich.

Panna   Cream (either whipped and sweetened for ice cream or pie; or heavy and unsweetened when included in pasta sauce).

Panzanella   A cold summery salad made of stale bread soaked in water and vinegar, mixed with cubed tomatoes, onion, fresh basil, and olive oil.

Pappa al pomodoro   A bready tomato-pap soup.

Pappardelle alle lepre   Wide, rough pasta tossed in hare sauce.

Parmigiano   Parmesan, a hard, salty cheese usually grated over pastas and soups but also eaten alone; also known as *grana*.

Pecorino   A rich sheep's-milk cheese; in Tuscany it's eaten fresh and soft, or *stagionato* (aged, sometimes with truffle or chilli).

Penne strascicate   Hollow pasta quills in a creamy *ragù* (meat-and-tomato sauce).

Peperonata   Stewed peppers and onions under oil; usually served cold.

Peperoncini   Hot chili peppers.

Peperoni   Green, yellow, or red sweet peppers.

Peposo   Beef stew with peppercorns.

Pesce al cartoccio   Fish baked in a parchment envelope.

Pesce spada   Swordfish.

Piccione   Pigeon.

Pici or Pinci   A homemade pasta made with just flour, water, and olive oil, rolled in the hands to produce lumpy, thick, chewy spaghetti to which sauce clings. This local name is used around Siena and to its south.

Piselli   Peas.

Pizza   Comes in two varieties: *rustica* or *al taglio* (by the slice) and *al forno* in a pizzeria (large, round pizzas for dinner with a thin, crispy crust). Specific varieties include *margherita* (plain pizza of tomatoes, mozzarella, and basil), *napoletana* (tomatoes, oregano, mozzarella, and anchovies), *capricciosa* (a naughty combination of prosciutto, artichokes, olives, and sometimes egg or anchovies), and *quattro stagioni* (four seasons of fresh vegetables, sometimes also with ham).

Polenta   Cornmeal mush, ranging from soupy to a dense cakelike version related to cornbread; often mixed with mushrooms and other seasonal fillings, served plain alongside game, with a stew, or sometimes sliced and fried.

Pollo   Chicken; *alla cacciatore* is huntsman style, with tomatoes and mushrooms cooked in wine; *alla diavola* is spicy, hot grilled chicken; *al mattone* is cooked under a hot brick.

Polpette   Small veal meatballs.

Polpo   Octopus.

Pomodoro   Tomato (plural *pomodori*).

Porcini   Large, wild bolete mushrooms, what the French call *cèpes*.

Porri   Leeks.

Ribollita   A thick, almost stewlike vegetable soup made with black cabbage, olive oil, celery, carrots, and whatever else *Mamma* has left over, all poured over thick slabs of bread.

Ricotta   A soft, fluffy, bland cheese made from the watery whey (not curds, as most cheese) and often used to stuff pastas. *Ricotta salata* is a salted, hardened version for nibbling.

Risotto   Rice, often arborio, served sticky.

Rombo   Turbot fish.

Salsa verde   Green sauce, made from capers, anchovies, lemon juice and/or vinegar, and parsley.

Salsicce   Sausage.

Saltimbocca   Veal scallop topped with a sage leaf and a slice of prosciutto and simmered in white wine.

Salvia   Sage.

Sarde   Sardines.

Scaloppine   Thin slices of meat, usually veal.

Scamorza   An air-dried (sometimes smoked) cheese similar to mozzarella; often sliced and grilled or melted over ham in a casserole, giving it a thin crust and gooey interior.

Schiacciata   See "Focaccia."

Scottiglia   Stew of veal, chicken, various game, and tomatoes cooked in white wine.

Semifreddo   A cousin to *gelato* (ice cream), it's a way of taking nonfrozen desserts (*tiramisù, zuppa inglese*) and freezing and moussing them.

Seppia   Cuttlefish (halfway between a squid and small octopus); its ink is used for flavoring and coloring in some pasta and risotto dishes.

Sogliola   Sole.

Spezzatino   Beef or vealstew, often with tomatoes.

Spiedino   A shish kabob (skewered bits of meat, onions, and slices of tomato or peppers grilled).

Spigola   A fish similar to sea bass or grouper.

Stracciatella   Egg-drop soup topped with grated cheese; also a flavor of ice cream (vanilla with chocolate ripple).

Stracotto   Overcooked beef, wrapped in bacon and braised with onion and tomato for hours until it's so tender it dissolves in your mouth.

Strozzapreti   Ricotta-and-spinach dumplings, usually served in tomato sauce; literally "priest chokers." Also called *strangolaprete*.

Stufato   Pot roast, usually in wine, broth, and veggies.

Tagliatelle   Flat pasta.

Tartufo (1) Truffles; (2) An ice-cream ball made with a core of fudge, a layer of vanilla, a coating of chocolate, and a dusting of cocoa; order it *affogato* (drowning), and they'll pour brandy over it.

Tonno Tuna.

Torta A pie. *Alla nonna* is Grandma's style and usually is a creamy lemony pie; *alle mele* is an apple tart; *al limone* is lemon; *alle fragole* is strawberry; *ai frutti di bosco* is with berries.

Torta al testo A flat, unleavened bread baked on the hearthstone and often split to be filled with sausage, spinach, or other goodies.

Tortellini Rings or half-moons of pasta stuffed with ricotta and spinach or chopped meat (chicken and veal). Sometimes also called *tortelli* and *tortelloni*.

Trippa Tripe (cow's stomach lining). Served *alla fiorentina* means casseroled with tomatoes and onions, topped with grated Parmesan cheese.

Trota Trout.

Vermicelli Very thin spaghetti.

Vitello Veal. A *vitellone* is an older calf about to enter cowhood. *Vitello tonnato* is thinly sliced veal served cold and spread with tuna mayonnaise.

Vongole Clams.

Zabaglione/zabaione A custard made of whipped egg yolks, sugar, and Marsala wine.

Zampone Pigs' feet, usually stewed for hours.

Zuccotto A tall liqueur-soaked sponge cake, stuffed with whipped cream, ice cream, chocolate, and candied fruits.

Recommended Books & Films

Books

GENERAL & HISTORY *Florence, Biography of a City* (1993) is popular historian Christopher Hibbert's overview on the city of the Renaissance, written in accessible prose. Hibbert is also author of *House of Medici: Its Rise and Fall*, a group biography of Florence's most famous rulers.

Frances Stonor Saunders' *Hawkwood: Diabolical Englishman* is more than just the story of the English mercenary's brutal Tuscan campaigns; it's also the most comprehensive account of medieval life and power politics in pre-Renaissance Tuscany.

Stones of Florence contains Mary McCarthy's often scathing, but usually fond, views on contemporary Florence (written in the early 1950s). It's also an indispensable art- and architecture-historical companion.

The only favorable sequel to McCarthy's classic is *City of Florence* by Yale professor R. W. B. Lewis.

More recently, a few literary histories set in Florence have enjoyed wild success. Ross King's slim tome *Brunelleschi's Dome* tells the fascinating story behind the building of Florence's Duomo. Dava Sobel's *Galileo's Daughter* uses the scant documents available to re-create the relationship between the great Pisan scientist and one of his illegitimate daughters, and his fight against the blasphemy charges, which nearly got him killed.

More recent history is covered by Iris Origo in *War in Val d'Orcia*, her personal diary of life on a

Tuscan farm (and the front line) in 1943 and 1944.

ART & ARCHITECTURE   The first work of art history ever written was penned in 1550 (with a later, expanded edition published in 1568) by a Tuscan artist. Giorgio Vasari's **Lives of the Artists, Vols. I and II** is a collection of biographies of the great artists from Cimabue to Vasari's 16th-century contemporaries.

For a more modern art-history take, the indispensable but expensive tome/doorstop is Frederick Hartt's **History of Italian Renaissance Art.** An easier, more colorful introduction, complete with illustrations, is Michael Levey's **Early Renaissance** and his **High Renaissance.** There is no better book on Sienese art from Duccio to Francesco di Giorgio than the affordable **Sienese Painting,** by Tim Hyman.

Michelangelo, a Biography by George Bull is the classic scholarly take on the artist's life. For a livelier look, try Irving Stone's **Agony and the Ecstasy.** Written as a work of historical fiction, it takes some liberties with the established record, but it's a good read.

LITERATURE & FICTION   No survey of Tuscan literature can start anywhere but with Dante Alighieri, the 14th-century poet whose **Divine Comedy,** also published separately as **Inferno, Purgatorio,** and **Paradiso,** was Italy's first great epic poem since antiquity and the first major work to be written in the local vernacular (in this case, Florentine) instead of Latin. Allen Mandelbaum's edition of **Inferno** has the Italian and English side by side.

The next generation of Tuscan writers produced Giovanni Boccaccio, whose **Decameron,** a story of 100 tales told by young nobles fleeing the Black Death, is Italy's *Canterbury Tales.*

Tuscany also came up with the third great medieval Italian writer, Francesco Petrarca (Petrarch), whose **Selections from the Canzoniere and Other Works,** in a brand new translation, gives you a taste for lyrical poetry.

Even more real-world practical was Niccolò Machiavelli, whose handbook for the successful Renaissance leader, **The Prince,** won him fame and infamy simultaneously.

If you don't have time to read all of the above, pick up a secondhand copy of the **Italian Renaissance Reader,** edited by Julia Conaway Bondanella and Mark Musa, with selections from Boccaccio's *Decameron,* Petrarch's *Canzoniere,* Leonardo da Vinci's notebooks, Benvenuto Cellini's *Autobiography,* Machiavelli's *Prince,* Michelangelo's sonnets, and others.

E. M. Forster's **A Room with a View,** half of which takes place in Florence, and **Where Angels Fear to Tread,** set in San Gimignano, are perfect tales of uptight, middle-class British Edwardian society and how it clashes with the brutal honesty and seductive magic of Italy. More recent, Mark Mills' part-1950s, part-Renaissance murder-mystery, *Savage Garden,* is an atmospheric and at times charming read. Michele Giuttari's hard-edged police thrillers, **A Florentine Death, A Death in Tuscany,** and the **Black Rose of Florence** take a more sinister look at central Italy.

For kids, the Tuscan classic is *Pinocchio,* by Carlo Collodi.

TRAVELOGUE   Wolfgang von Goethe was, by most reckonings, the world's first famous Grand Tourist, and he recorded his traipse through Italy in **Italian Journey.**

Mark Twain became internationally famous for his report on a tour of Europe and Palestine called **The Innocents Abroad,** a good quarter of which is about Italy. Henry James's **Italian Hours** pulls together travel essays written by the young author.

A Traveller in Italy (Methuen, 2006) is the informed account H. V. Morton wrote of his trip through the peninsula in the 1930s, with gorgeous, insightful prose by one of the best travelogue writers of the last century.

Frances Mayes' **Under the Tuscan Sun,** and its sequel **Bella Tuscany,** chronicle her experience of buying and renovating a house outside Cortona (where the book remains controversial). It spawned a huge industry of "I bought a house in Tuscany/Umbria/Sicily/wherever and renovated it and here's the charming story of how I learned to fit into Italian society" books—or, rather, it breathed new life, and a more prominent placement on the bookshelves, into a largely ignored genre that had already been claimed (and done much better) by Tim Parks (in the Veneto) and the late Barbara Grizzuti Harrison (in Sicily).

Films

Tuscany's countryside and hilltowns have served as backdrops for everything from Kenneth Branagh's *Much Ado About Nothing* to 1999's *A Midsummer Night's Dream* and Zeffirelli's *Tea with Mussolini.* And, in *The English Patient,* Ralph Fiennes convalesces in the monastery at Sant'Anna in Camprena, south of Siena, and there are cameos from Montepulciano and Pienza. *Stealing Beauty,* starring Liv Tyler, was filmed on the Brolio estate, near Gaiole in Chianti.

The Taviani brothers' **Fiorile (Wild Flower)** is a story within a story, reviewing the last 100 years of Italian history as a father details the lineage of a family curse.

James Ivory's **A Room with a View** is based on the E. M. Forster novel (see above). Although only half the film is actually set in Florence, it's the sharpest glimpse into the 19th-century British infatuation with Tuscany. *Hannibal,* the further grisly adventures of Anthony Hopkins' Oscar-winning character from *The Silence of the Lambs,* is set partly in Florence. The biggest recent blockbuster to come out of the region is **Twilight: New Moon,** the film adaptation of the second in Stephanie Meyer's *Twilight* trilogy of teen-vampire novels. Although Meyer sets the crucial scenes of her tale in Volterra, it was actually filmed in Montepulciano.

The greatest native talent to come out of Tuscany in the past few years is actor, director, writer, and comedian Roberto Benigni, creator of several slapstick mistaken-identity romps *(Johnny Stecchino, Il Mostro).* Then, in 1998 this Tuscan native won three Oscars, including Best Foreign Film and Best Actor (only the second non-English-speaking actor to do so)—with **La Vita è Bella (Life Is Beautiful),** an unlikely tragicomic fable set partly in Arezzo of one Jewish father trying to protect his young son from the horrors of the Holocaust by pretending the concentration camp they've been sent to is part of a big game.

Index

See also Accommodations and Restaurant indexes, below.

Photo **Credits**

Photo Credits

p 113, bottom: © Kirsten Scully; p 114: © Vanessa Berberian; p 115: © Kirsten Scully; p 117, bottom: © Vanessa Berberian; p 117, top: © Vanessa Berberian; p 118: © Riccardo De Luca; p 119: © Riccardo De Luca; p 120: © Riccardo De Luca; p 121: © Riccardo De Luca; p 123: © Vanessa Berberian; p 125: © Vanessa Berberian; p 126: © Riccardo De Luca; p 127: © Kirsten Scully; p 129, top: © Riccardo De Luca; p 129, bottom: © Riccardo De Luca; p 130: © Riccardo De Luca; p 131: © Kirsten Scully; p 133: © Vanessa Berberian; p 134: © Riccardo De Luca; p 135: © Vanessa Berberian; p 136: © Vanessa Berberian; p 137, top: © Vanessa Berberian; p 137, bottom: © Vanessa Berberian; p 138: © Kirsten Scully; p 139: © Vanessa Berberian; p 141: © Kirsten Scully; p 143, bottom: © Riccardo De Luca; p 143, top: © Vanessa Berberian; p 144: © Alden Gewirtz; p 145: © Kirsten Scully; p 147, bottom: © Vanessa Berberian; p 147, top: © Riccardo De Luca; p 148: © Vanessa Berberian; p 149: © Kirsten Scully; p 150: © Riccardo De Luca; p 152: © Riccardo De Luca; p 153: © Vanessa Berberian; p 154: © Kirsten Scully; p 157: © Sandro DiFatta; p 158, top: © Kirsten Scully; p 158, bottom: © Sandro DiFatta; p 161: © Sandro DiFatta; p 162: © Vanessa Berberian; p 163, top: © Kirsten Scully; p 163, bottom: © Vanessa Berberian; p 164: © Vanessa Berberian; p 165: © Courtesy Hotel L'Antico Pozzo; p 168: © Vanessa Berberian; p 169: © Vanessa Berberian; p 170: © Kirsten Scully; p 171: © Vanessa Berberian; p 172, top: © Vanessa Berberian; p 172, bottom: © Jennifer Reilly; p 174: © Courtesy Palazzo Ravizza, Photo by Bruno Bruchi; p 175: © Courtesy Da Divo; p 177: © Sandro DiFatta; p 178: © Sandro DiFatta; p 179: © Sandro DiFatta; p 181: © Sandro DiFatta